Praise for William F. Roemer's accounts of organized crime

Roemer: Man Against the Mob

"A high-speed journey through mob-land's inner sanctum, with wiretaps, payoffs, shootouts, double-dealing and instant death. . . Fascinating."

—*People*

"Roemer does an admirable job of bluntly recreating the inner workings of Chicago's underworld and the FBI's methods of fighting them. . . . A revealing memoir that pulls no punches in recalling the triumphs—and, at times, the foul-ups—that characterized Mr. Roemer's remarkable career."

—*The New York Times Book Review*

War of the Godfathers

"Exciting reading. . . Roemer's experience has left him with some fascinating tales, and this is one of them."

—*Kirkus Reviews*

"A unique contribution to U.S. crime history."

—*Publishers Weekly*

By William F. Roemer, Jr.
Published by Ivy Books:

ROEMER: MAN AGAINST THE MOB
WAR OF THE GODFATHERS
THE ENFORCER
ACCARDO: THE GENUINE GODFATHER

THE ENFORCER

Spilotro: The Chicago Mob's Man Over Las Vegas

William F. Roemer, Jr.

IVY BOOKS • NEW YORK

An Ivy Book
Published by The Ballantine Publishing Group
Copyright © 1994 by William F. Roemer, Jr.

http://www.randomhouse.com

Library of Congress Catalog Card Number: 93-74484

ISBN 0-8041-1310-6

This edition published by arrangement with Donald I. Fine, Inc.

Manufactured in the United States of America

First Ballantine Books Edition: May 1995

OPM   20 19 18 17 16 15 14 13 12 11

Acknowledgments

I want to express my appreciation to the staff at Donald I. Fine, Inc.: Don Fine himself, a legend in the publishing industry; Larry Bernstein, Production Director; Jason Poston, Assistant to the Publisher; Bob Gales, Sales Director; and Larry Kramer, the accountant for Donald I. Fine, Inc.

Also I thank Jeannie, my wife, who gives me daily inspiration and gave this work its first editing. I couldn't do anything without her.

I give a great deal of appreciation to Roy Suzuki, my researcher. Roy's story is a great one. A Japanese-American who was interned with his fellow citizens of Japanese descent following Pearl Harbor, Roy became one of the top IRS agents in Chicago during my days as an FBI agent. Following his retirement, he was one of the founders and first officers, as he still is, of Courtwatchers, the Chicago chapter of Court Buffs of America, the group of observers of almost all the mob trials. Not only does Roy keep me up to date on what is going on in Chicago throughout each year, but he did much of the research on this book. I couldn't have done this book without him!

Ron Asher of the Nevada Gaming Control Board was a big help.

So was Greg Kowalick of the Division of Gaming Enforcement, New Jersey Casino Control Commission.

Bill Ouseley, the former FBI agent in Kansas City who was the case agent on the Strawman cases there, was invaluable.

Lee Flosi, who also worked on the Strawman cases as an FBI agent in Kansas City, helped as well. He later became the supervisor of an organized crime squad of the FBI in Chicago and is now retired from the Bureau, working as the director of security for the World Cup soccer organization.

Pete Wacks, an FBI case agent on the Pendorf case in Chicago and arguably the top field agent in the FBI today, was a great help. So was our buddy, Art Pfizenmayer, who worked with Pete on Pendorf in Chicago and then became the supervisor of the organized crime squad of the FBI in San Diego. He supervised the investigation leading to the conviction of the Chicago mob bosses John "No Nose" DiFronzo and Donald Angelini in San Diego in early 1993. Sam Carlisi was also indicted in that case but he was acquitted.

I thank my many informants inside the mob who I cannot name. I thank those I do name, such as Gerardo Denono.

My gratitude to Bill Branon, the Special Agent in Charge of the Chicago office of the FBI as I wrote this. And to Bob Walsh, the Assistant SAC there then, now an Inspector in Washington.

How could I fail to thank Mike Simon, the FBI case agent on the Spilotro investigation in Las Vegas for years?

May God bless Duncan Everette, the FBI case agent on Anthony Spilotro for years in Chicago with whom I worked. RIP, Dunc!

And may God bless my close pal Bill Duffy, the Deputy Superintendent of the Chicago Police Department, whose Intelligence Unit he personally supervised. He investigated Spilotro for decades.

Thanks to Joe Yablonsky, the SAC of the FBI office in Las Vegas during three of Spilotro's most tumultuous years in the early 1980s, and the FBI agents Chuck Thomas, Tommy Parker, Warren Salisbury and Al Zimmerman, who investigated Spilotro in Vegas for years.

My special thanks to all my fellow FBI agents on Criminal Squad Number One, known as C-1, in Chicago, the most highly regarded organized crime squad in the FBI during the years I happened to be a part of it. They investigated Spilotro throughout his criminal career. I'll not name them here since I do in the text of this book.

I thank Lou Spalla, recently retired from the Arizona Department of Public Safety, and our pal there, Leo Jacques. Both worked closely with me when they were with the Pima County Drug Control Agency. Both have been most helpful since.

My thanks to my colleagues in the Chicago Crime Commission: Bob Fuesel, Jeannette Callaway and Jerry Gladden.

My appreciation to my nephew Pat Roemer, and to Scott Hanson of Goreville, Illinois, who keep me abreast of what appears in Chicago's press.

I thank Fred DeBartolo of the Cook County Public Defender's Office for keeping me current on activity in Chicago.

I give my thanks to Tom Carrigan, the former Chief of Investigation and Enforcement of the Nevada Gaming Control Board, for his help for so many years.

God bless Jim Mansfield, who studied with me at Notre Dame, served with me in China in the Marine Corps and worked with me in the FBI in New York. A guy can't have a better pal than that. RIP, Jim.

My gratitude to Larry Heim, the editor of the Grapevine, the organ of the Society of Former Agents of the FBI, and to Jim McFall, the Executive Director of the Society.

I thank Jim Fox, the recently retired Assistant Director in Charge of the New York office of the FBI, and Doug Lintner, one of the top organized crime agents in that office.

My thanks to Miles Cooperman and Jim Bredican of the Cook County Sheriff's Office.

Larry Whelan, formerly of the Nevada Gaming Control Board, gave me a lesson on the mechanics of skimming years ago. Thanks, Larry.

Also, my gratitude to many members of the Fourth Estate who have been so helpful through the years, including John O'Brien, John Drummond, Sam Meddis, Steve Neal, Irv Kupcinet, Bruce Frankel, Jerry Seper, Rosalind Rossi, Matt and Phil O'Connor, Al Tobin, Marnie Inskip, Patricia King, Mike Goodman, Ken Miller, Sandy Smith, Art Petacque, Ron Kozial, Phil La Velle, Ralph Blumenthal, Chuck Goudie, Jim Agnew, Rich Lindberg, Nate Kaplan, John Binder, Denny

Walsh, Mark Kiesling and Jim Drinkhall. My relationship with all of them has been a two-way street, and I appreciate that curve in the road that bent toward me.

I also appreciate the help that Bill Hartnett of Here's Chicago, the tourist attraction, has extended to me since 1950. We were recruits at the FBI Academy in Quantico, Virginia, and agents in the New York office together. He has been at my side since.

I can't forget Ralph Salerno, the former Chief of Detectives in the Intelligence Unit of the New York City Police Department for many years. I owe him for his recitation of the activities of many of the New York mobsters, like Meyer Lansky, Frank Costello, Bugsy Siegel and Lucky Luciano who figure in this story.

I also wish to acknowledge two guys who don't wish to be acknowledged. But then I guess one is known by his adversaries. Rocky Infelice was one of them. Rock is an unusual mobster. Before he became "made" as the underboss of the Chicago mob years ago but after I had retired to Arizona, Chuckie English, another high level Chicago mobster before his own people whacked him, came out to see me. The mob was concerned at the time, during the days when Tony Accardo was the *consiglieri*, who sat at the top no matter who the boss actually was, because Rocky had been convicted decades before of a narcotics violation. Dealing in dope was a real violation of *omerta* in those days under Accardo. It was Chuckie's mission to find out from me the circumstances of Rock's arrest. I told him I had no such knowledge, that it was a DEA case, not an FBI investigation. I told Chuck, however, that I had no knowledge that Rock had dealt in any dope after he had been inducted as a formal member of La Cosa Nostra. I also told English that I had a certain respect for Rock due to his background. Infelice did not duck the draft during World War II like almost all his colleagues. In fact, Rock volunteered for the paratroopers. He became a member of the Screamin' Eagles, the 101st Airborne, the highly respected fighting unit which became known as the Bastards of Bastogne when they fought against all odds against the best Hitler had in the Battle of the Bulge. Successfully.

In any event what English took back to Chicago from his visit to me in Arizona must have served Rocky's cause because soon after that he was elevated to the underboss spot, the second most important job in the Outfit.

Now it was January 9, 1992. Rocky and four of his key lieutenants were on trial for a violation of the RICO statute in federal court in Chicago. They had murdered two guys and engaged in many other instances of racketeering. The government introduced its Exhibit 446T that day. Exhibit 446T was a tape recording of a conversation between Infelice and another of his top aides, "B. J." Jahoda. Jahoda, unknown to Rock, was carrying a wire, wearing a body mike, on the day he conversed with Infelice. Jahoda was cooperating with the government in its investigation of Infelice and the Chicago mob. As recorded on Jahoda's body mike, Infelice was heard to ask Jahoda if he had read "Roemer's book." Jahoda indicated he had not. Infelice then informed Jahoda that "He's pretty accurate in most of his stuff. He didn't lie. You remember, he was 'G guy' here for more than twenty years. A capable man."

So, thanks, Rock. You didn't expect to be acknowledged in this book and had no idea your remarks were to be recorded for posterity so I guess that makes them all the more interesting.

In the same vein, another guy I should acknowledge is John "No Nose" DiFronzo. In the early 1990s DiFronzo and Sam "Wings" Carlisi (more about them later) ran the Chicago Outfit in tandem until January of 1992 when DiFronzo was arrested by FBI agents in his home in Long Grove, Illinois, a western Chicago suburb. Under the authority federal agents have when making an arrest, they searched his house "incidental to the arrest." They found he was not much of a reader of heavy literature. However, he did have one book—*Roemer: Man Against the Mob*—my autobiography. Actually, due to the circumstances, I may not have been too honored by the FBI's discovery. They found the book on the nightstand of "No

Nose." Right next to his bed. Pete Wacks, one of the members of the FBI search party that day, joked to me: "It probably put him to sleep at night." Even so, I'll thank DiFronzo here. At least he bought my book. Or did he steal it? Thanks anyway, "No Nose."

Most of all, I thank my God, in gratitude for giving me the enthusiasm, the ability, the courage, the energy, the intelligence, the strength and the ability to make up for many mistakes and a lot of ineptitude during my thirty years with the FBI so that I could hope to live up to my lifetime motto: Keep Punchin' and Keep the Faith!

Introduction

There are writers with much greater literary success than mine who are writing the story of Las Vegas, authors who I like and respect. However, unlike many of them, I have "been there." I'm not writing about something I don't know. I knew Tony Spilotro, I know Chicago and I know Las Vegas.

I was an FBI agent for thirty years. I spent twenty-four of those years working in Chicago, twenty-one of them on Spilotro and his associates. Much of the information I developed concerned the interests of the Chicago Mob in Las Vegas. I guess I've made some twenty-five visits to Vegas investigating mob activity.

I was never actually the case agent on Spilotro, the agent to whom his investigation was assigned. However, I worked in harmony and close association with those agents, particularly Duncan Everette and Mike Simon. In addition, for much of the time Spilotro was active in organized crime, I was the coordinator of what the FBI calls the TECIP, the Top Echelon Criminal Informant Program, in Chicago. In addition to my personal development and maintenance of most of the CTEs, Top Echelon Criminal Informants, I monitored and coordinated those developed by other Chicago FBI agents. Therefore, I was very much aware, during Spilotro's entire crime career, of what was being developed from all our informants, not only those furnishing information on his activity but on all of his fellow mobsters.

Furthermore, I was the case agent on two of the four elsurs, electronic surveillances, that furnished reams of information on the Chicago family of La Cosa Nostra. I monitored all four on a daily basis from the time we installed those bugs in 1959, until we were ordered by Lyndon Johnson in 1965 to remove them because they were allegedly violating civil rights. They were in the four most strategic meeting places of the Chicago mob, including their general headquarters and the special headquarters of the mob boss, Sam Giancana. Almost daily, mobsters conferred about their interests, and the interests of mobs in other cities, especially Las Vegas.

I have researched this book in my personal archives, and read volumes of material located at the Chicago Crime Commission, where I serve as a Special Consultant on Organized Crime.

One thing more I'd like to make clear before you read this effort. I have reconstructed some dialogue. I have done so based on information from our hidden mikes, or from informants who were there and who reported it to me. Although I heard some of it directly, firsthand, I don't recall all of it verbatim. I remember the gist of the conversation. I remember who was speaking and who was present. I can reconstruct some of it word for word from the sources I've described above. But I am not going to tell you that every sentence quoted here was spoken in exactly those words. I will tell you, however, that I have conversed personally with over a hundred, maybe two hundred, highly placed and lowly placed mobsters on perhaps a thousand occasions. I have also conversed with informants high up in the mob on hundreds of occasions. I have listened to conversations of mobsters for thousands, perhaps tens of thousands, of hours. I believe I have a clear idea of how particular mobsters at all levels talk and what they talk about. I tell you this up front, and honestly.

I don't want to fly under false colors. Some of the dialogue is verbatim, obtained from identified sources. But some is not. But that which is not is based on my unique vantage point, something no other author I know has had the advantage of in writing this story. I was there.

There are photographs in this book of the characters I discuss. Some of them are FBI surveillance photos, some are mug shots, and all are from my personal library. I utilized almost all these photos for surveillance purposes during my career as an FBI agent and believe that including them makes for a much more enjoyable book.

THE CHICAGO FAMILY

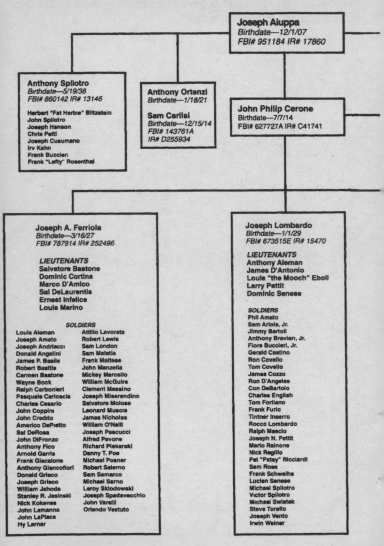

Joseph Aiuppa
Birthdate—12/1/07
FBI# 951184 IR# 17860

Anthony Spilotro
Birthdate—5/19/38
FBI# 860142 IR# 13146

Herbert "Fat Herbie" Blitzstein
John Spilotro
Joseph Hanson
Chris Petti
Joseph Cusumano
Irv Kahn
Frank Buccien
Frank "Lefty" Rosenthal

Anthony Ortenzi
Birthdate—1/18/21

Sam Carlisi
Birthdate—12/15/14
FBI# 143761A
IR# D255934

John Philip Cerone
Birthdate—7/7/14
FBI# 627727A IR# C41741

Joseph A. Ferriola
Birthdate—3/16/27
FBI# 787914 IR# 252496

LIEUTENANTS
Salvatore Bastone
Dominic Cortina
Marco D'Amico
Sal DeLaurentis
Ernest Infelice
Louis Marino

SOLDIERS

Louis Aleman	Attilio Lavorata
Joseph Amato	Robert Lewis
Joseph Andriacci	Sam London
Donald Angelini	Sam Malatia
James P. Basile	Frank Maltese
Robert Basitis	John Manzella
Carmen Bastone	Mickey Marcello
Wayne Bock	William McGuire
Ralph Carbonieri	Clement Messino
Pasquale Carioscia	Joseph Miserendino
Charles Cesario	Salvatore Molose
John Coppini	Leonard Muscia
John Credito	James Nicholas
Americo DePietro	William O'Neill
Sal DeRosa	Joseph Pascucci
John DiFronzo	Alfred Pavone
Anthony Fico	Richard Piekarski
Arnold Garris	Danny T. Poe
Frank Glacalone	Michael Posner
Anthony Giancofiori	Robert Salerno
Donald Grieco	Sam Samarco
Joseph Grieco	Michael Sarno
William Jahoda	Leroy Skiodowski
Stanley R. Jasinski	Joseph Spadavecchio
Nick Kokenas	John Varelli
John Lamanna	Orlando Vestuto
John LaPlaca	
Hy Larner	

Joseph Lombardo
Birthdate—1/1/29
FBI# 673515E IR# 15470

LIEUTENANTS
Anthony Aleman
James D'Antonio
Louis "the Mooch" Eboli
Larry Pettit
Dominic Senese

SOLDIERS
Phil Amato
Sam Ariola, Jr.
Jimmy Bartoli
Anthony Bravieri, Jr.
Fiore Buccieri, Jr.
Gerald Castino
Ron Covello
Tom Covello
James Cozzo
Ron D'Angeles
Con DeBartolo
Charles English
Tom Fortiano
Frank Furio
Tintner Inserro
Rocco Lombardo
Ralph Mascio
Joseph N. Pettit
Mario Rainone
Nick Regilio
Pat "Patsy" Ricciardi
Sam Rosa
Frank Schweihs
Lucien Senese
Michael Spilotro
Victor Spilotro
Michael Swiatek
Steve Torello
Joseph Vento
Irwin Weiner

Anthony Accardo
Birthdate—4/28/06
FBI# 1410106 IR# D83436

Gus Alex
Birthdate—4/1/16
FBI# 4244200

Dominic Blasi
Birthdate—9/9/11
FBI# 635770 IR# E8187

Willie Messino
Birthdate—1/7/17
FBI# 922367 IR#55433

Angelo LaPietra
Birthdate—10/30/20
FBI# 1777469 IR# D48410

LIEUTENANTS
Frank James Calabrese
Frank Caruso
John Fecarotta
James LaPietra
John Monteleone

SOLDIERS
Joseph Albano
Ernest Amodei
Frank Bruno Barbara
Sam Bills
Anthony Bova
Frank Butera
Frak Michael "Mike" Caruso
Rich Catezone
Charles DiCaro
James DiCaro
Paul DiCaro
Sam Gallo
Morton Geller
Jerome Gralla
Anthony Imparata
Angelo Imperato
Vincent Inserro
Joseph LaMantia
Richard LaMantia
Anthony Maenza
Nick Montos
Dominic Palermo
Flor Piccinini
Aldo J. Piscitelli
James Quarello
Carmen Russo
Terry Scalise
Tom Scalise
Nikolic Slobodan
Michael Talarico

Vincent A. Solano
Birthdate—10/12/19
FBI# 1995437 IR# D4182

LIEUTENANTS
Joseph Arnold
Joseph DiVarco
Michael Glitta

SOLDIERS
Anthony Armieri
Dan Bartoli
Ray Caccamo
Thomas Campione
Jasper Campise
Orlando Catanese
Anthony Cipriano
Anthony Cingnani
Frank DeMonte
Sal Dodero
Sid Finzelbar
Sal Gruttaduaro
Murray Jans
Walter Micus
Joseph Morici
Daniel Morsovillo
Nick Nitti
Frank Orlando
Leonard Patrick
Mike Patrick
Frank Paula
Sam Sarcinelli
Christ Seritella
Morton Shapiro
Calvin Sirkin
George Sommer
Anthony Spadafore
Ray Spencer
Arnold Taradash
Frank Tornabene
Len Yaras

Albert Caesar Tocco
Birthdate—8/9/29
FBI# 296484

LIEUTENANTS
Joseph Barrett, Jr.
Tony "Dago Tony" Berretoni
Richard Guzzino
Chris Messino

SOLDIERS
Douglas Aldridge
Harry Ansel
Daniel Bonneta
Roy Bridges
Clarence Crockett
Frank D'Andrea
Gerry Ferraro
Sheldon Flahman
Joseph Marek
Gino Martin
Seymour Miller
Tony Pelligrino
Joseph Jerome "Jerry" Scalise
Jerry Scarpelli
Eric Schmidt
Al Troiani
William Zanon
Richard Zink

Prepared by William Lambie of the office of the Attorney General, State of Illinois, with the assistance of the author, a Special Consultant on Organized Crime to the Chicago Crime Commission, then and now. Introduced by the author during his testimony on March 4, 1983, before the U.S. Senate Permanent Subcommittee on Investigations

Prologue

Sam Giancana was displeased. The head of the Chicago family of La Cosa Nostra was looking for a new *representato* in Las Vegas. Years earlier, Al Capone had sent Johnny Roselli, but there had been problems. So Marshall Caifano was sent to take over. But the first thing he does is change his name to John Marshall, and then . . . Well, there were problems.

A low profile was needed in Las Vegas. It was not responsible for the Chicago "rep" in Vegas to stick out. The function of that rep was to be the "Mr. Outside" for the mob. Outside the casinos. The mobs had dozens of men inside directing the skim, the reason for the mob being there in the first place. Mr. Outside made sure all the Mr. Insides stayed in line. If one of the inside casino bosses for the Chicago mob had any kind of a problem, it was Mr. Outside he consulted to make sure the recalcitrant shaped up. Or else. He was the muscle. He had the brains. There was no doubt who was the boss. Nobody—and I mean nobody—fooled with the Chicago *representato* in Las Vegas. There was nobody more powerful than he. Even the "godfather of Las Vegas," Moe Dalitz, didn't screw around when in the presence of that guy.

As if changing his name gave him a certain cachet, finesse and elegance, Caifano in his early days as Chicago's man in charge of affairs in Vegas handled things very softly and very quietly. Although Giancana, with his hyperaggressive personality, was no one to be conducting lessons on maintaining a reserved presence, there was one guy in Chicago who was above Giancana. No matter who the boss in Chicago was, there was one guy who stood above him, looking over his shoulder.

1

There was one guy who had done it all. He had been the bodyguard of Al Capone in the Twenties. He had been one of the triggermen in the St. Valentine's Day Massacre of 1929 when he helped Capone wipe out his rivals, the members of the Bugs Moran Gang. He had been a capo, a captain of the La Cosa Nostra under Frank Nitti in the Thirties. He had been the underboss, the number two man in the Outfit, under Paul "The Waiter" Ricca in the early Forties. He had succeeded Ricca as the top boss in Chicago in the mid-Forties. He had remained the Chicago boss until 1957 when he voluntarily stepped down and selected Giancana to succeed him. He had remained active in mob affairs, however, as *consiglieri*, the advisor and counselor to the Chicago Outfit. Now in the Sixties he was still "The Man." As powerful as Giancana was, this guy was more so.

His name was Tony Accardo. The press called him "The Big Tuna." His colleagues called him "Joe Batters," a name Al Capone had given him after Accardo battered two of Capone's foes to death with a baseball bat. "This guy is a real Joe Batters," Capone had exclaimed. The name stuck.

Although Giancana would not caution Caifano to keep a low profile, Joe Batters did. "Keep your head down" was his instruction. "You make noise out there and everybody will know we're out there. We had a president one time who said 'speak soft and carry a big stick.' That's what we want you to do. A problem comes up, you handle it. But nobody gets hit in Las Vegas. You decide somebody gotta get whacked, you talk to us. If we agree, you snatch them, take them out to the desert and hit them there. We don't want to scare the tourists. If it wasn't for the suckers who come there to make a play at our tables and the old ladies who pull the levers on our slots we couldn't get no skim. Without the skim we got no reason to be out there. So don't be scaring the fuckin' players. Keep your head down. That's what we did with that Gus Greenbaum at the Flamingo. He hada be whacked, we did it in Phoenix, not Las Vegas. Same thing with Russian Louie. They never found his body out in the desert where Johnny buried him. Above all else, you do nothing to alert that Gaming Board out there that any fuckin' mob is out there, certainly not us. All the people inside the casinos know who you are and what you are. You don't have to tell them. They know you are the guy with the ape on your shoulder. You don't have to scare them—they're already scared. Every guy we got out there has been put out there by us. They know what happens they get outta line. And they know you're the guy with the gun. But you don't do nothin' to alert the gamers that you're who you are. Keep your fuckin' head down!"

It was good advice, of course. It came from Joe Batters. He who had done it all.

But did Johnny Marshall heed that advice? Did he know better than to strut around the Strip and Glitter Gulch? Hardly. He was a man selected by Giancana, the loudmouth, not personally by Accardo, the suave, reserved thinker. In fact, we were well aware why Giancana selected Caifano to go out west. Giancana had a thing for Darlene, Caifano's beautiful wife. Darlene may have been a hillbilly from Kentucky, but, like her role model, Virginia Hill, Bugsy Siegel's paramour, once she arrived in Chicago she learned quickly where her bread could be buttered. In the early days of the FBI's Top Hoodlum Program, I worked with Ralph Hill, my partner. While I had two top Chicago mobsters assigned to me as my special targets, Ralph had Giancana. Starting in early 1958, we followed Giancana and, though we were very surreptitious and kept our distance, we were able to stay with him most of the time. We found out that almost every Friday night Giancana kept a rendezvous at the Thunderbird Hotel in Rosemont, what was then a slow, lazy western suburb of Chicago. Who do you think Giancana rendezvoused with in those days? Darlene! The mob boss was stealing the delights of the wife of one of his underlings. It suddenly made sense that he felt it would be nice if that guy would spend most of his time thousands of miles away, that he should keep his residence and his wife in Chicago but spend almost all his time in Las Vegas. Ralph alerted Caifano to the situation with Darlene, but we found we were dealing with a different culture. Caifano was actually very pleased that Darlene interested his boss. That was fine as long as the trade-off was a big step up for him in the Outfit. We thought we were causing trouble for Giancana, that his man in Vegas might come over to our side ("flip" in FBI lingo) and inform on Giancana and his other mob associates, especially about their interests in Las Vegas. We found that Caifano apparently already knew the score. He obviously had made his own deal, giving Giancana Darlene in exchange for Las Vegas. Caifano felt such a deal offered more than he could win at any blackjack table in Vegas.

Perhaps it was because of his deal with the devil that Caifano got carried away. In Las Vegas parlance, Darlene was his ace in the hole. It was Caifano's lifeline. Or so he thought. He began to disregard the instructions that Accardo had given him. His rabbi was Giancana; he had hardly ever met with Accardo. He began to strut around Las Vegas as if the city was his own private domain. He made noise when confronted by local authorities and, in general, went out of his way to make his presence known to the world.

Meanwhile, the situation in Chicago was rapidly changing. We finally got Giancana, sending him to prison for contempt of court. When he came out, Sam recognized the animosity against him among his own people and voluntarily abdicated. He fled to Mexico, and stayed away from the States for eight years. When he finally came back, his own people, maybe even his closest pal, killed him. After we put Giancana's next three successors away, the mob reached up to its finest resource and brought Tony Accardo back. Insisted on it.

Now that Accardo was back in power, he quickly acted to remove the idiot who had been representing the Outfit in Las Vegas. He recalled Marshall Caifano. No longer did Caifano have his rabbi.

But who would be a suitable replacement for Caifano? Had to be a ruthless guy, a tough guy, a guy who could handle the disciplinary work, handle all the Mr. Insides. But a guy with some smarts, too.

Who would this guy be?

PART ONE

1914 to 1971
FORMATION

The Top Moper

1   Little did he know when he emigrated to the United States from his native Triggiano, Italy, at the age of fifteen that he was carrying a plague in his genes.

Pasquale Spilotro arrived at Ellis Island in 1914, destitute and with almost nothing going for him. He had no education, no money, no particular skill. He did have one thing, however, that would stand him in good stead in his adopted country. He had the work ethic.

Pasquale, who would soon be called Patsy by his fellow Italian-Americans, shared with many of his countrymen the desire to learn and to work hard. Little did he realize, then, that his family had the fault that a small fraction of his countrymen carried. Almost all Italian immigrants would thrive in their adopted land and make all who came in contact with them proud and glad that they had come. Ninety-nine and forty-four one-hundredths percent fell into this category. Without them the United States would be less of a country.

But Patsy carried the gene.

He traveled from New York to Chicago. Soon afterwards, he settled on the far west side of Chicago, putting down a small sum and buying a modest two-story home at 2152 North Melvina. It was gray and constructed of clapboard like so many other houses in that neighborhood.

Somewhere along the way, Patsy met the girl of his dreams. Her name was Antoinette, and soon she became his wife, the woman with whom Patsy would spend the rest of his life. Patsy and Antoinette were devout Catholics. They worshipped at St. John Bosco Catholic Church with many of their neighbors, attending mass weekly and taking communion each Sunday.

Soon Patsy learned a very useful skill. He discovered he had a natural talent for cooking and began to make a favorite meal of his fellow countrymen—pasta with a great meatball sauce. He opened a small restaurant in the heart of one of Chicago's two Italian neighborhoods and named it Patsy's.

Unlike Patsy Spilotro, most Italian immigrants settled in The Patch when they came to Chicago. The Patch was located around the intersection of Taylor and Halsted on the near southwest side of the city, about a mile or so from the Loop. This was where most of the mobsters would grow up, such men as Sam Giancana, Sam DeStefano, Willy Daddano, Philly Alderisio, Marshall Caifano and Sam Battaglia, those who would become top leaders of the Chicago family of La Cosa Nostra in later years.

Instead, Patsy opened his restaurant in the other Italian neighborhood in Chicago in those days, the one located on the west side, a couple of miles north of The Patch, around the exact intersection where Patsy opened his restaurant—the corner of Grand and Ogdon Avenues. Whereas Italian-Americans from The Patch would form The 42 Gang, their counterparts from Grand-Ogdon would form the Circus Cafe Gang. Tony Accardo, who grew up in this neighborhood, would become a leader of this group, waiting to graduate to The Outfit, to join Al Capone and Frank Nitti.

Patsy worked hard. He made a great veal cutlet and his spaghetti became well known. In those days the neighborhood was relatively safe and, being close to the Loop and especially close to the Civic Opera, many who enjoyed Caruso there would end their evening by slumming at Patsy's.

It wasn't much, but the food was great. For a while, Patsy ran the whole restaurant almost single-handedly. He did all the cooking and he worked there seven days a week, starting at four-thirty in the morning when he began to prepare the food fresh for breakfast and remaining through lunch and dinner until midnight when the last theatergoer left.

It was an exhausting life. He had always been a frail man,

very small and slender, not even five foot six inches and not even one hundred and thirty-five pounds. His own food, his pasta, was about all he ate and, though he ate a lot of it, the hard work and the long hours kept him slender.

Patsy and Antoinette had six children, all boys—Vincent, Victor, Pasquale, Anthony, John and then Michael. While Patsy was overwhelmed, Antoinette did her best to raise them, unruly, hard-to-handle and undisciplined as the boys were. Anthony, the fourth, was born on May 19, 1938. He would become the worst of the litter. But almost all would have their problems with the law. Something was in Patsy's genes, apparently.

The boys were all made to pitch in and attempt to alleviate some of the burden at Patsy's. Vincent and Pasquale, Jr., an intelligent boy called Pat by most, made more of an effort and were a great help to their parents.

Anthony, called Tony by his neighbors, attended Burbank Elementary School, not St. John Bosco, the Catholic school in the neighborhood. Later, the nuns at St. John Bosco would be happy he had not been one of theirs, though perhaps it would have made a difference.

But six boys were a lot to look after and take care of, even if Patsy and Antoinette hadn't owned a restaurant that required so much of their attention. Several of their sons began spending time with the wrong crowd, with older boys who had more money and glamour than those who were harder-working and law-abiding. The allure of the easy life was there, and young impressionable boys like Tony Spilotro were taken in by it. Slowly, he chose to be corrupted.

Soon Patsy began to realize what he and Antoinette were raising. A bunch of young toughs who skipped from one problem to another. Patsy attempted to keep them busy at the restaurant, but most of them had no desire to learn the business, especially not in the hot kitchen. They waited on tables and washed the dishes but, except for Pat, that seemed to be the extent of their ambitions—and their ability.

Tony entered Steinmetz High School, the neighborhood school, in 1953. He had long admired the high school boys and finally he was there. He soon set about making a reputation for himself as a real tough guy, someone you didn't want to mess with. A bully. But he wasn't a large boy, barely taller than his father and no heavier. He couldn't intimidate anyone with his stature since most of the Poles and the other Italians who made up the majority of the student body were bigger than he was, especially the upperclassmen.

Finally, in 1954, the pace and the anxiety became too much for Patsy. At the age of fifty-five he suffered an aneurysm—a blood vessel in his brain ruptured and he was dead as he hit the floor.

Now there were few restraints on Tony. Although his father had rarely been at home, devoting most of his time to the restaurant for the desperately needed income it produced for the family, Patsy was the only real authority figure that young Tony had in his life. In his sophomore year at Steinmetz at the time of his father's death, Tony never found anyone there to take his place. Or maybe he just never looked very hard. The only person who might have had a chance was his brother Pat. Just a year or so older than Tony, Pat had a lot going for him. In fact, in later years he would become a captain in the Air Force and then a dental surgeon, a fine one. During high school, Pat attempted to use his influence on his kid brother but most of the time he was fighting a losing battle.

Even at that early age Tony was arrogant, vicious, unruly and incorrigible. He swaggered through the hallways, bumping the smaller students, especially the girls, out of the way. He knew enough to stay out of the way of the football players and the other athletes at Steinmetz but he looked to find the weak and prey on them, again especially the girls. He became the terror of the freshmen.

Tony never got involved in any of the extracurricular activities at Steinmetz. He had no discipline and he thought sports were dumb. Steinmetz had a fine debating team and a theatrical group but Tony never gave such activities a passing thought. That stuff was not for him either.

Neither were studies. It wasn't long into his sophomore year that Tony dropped out. He would never again in his life open a serious book.

Now Tony sought the company of other dropouts in the neighborhood. One was Joey Hansen. Another was Frank Cullotta. They were of the same stripe, dropouts with too much time on their hands.

For a couple of years, Tony had been engaged in petty crimes like shoplifting and purse-snatching. Several elderly ladies in the neighborhood had been robbed by the young tough. Some of the young girls had been accosted but none ever filed a rape complaint with the police. More and more of the neighborhood parents warned their young children—boys and girls alike—to beware of that young Spilotro.

But it wouldn't be long before Tony got caught. On January 11, 1955, at the age of sixteen, Tony suffered his first arrest—the first of dozens. He had gone into a store in River Forest, a ritzy suburb just west of Chicago, and attempted to steal a shirt. He was apprehended and arrested for larceny. The lenient Judge Salter, not knowing what monster his benevolence would help to create, fined him ten dollars and put him on probation.

Other arrests in Chicago and such suburbs as Oak Park and Evanston would follow. Soon the officers of the 16th District of the Chicago PD would pick him up on sight—for "investigation." During the Fifties this was a common practice for Chicago cops. When they spotted an antisocial young punk just hanging around the neighborhood, they threw him into their squad car. Sometimes they cuffed him around in the car and let him go. Sometimes they took him to the squad room and did it. Rarely did they book him. As Bill Duffy, the great former Deputy Superintendent of the Chicago PD would say: "We got him for mopery." Mopery was a catchall for the cops. Any suspicious guy could be hauled in under that charge. Even "intent to mope" was sufficient. No one ever went to court for mopery but some received a bloody nose and bruised ribs for it. And even more than that for resisting a street arrest for mopery.

By the end of the Fifties, Tony had been arrested thirteen

times on the record, not counting the dozens of times he had
been picked up for mopery. His crimes included possession of
burglary tools and larceny, but mostly "investigation." The famous team of Hanhardt and Hinchy even pinched him a couple times. They were legendary Chicago cops. No burglar or
thief was safe from them. That they made Tony one of their
targets is significant; they didn't waste their time on punks.
Even though he was a youngster, Hanhardt and Hinchy realized this was one bad dude. They attempted to deal with him
in a significant manner long before he achieved notoriety. Bill
Hanhardt would also pinch Frank Cullotta and other future associates of Spilotro, trying to cure them before they graduated
to bigger and worse things.

These were the formative years for young Tony Spilotro.
This was his education. From a grade and high school bully to
a common, petty thief. Until he attained the stature where, on
sight, experienced cops would bring him in for mopery. In
Tony's culture that was real status, something to brag about.
"Those bigtime cops, they know who I am," he would boast.
"They worry about me. They don't waste their time on
punks." Thanks to Hanhardt and Hinchy, Tony had neighborhood bragging rights. He had become a top moper.

2 Mad Sam

He was the worst torture-murderer in our history. Not
only in Chicago but anywhere.

If Tony Spilotro, the kid, was a sadistic bully, then this guy
was a grand master. He would as soon stick you in the balls
or throat with his ice pick as carry on a conversation with you.

Sam DeStefano was known to one and all as Mad Sam. He

was just that. He was demented. Sam lived with his attractive wife, Anita, and their three children, a boy and two girls who were twins, in a nice, expensive house on Sayre Avenue in a tree-lined, upper-middle-class neighborhood on the far west side. The family lived upstairs while downstairs, in the basement, Sam had built a torture chamber. All kinds of horrors took place there. If only their nice neighbors could have heard the screams that echoed in that basement!

Although it was a nicer neighborhood than Tony's, it wasn't far away, just about ten blocks. So it was only natural that the reputation of Mad Sam was known to Tony Spilotro. And since Sam was always on the lookout for young recruits, to assist him in his business, it wasn't long before young Tony came to Mad Sam's attention in the very early Sixties.

Sam DeStefano grew up downstate but his family moved to Chicago when Sam was a teenager. He quickly came to the attention of the leaders of the 42 Gang, the gang of young toughs in The Patch. Early on he was arrested for a gang rape and for many other things just as young Tony would be years later. Except that Sam served some time in prison while Tony did not. Society had changed in the years between the youth of DeStefano and that of Spilotro. Crimes that merited jail in the Thirties and Forties no longer did in the Fifties and Sixties.

When members of the 42 Gang graduated from minor crimes they ordinarily became "made," inducted into the Chicago family of La Cosa Nostra, the Outfit. Such was the path of Sam Giancana, Sam Battaglia and Phil Alderisio, all of whom in turn would eventually become the absolute boss of the Chicago LCN. Others, like Marshall Caifano, would go on to serve in other places.

But Sam did not climb up the mob ladder. He was too undisciplined. The guy was nuts, too uncontrollable even for the Outfit.

However, DeStefano had come to the attention of some of the elder statesmen of the mob, such as Tony Accardo, aka Joe Batters, and Paul "The Waiter" Ricca. Ricca took a particular shine to Sam. First he got him a payroll job. A payroll job in Chicago jargon is a job on the city payroll where one is excused from any real labor. In fact, if the recipient shows up at all to sign in on any given day the city is ahead of the game. Sam's was a ghost job with the Streets and Sanitation Department through the auspices of the regular Democratic organization of the First Ward of the City of Chicago. I have testified before the U.S. Senate Permanent Subcommittee on Investigations that that organization has been for decades the conduit for the orders of the leaders of the Chicago mob to those public officials who are "on the pad," who are corrupted to provide favorable treatment for the mob. Since Ricca was firmly in a position to dispense orders to the functionaries under his control in the First Ward, it was easy to find something for Sam DeStefano.

Sam held this job for many years until that era's ace newspaper reporter, Sandy Smith of the *Tribune*, exposed him and caused Streets and Sanitation to fire him due to the bad publicity. Sadly, this tradition has continued. As late as 1993, a payroller from the same department was found to be chauffeuring mob boss Joe Lombardo around town during the employee's so-called working hours.

Getting caught made little difference to Sam, except that suddenly he had no cover when he filed his income tax returns.

The reason it didn't make much difference is that Sam had been given another concession by Ricca and Accardo, one large enough to support his manner of living. He got the authority from them to put money on the street. To be a juice man. In New York they call it loan-sharking. Shakespeare called it shylocking. In Chicago they call it juice and in order to put money out on the street you had to be cleared by the Outfit.

Sam, like other juicemen, put his money on the street "six-for-five." Each week a borrower had to make payments on his loan, six dollars for every five he borrowed. Let's say you are a well-known burglar and thief but not one of the best. You have trouble supporting your wife and kids with what you can steal. You are frequently between scores. You decide to go to a "shy," a shylock, a loan-shark, a juice man. At first, since you have some type of credit with them, you go to an Outfit guy. But soon you fall behind in your payments and lose that credit. Now you have just one guy to turn to. One guy who will take you on as a client. That guy is Sam DeStefano. It's well known that he will loan money to just about anybody. But it's also well known that he is ruthless. You'd better pay the "vig," the vigorish or interest, every week, right on time, or you'll wind up down in his basement. And that is a fate that shouldn't befall anybody—bad thief or altar boy.

Suppose you borrow $10,000 from Mad Sam. Like most thieves, you feel sure the next big score is just around the corner and that when the vig falls due in one week you'll have enough to at least pay that much, if not the whole $12,000. Because that's what you'll owe if you borrow $10,000 at six-for-five. At minimum, you'll have to pay $2,000 vig every week, come hell or high water. Even if you pay off $9,999, you've got to pay the full vig of $2,000 per week on a $10,000 loan. If you don't, one of Sam's collectors will come after you and haul you into the basement. There you will meet a gleeful Sam DeStefano with his infamous ice pick and a couple of other guys to hold you while he applies it to the most sensitive parts of your body.

Most of those on juice loans were high risk. If they weren't they'd go to a legitimate lending institution like a bank or savings and loan. But some businessmen and most thieves and burglars had no credit. They lived from sale to sale or from score to score. Most of those people went to Outfit juicemen. Most wouldn't go near Sam DeStefano even if their lives depended on it. But some were so desperate, such high risks, that the other juicemen in Chicago would not touch them, would not lend them as much as a quarter.

But Sam DeStefano would. He welcomed those highest of risks because he knew they probably *wouldn't* pay on time. Then he could have his men haul them into his basement every week and go to work on them with his ice pick. This is what Mad Sam lived for.

I had joined the FBI in 1950 after obtaining a law degree. Initially stationed in field offices in Baltimore, New Haven and New York City, I was assigned to Chicago in 1954. Those were years before the Bureau actively investigated organized crime. J. Edgar Hoover did not think the Bureau had jurisdiction because he did not recognize that there was any participation across state lines; for instance, involvement of the mob in New York with the mob in Chicago. Since interstate character is what gives federal law enforcement its jurisdiction, Mr. Hoover, justifiably in my opinion, did not send his troops into the battle against the local mobs, except on rare occasions when some mobsters became involved in federal crimes, such as the acid attack on Victor Reisel, the syndicated columnist whose columns were published in scores of newspapers around the country.

However, in November 1957, eighty leaders of organized crime from all around the country, from California to Boston, from New Orleans to Buffalo, convened to confer with each other in Apalachin, a small village in western New York state. They were discovered by a sergeant on the New York State Police, identified, and rounded up. The press raised a hue and cry. Public hearings were scheduled. Hoover now found the evidence he needed to initiate an investigation, officially, of organized crime, of the mobs. He sent out a directive to all FBI field offices on November 27, 1957 entitled The Top Hoodlum Program. It instructed each field office to target the top ten "hoodlums" in each territory and to determine whether they were engaging in criminal activity within the jurisdiction of the FBI. Hoover assigned me to the Program in Chicago. During my years with the FBI, I had had some success in planting bugs—microphones—inside the meeting places of members of the Communist Party. Investigation of Communism was the highest priority of Mr. Hoover during most of the Fifties. Now his highest priority would gradually shift from Communist investigations, as we won that battle, to the investigation of Organized Crime.

In 1959, I was perhaps the youngest agent on Criminal Squad Number One in the Chicago office, the major case criminal squad known as C-1. We handled all the major criminal cases along with the Top Hoodlum Program. All bank robberies, extortions, kidnappings and other major federal crimes within the jurisdiction of the FBI were assigned to C-1. It was a real honor to be assigned there.

Richard B. Ogilvie, who would later become the governor of Illinois, was then the chief of the Midwest region of the Attorney General's Division of Organized Crime. He was investigating the mob's involvement in the nightclub business in Chicago. He subpoenaed several nightclub owners to testify. One, named Arthur Adler, was the owner of a club in the Rush Street area of Chicago, then the major nightlife district. Shortly thereafter, Artie disappeared. Now, ordinarily we wouldn't investigate the disappearance of a local citizen. Lacking some evidence of a kidnapping, that would not be considered a federal crime. But Adler had been a federal witness and his disappearance might constitute obstruction of justice and give us jurisdiction.

The case was assigned to me. I soon found out that Adler had been on juice to somebody named Sam DeStefano. I had little idea of who this guy was. But all other logical leads had evaporated by the time the body of Adler was found naked in a sewer near North and Harlem on the far west side. (I found out later that Adler's death had been, technically, an accident. He had been hauled into Sam's basement, stripped naked and gouged with Sam's ever-present ice pick. But right in the middle of the torture he had suffered a heart attack and died. "Take him out of here," Sam ordered his underlings. "Find a sewer and throw him in." (That's what they did, just a few blocks from the 1600 block of North Sayre where Sam lived. It was the dead of winter so the icy cold preserved the body for weeks. But when the spring thaw arrived and the water began to flow, the sewer blocked up. Streets and Sanitation was called by the neighbors and Artie's bloated body was discovered.)

A fellow squad member and I went to have a talk with Mad Sam. We found him at home, not in his basement but on the first floor. Eventually, I hit him with the accusation. Did he kill Artie Adler? Sam called his wife, Anita, his three kids and two of their teenage guests into the family room. Calmly he explained to them just who we were, "agents of the Fed-er-al Bureau of In-ves-ti-ga-tion! They have come to accuse me of killing Arthur Adler." I remember that he paused for ten or twelve seconds as he looked each of his family members and their guests in the eyes. Then he very calmly walked over to them. And immediately lost his calm. He exploded! "If I killed Arthur Adler then let God above come down! Right now! And put cancer in the eyeballs of you and you and you and you and you!" He actually began to foam at the mouth as he stuck his finger into the face of each of them. Soon we departed. We guessed that Sam expected us to believe that he would not call the wrath of God on his wife, kids and their guests if in fact he was guilty. That was my introduction to Mad Sam DeStefano.

I had about a dozen more meetings with him. I decided, after I had done some more checking on Sam, that he might be so off the wall he might serve as a good source on such people as Accardo and Ricca and even the guys he palled with in the 42 Gang who were now top leaders of the Outfit. I would usually arrive at his house around nine in the morning. He would still be sleeping, but Anita would rouse him and he would come downstairs, always in his pajamas with his fly open, with his penis fully exposed. Anita would serve breakfast and coffee and we would talk, usually winding up again in the family room, which was fully mirrored on each wall so that as Sam talked he could walk around the room admiring his tallywacker. Before I got somewhat used to it, I remarked to Anita that her coffee had a very distinctive taste. Sam explained that the flavor was produced by the Italian coffee beans with which Anita brewed the coffee.

On a couple of occasions, sometimes as I arrived but usually as I was departing, I noticed a young lad either hanging around the street or in a car parked near Sam's house. I didn't recognize this young fellow and paid little attention to him.

After a dozen or so such visits to Mad Sam's house, which were somewhat productive since Sam was most voluble and somewhat indiscreet in discussing his associates, I got a call from Bill Duffy, a close friend and the Deputy Superintendent of the Chicago Police Department, the department's top authority on organized crime.

"Bill," he asked me, "have you been going out to Sam DeStefano's house?"

"Why?" I said.

"Well, you dummy, he's been pissing in your coffee!"

Italian coffee beans, my rear end! I decided to end my visits to the home of Mad Sam. To this day I can't drink coffee. I have a mental block, even if Jeannie makes it for me. Perhaps Sam did me a favor.

I saw Mad Sam only once more after that. Several years later I was coaching a team of college baseball players, All-Stars home for the summer, playing in the Northern Illinois Collegiate League. My son, Bob, who was captain of the Notre Dame team and who would soon sign with the Pittsburgh Pirates, was the catcher. We were playing an exhibition game at the Illinois State Penitentiary, Stateville, in Joliet. I was in my baseball uniform, coaching third base. All of a sudden a cry went out, in a deep, guttural voice. "Fuck the FBI! Fuck J. Edgar Hoover! Fuck Mr. Roemer!" I recognized the voice immediately. I turned. There staring down at me from the grandstand was Sam DeStefano. Soon the entire inmate population took up the chant. The guards had to run up into the stands with their night sticks to calm them down.

I don't believe Tony was involved in the death of Arthur Adler. He had only just begun working for Mad Sam and wasn't yet important enough to be implicated. But this was the kind of behavior Mad Sam was known for, and Tony actively tried to be a part of it. Mad Sam was the role model he chose for himself—one who couldn't have been more different from his father.

3 Tony's Honeymoon

Tony had already become a top moper. Soon he was on his way to becoming a Top Jewel Thief. The Top Jewel Thief Program of the FBI was targeted, as the name implies, at the major thieves and burglars. In Chicago this program was assigned, not to us on C-1, but to the agents who worked under Supervisory Agent Kenny Grant on Criminal Squad Number Two, known as C-2. This is how it came about.

Agostino's was a very nice restaurant just off Rush Street. It was a hangout for many of the mid-level mobsters and many top thieves and burglars in Chicago. One of the favorite waitresses of its patrons was a pretty but slight girl of twenty-two named Nancy Stuart. Tony needed short girls to date since, at just over five foot five, he was very short himself. Just over five feet, Nancy fit the bill. A good match for Tony.

Nancy wasn't Tony's first girl but the attraction soon grew to love and on January 15, 1960 they were married at Tony's parish, St. John Bosco. Even though he never went to mass there, it was Tony's parish church because it covered the area in which he lived. It was a tradition in the parish for the Spilotros to be married there—Vincent, Victor and Pat had already done so.

Then Tony and Nancy took a delayed honeymoon in Europe. They went with John Cook and his wife, Marianne. Cook was already designated a Top Jewel Thief by Grant and his guys.

The Spilotros and Cooks rented a Mercedes-Benz when they arrived in Antwerp, Belgium, the diamond capital of Europe. Unknown to Spilotro and Cook, Interpol had been alerted by C-2 when Cook, under constant surveillance by C-2, had applied for a passport. When the pair got to Belgium, Interpol was right with them. They alerted the Belgium gendarmes and when the pair was spotted casing jewelry stores, the police moved in and arrested them. In their possession the police found all kinds of burglary tools including passkeys and crowbars. No charges were filed but the foursome was ordered out of Belgium. What a way to start a honeymoon!

As they progressed through Switzerland and into Monaco, Interpol was tracking them, albeit unknown to Tony and John Cook. Then in Paris, Interpol swooped down once again. This time they found a couple of dozen lock-picks on Tony.

Tony, Nancy, John and Marianne decided at this point that the honeymoon was over. They flew back to O'Hare Airport in Chicago, but on the way made another side trip to Monaco, thereby temporarily losing Interpol.

By the time they arrived at O'Hare, Interpol had them once again under surveillance and had alerted U.S. Customs. Their baggage was searched, and, lo and behold, loads of the most expensive diamonds were found, including two that Tony had sewn into his wallet. More lock-picks and other burglary tools were also confiscated from the honeymooners and their friends.

Months later Tony and John were convicted *in absentia* in Monaco for the theft of jewels from a major jewelry store. The sojourn there had been profitable—at least for a couple of days. Both were sentenced to three years—should they ever show their faces in Monaco again. They were also sentenced on charges that they had stolen some $200,000 from the Monaco hotel room of a wealthy matron who was visiting from New York with her young boyfriend, a male "model." Very embarrassing for her—and for Tony and John when they were convicted.

Although those of us on C-1 hadn't done much to impede the progress of Tony Spilotro as he upgraded his status from Top Moper to Top Jewel Thief, the agents on C-2 were very much aware of just who he was.

* * *

Tony was about to get more attention from C-1, however, and the connection would be Mad Sam.

I may have given up on my plan to convert Sam as a source, but I was still looking for someone else and decided to develop as a PCI, a potential criminal informant, someone who was close to him. Each FBI agent is judged on his PCIs, his CIs and especially his CTEs—Top Echelon Criminal Informants, those highly placed in the mob and fully developed as reliable informants. I had learned that a guy I will call Rudy was a juice collector for Sam. Rudy had run off with some of his collections but had been located in Milwaukee and brought back to Chicago in the trunk of a car. He had been taken to the upstairs room of a restaurant in Cicero called Mario's, operated by and named after Sam's kid brother. There he had been stripped naked and handcuffed to a hot radiator. Sam then called Rudy's mother and father, wife and children. "Rudy has returned to us," he told them, "and I am throwing a party for him Saturday night at Mario's. You are invited." When they arrived, Rudy was still upstairs, naked, cuffed to the hot radiator. But when the meal was over, down he was dragged, still naked, smelling badly from his burned flesh. He was thrown at the feet of his parents, his wife and children. Then Sam made them all urinate on him! That would serve Rudy!

Thinking that Rudy might well have the motivation to become a PCI and inform on Sam, I stopped at his apartment one morning. But his wife informed me that he had already departed. He'd be back the next day. I'd be there, I told Rudy's wife.

However, the next day Ross Spencer, my supervisor, called a hastily arranged squad conference, requiring the presence of all C-1 agents. I was included and I had to postpone my plan to interview Rudy.

Agents are not to be disturbed during squad conferences except for the most important reasons. But in the middle of the conference, Phyllis Barton, the C-1 secretary, hurried into the room.

"Mr. Roemer," she said, very embarrassed, "there is a man

on the phone who is screaming at me that I must get you, that it is very important. I know it's very unusual, but would you take this call?"

I took it. Right in the squad room with twenty or so other C-1 agents listening to my end of the conversation. This is what I heard:

"You got no guts, Mr. Roemer! You're a dirty coward, Mr. Roemer!"

I immediately recognized the voice. It was Mad Sam! He went on. "You were supposed to come out to Rudy's house this morning, weren't you, Mr. Roemer. But you didn't show, did you, Mr. Roemer! You're a fucking coward, Mr. Roemer! You suspected I might be here, didn't you, Mr. Roemer! And you were right. I was there, Mr. Roemer! And I had Tony Spilotro and Leo Foreman with me, Mr. Roemer! But you didn't show, did you, Mr. Roemer, you got no guts, Mr. Roemer!"

I lost my cool. "Where will you be in one hour, Sam?" I asked. He replied he'd be at home. "OK," I said, "I'll be there. And, Sam, then we'll find out who the best man in Chicago is!" Sam told me at one of our coffee klatches at his home that he was the best man in Chicago with a gun, that he had once challenged an "Outfit guy" to "go belly to belly, gun to gun" with him on Cicero Avenue to "find out who the best man in Chicago is." I challenged him now so that we'd find out who the best man in Chicago really was.

Much to the dismay of Ross Spencer and my fellow C-1 members, I threw down the phone, checked my gun and prepared to leave the office. But now Phyllis Barton came running again.

"Now there's a lady on the phone, Mr. Roemer! She's almost hysterical. She says it's a matter of life or death that she talk to you!"

I picked up the phone. It was Anita. "Please, Mr. Roemer, don't come out here. He means it. He will kill you. Then he'll be in big trouble."

He'd kill me and then *he* would be in big trouble! I thought for a second or two. "OK, Anita, I won't come. But on one condition. You must tell him I'm not coming because I'm letting him hide behind his wife's skirts!"

But I had been alerted that there was someone named Tony Spilotro out there someplace. And that if he was a henchman of Mad Sam DeStefano he was somebody I should be on the lookout for. In fact, on the morning of Sam's call to me, I suggested to Ross Spencer that we ought to open up a 92 case on this guy Tony Spilotro and find out how he fit in. A 92 case is an intelligence-type case calling for investigation to find out just who a person is and what he might be involved in. If merited, then a more substantive type case is opened, such as a RICO case, an Interstate Travel in Air of Racketeering case or any other investigation that might be warranted. Spencer agreed with me. The 92 case was opened.

When this was done, C-2's Top Jewel Thief investigation of Tony Spilotro would be superseded by C-1's Case Number 92-2563, our Anti-Racketeering case. C-2 would continue their investigative interest in Tony, but with not nearly the attention and manpower that C-1 would assign to him.

Tony Spilotro had come to the attention of the FBI. Little did we know then, as a new decade was beginning, just how much investigative interest we would have in this guy during the next twenty years. And not only in Chicago.

4 Mayhem With Mad Sam

As the new decade of the Sixties dawned, Tony joined Mad Sam. DeStefano had learned of Tony's reputation as a young slugger, as a top moper and as a Top Jewel Thief. It was a marriage made in hell, the elder of the church of torture with the young acolyte. Sam needed a crew of collectors, a band of toughs who would use muscle to collect what was owed. That was the easy part.

During his first couple of years with Mad Sam, most of Tony's responsibilities were fairly simple ones. Sure, there was some rough stuff once in a while. There were a few debtors who didn't pay up on time. In such cases it was often Tony who grabbed them by the scruff of the neck with one hand while the other held a gun and hauled them into Sam's basement where he joined in on the fun. And Sam had frequent fun during this time, though some cases were more noteworthy than others.

I'm not sure whether Tony was involved in one of the most famous of all Chicago mob killings, which occurred in 1961. The reason it was very possible that Tony was involved was that Sam got credit in some responsible quarters of law enforcement and the media for the deed. I'll tell you up front, however, that I don't believe either Sam or Tony was involved, but since so many think so, let me tell you about it.

William "Action" Jackson was a mob juice collector. I don't think he worked all that much for DeStefano, but he did do *some* business for him. I understood that Action worked for Willie "Potatoes" Daddano, a mob capo who had some money on the street although that was not his main function in the mob. In any event, I grabbed Action Jackson one day, probably in 1960, on a street corner, Roosevelt and Ashland as I recall. I tried to get Action to sit down with me by inviting him to lunch, a practice I used frequently in those days, attempting to develop Action as a PCI. But Jackson resisted my attempt. He wouldn't go anyplace with me and he was most reserved, not abusive, but he made no bones that he did not want to be seen with me anyplace, at any time. That was the end of it. Or so I thought.

But then a couple of other ace agents on C-1, Denny Shanahan and Johnny Roberts I believe, developed another PCI, a bartender in a joint frequented by many soldiers in the Outfit and by thieves and burglars. Action Jackson was one of the most frequent visitors to this bar. He said some things to the PCI, some indiscreet things, things that only Action Jackson would know, about his activity on behalf of the mob.

Now when an informant gives us information, we protect that source. We don't handle the information in any way so that it might splash back on the informant, to compromise him. That is the cardinal rule with us. We never use the information to make a case if in doing so the informant might be identified. That is a given in the FBI. Once in a blue moon we screw up, but never on purpose, and never have I been guilty of that. But here the information didn't come from Action Jackson. He had rebuffed my effort to "make" him, to develop him. But apparently we used the information which had originated from him, through his bartender, the real PCI, in such a way that when it came to the attention of the Outfit, it splashed back on Action.

Whoever it was, they grabbed Action and took him to a meat-rendering plant on the south side. There they hoisted his three-hundred-pound body onto a meat hook. They smashed the meat hook through his rectum and tied him there so he wouldn't fall off. While he was in excruciating pain, they went further. They beat him in the kneecaps with a hammer. Nice. Now they questioned him. Was he a snitch for Roemer? Was he a stool pigeon? Was he a rat?

Action couldn't comply with their demands because he *wasn't* an informant. He couldn't admit he snitched to Roemer because he hadn't. But the torturers weren't satisfied. They now went further. They applied a cattle prod to his penis. They juiced it up and when Jackson screamed and screamed in the greatest pain from all that these men were doing to his body, they went further. They poured water on the cattle prod, causing even more of an electric shock. This did it. Action Jackson passed out, never again to regain consciousness. They left him on the meat hook for three more days until he expired. He was then "trunk music," in the parlance of the mob. He was thrown into the trunk of his Cadillac, driven to lower Wacker Drive in the Loop and left until the stench of his decomposing body alerted the public.

Years later we would put a hidden mike into the headquarters of a hit crew from Chicago that was in Miami to kill a labor leader there. They would discuss the Action Jackson murder and in doing so it appeared to us that they were taking credit for it. However, as I say, many qualified people in Chicago attribute it to Mad Sam DeStefano. We'll probably never know for certain.

I recall that one of the matters I discussed with Sam on one of my frequent visits to his home was the brutal murders of Billy McCarthy and Jimmy Miraglia. The bodies of these twenty-four-year-old burglars were found on May 15, 1962 in the trunk of a car on the southwest side of Chicago, badly beaten with their throats slit from ear to ear. The car had been parked on 55th Street for two weeks before neighbors complained of the stench emanating from the trunk and called Streets and Sanitation. I recall the situation came up because Sam told me that the coppers had been to his house to question him about the killings, the word being that McCarthy and Miraglia had been on juice to him. The newspapers were calling the murders the M & M Murders.

Actually, Sam *had* been involved. And even more so had Tony. Here's what happened, as we would learn many years later when one of those involved would testify in court. McCarthy and Miraglia had attempted to rob three legitimate businessmen in Elmwood Park, a suburb located just across Harlem Avenue, the dividing line between Chicago and the suburbs at North Avenue. When the businessmen resisted, M & M killed them. In Elmwood Park. Now every thief in Chicago knew that Elmwood Park and River Forest were off-limits in those days because so many of the top leaders of the Outfit lived there. The mob ordered that those two bedroom communities of Chicago were to be kept clean so that the police could not swoop down on the mobsters in their homes and embarrass them in front of the neighbors and their kids. So when M & M did their thing in Elmwood Park they were in big trouble.

The mob learned quickly that M & M were on juice to Sam. How easy it would be to have one of Sam's collectors grab

them for the Outfit and bring the two to them. Sam assigned
the job to Tony.

Now at that time, the two hitters for the Outfit were Felix
"Milwaukee Phil" Alderisio and Chuckie Nicoletti. They handled the "heavy stuff" for the mob. Anybody who got bollixed
up with the mob in any way had to pay for it by being beaten
or killed, usually the latter, by Alderisio and Nicoletti.

On the evening before Jimmy Miraglia disappeared, May 2,
1962, police from the old Racine Avenue district came across
Alderisio and Nicoletti at 1750 West Superior on the west side.
They were sitting in a late model Ford and it later became evident that they were casing the job. After they failed to re-
spond adequately when questioned, they were arrested and the
Ford was impounded. On inspection, it was found to have
been outfitted with hidden gun compartments and an array of
electrical gadgets and switches, all of which made the police
well aware they were looking at the classic mob work car. It
was reinforced on the sides with extra metal and equipped
with extra shocks and bulletproof windows. The license plates
were made to flip up to avoid observation. And the engine was
souped up.

Alderisio and Nicoletti were released from police custody
the next day, charged only with fictitious registration of the
Ford, which was found to be registered to a vacant lot.

Tony found Billy McCarthy quickly, but couldn't locate
Jimmy Miraglia. So Tony, Sam and the Outfit heavy guys tortured Billy. They put Billy's head in a vise and squeezed it.
Tighter and tighter, all the time cursing him while he refused
to give up the whereabouts of Jimmy. Finally one of his eyes
popped out from the pressure. It was only then that he gave up
Jimmy. Then they slit Billy's throat.

They soon located Jimmy. No need to torture him despite
the protestations of Mad Sam who wanted more fun. As another of Sam's collectors would tell us years later, Sam actually drooled, foam flowed from his mouth and he flew into
ecstasy when torturing somebody. But Jimmy was killed
quickly, his throat slit from ear to ear. I don't know who actually performed those deeds on the M & M boys, whether it

was Sam, Philly, Chuckie or Tony. All were involved but I never have learned who actually twisted the knife.

In any event, Tony had now gotten his feet wet. He had "made his bones," he had come to the attention of real Outfit guys, real heavy guys in the Chicago family of La Cosa Nostra. They didn't get any "heavier" than Milwaukee Phil Alderisio and Chuckie Nicoletti. Tell me about it!

Tony had served a long apprenticeship. He had not only come to the attention of the mob hit men, but had performed with them. Very creditably, in their eyes. It was time to move up. Time to leave one mentor for another, this one much more highly placed than Mad Sam.

5 Milwaukee Phil

Without question, the two deadliest shooters in the history of the Chicago Outfit were Felix "Milwaukee Phil" Alderisio, known as Philly to his confederates, and Chuckie Nicoletti. In the late Fifties and throughout the Sixties, they were the guys who performed the contracts sanctioned by the mob bosses of the day, particularly Sam Giancana.

Philly had spent some of his youth in Milwaukee, hence his nickname. He was one bad-ass. Not a particularly big guy, about five-ten, and not much of a face-to-face fighter, but he had no compunction about coming up behind a victim and giving him a shot in the back of the head. Or suddenly showing up in front of him and blowing his head off with a shotgun. A real nice guy.

I never got to know Philly real well. I ran into him from time to time, usually when he would make me on a surveillance and a couple of times at the Tradewinds, the nightclub on Rush Street where he hung out with his close pals, Marshall Caifano and Obbie Frabotta, with whom he shared a piece of the place in the name of their front, Steve Kosta.

We would bump into each other near the Tradewinds which, by a strange coincidence, shared a common wall with Jim Saine's Restaurant, an FBI hangout, right north of it. Across the street on one side of the Tradewinds, incongruously, was the Quigley North Preparatory Seminary, the school for young men studying for the priesthood. So going north you went from the sublime to the ridiculous to the superior.

When the Top Hoodlum Program was initiated, none of us, of course, were known by sight or name to the mobsters we targeted. But the Tradewinds, being the hangout of so many of the mobsters, became one of the very first places we placed under surveillance. One of my partners, Ralph Hill, set up at the Tradewinds at least a couple of nights a week. Ralph loved the nightlife and the women, the wine and roses. He was just the kind of agent we needed as we initiated the Program, and he reveled in his assignments. He was the guy who introduced us all to Jim Saine, and we frequently used Saine's as our jumping-off spot and our retreat on Rush Street. The place is now called Luciano's and the old Tradewinds is now a bank. Quigley Seminary is still functioning at the same location. Thank God!

But soon the mobsters who hung out in the Tradewinds got to know the three of us who tailed them. Hill, Marshall Rutland and I were then the three musketeers. We worked closely together. Hill had Giancana and Caifano assigned to him, I had Murray "The Camel" Humphreys and Gussie Alex, while Rutland had Frank "Strongy" Ferraro, the mob underboss, their *sotto capo*, the number two man in the Outfit. About once a week I would conclude my day by spending three or four hours up until midnight assisting Ralph on the fisur, the physical surveillance, at the Tradewinds. And Alderisio was more often than not our top target. In those days, we had nothing much better to do than fisur. It wasn't until July 1959 that we put our first bug in and then a whole new world opened up for us as we were able to listen—almost minute by minute—to what the top echelon of the Outfit was planning. We were inside the skin of the mobsters and fisurs became obsolete. Our kindergarten days were over and we had jump-started our sophisticated investigation right over grade school, high school and even college right into post-graduate work.

But in 1957 and 1958, a tail on Philly Alderisio, to see who he was meeting with and who he might be targeting for his next kill, was big stuff for us neophytes. In those salad days, Philly was big stuff to us. Not that he wouldn't always be— just as we graduated, so would he.

I always assumed that it was Philly who harassed my wife and kids. As he and his associates began to know me by sight and name, Jeannie would get a call on the nights when they would make me at the Tradewinds. On some occasions tne caller would ask her who I was fucking that night. On others she would be told that they got me that night and that she would never see me again. Then they started following Bill and Bob, then six and eight, to school. Finally, they attempted to gain entry into our home when they told Jeannie I was changing the insurance policy on our household goods and they needed to appraise them.

So I never had any great love for Philly Alderisio. I felt he had taken it to a personal level and so I had no compunction when discussing him with his colleagues. I described him as a dirty killer, even on one occasion when I discussed him with Tony Accardo. I told Joe Batters that Philly had double-crossed him, going against his orders when handling Bernie Glickman. Glickman was the front for the Chicago mob, the fight manager who managed several world boxing champions such as Sonny Liston and Ernie Terrell, the heavyweight champions, and Virgil Akins, the lightweight king. All this got back to Alderisio. We heard him one time on a hidden mike we had planted in the Armory Lounge, the special headquarters of Sam Giancana when Giancana was the boss of the Outfit. He called me "the G's heavy," which I took as a compliment, I guess. Alderisio complained to Sam that I was spreading "bad things" about him. He felt that "if he's got the goods on me, pinch me, but don't bad-mouth me all over town." I got a kick out of that. He sounded like a little baby whining to his mommy.

The other mob heavy, Chuckie Nicoletti, wasn't my favorite person either. The first time I ever got together with him was about the time he was in his heyday as Alderisio's partner. Vinnie Inserra and I made arrangements with Chuckie to meet at a gas station on the corner of California and Lexington on the mid-west side. Vinnie and I wanted to develop him as a PCI, then hopefully into a CTE.

We arrived as scheduled at about ten in the morning. Chuckie didn't show for about fifteen minutes. He obviously cased the place to observe the lay of the land. But when he arrived he was cordial and suggested we meet him in the Cal-Lex Social Club, down the street on California Avenue. He preceded us and we arrived to find the club warm, obviously prepared for our sit-down on this cold winter day. It was empty except for Chuckie. We talked for a couple of hours, as I recall. He was quite open with us. Told us that he "showed" his income by being carried on the payroll as a salesman at a few suburban car dealers, which he named. We never threw him a hardball question because we didn't want to alienate or anger him. Our objective was to keep the door open for future friendly meetings when we could develop him further. It was a technique I would use frequently and successfully as the years went by. But not with Chuckie. We tried, unsuccessfully, on several occasions to get Chuckie to another sit-down. But he never showed again.

Years later, the mob gunned him down. Not quite his own people, I guess, but obviously with their sanction. Chuckie had gone up to Milwaukee and whacked a mob boss there. Most upset, the man's bodyguard had come into Chicago a few months later and retaliated. Got revenge for his boss. Although we never fully verified that scenario, if true it was unique that one family of the LCN would retaliate in such fashion against another. It was also unique because Milwaukee "belonged" to Chicago. The Milwaukee family of La Cosa Nostra, bossed then by Frank Balistrieri, was subservient to the Chicago LCN.

That is the reason why I say not quite his own people. They were and they weren't.

6 Mob Hits

Almost immediately upon leaving Sam DeStefano and joining Philly Alderisio—really the Alderisio and Nicoletti team—a very significant event occurred in Tony's life. He was "made."

Now, for a guy like Tony, that *is* significant. It meant that he was formally inducted into the Chicago family of La Cosa Nostra. At the time, in the early 1960s, the boss was Sam Giancana. The underboss was Frank "Strongy" Ferraro, whose real name was Sortino. The capos, or captains, were Frankie LaPorte, Ross Prio, Fiore "Fifi" Buccieri, Chuckie Englisi aka Chuckie English, Joe Amato, Willie "Potatoes" Daddano and Jackie Cerone. Butch Blasi, the top aide to Giancana, was equally important although not a capo. Other very important mobsters then were Murray "The Camel" Humphreys, the leader of the connection guys, which we called the corruption squad; Gus Alex, who had the Loop and was a connection guy; Ralph Pierce, who had the south side; and Lenny Patrick, who was about to move from Lawndale with most of his Jewish clientele to Rogers Park. These four were vital cogs in the machinery of the Outfit, but since they were not Italian they could not be made, could not be formal members.

In Chicago, being made is very informal. I remember Blasi talking in front of Mo, our hidden mike in Giancana's headquarters at the Armory Lounge. He talked about his induction. "I was called in by Jimmy Belcastro who had the Patch then.

He told me I was made and put me to work in one of his joints. That's all there was to it."

Chicago is unlike most of the twenty-four families in the LCN in this regard. I remember our field office in Boston put a bug in the headquarters of the Patriarca family there. They actually overheard an entire induction ceremony. First the finger of the inductee was pierced, as was that of his sponsor, an old-time made guy. Then they put a holy card, the card of a Catholic saint, in his palm. They mingled the blood of the inductee with that of his sponsor and then they burned the holy card in the hand of the inductee. They made him repeat a lengthy oath, the infamous oath of *omerta*. He pledged that he would never break the vow of silence, never talk to any outsider about the existence of La Cosa Nostra, never become an informant, never covet the wife or girlfriend of another made guy or his daughter if his intentions were dishonorable and, in general, never do anything against the best interests of the organization he was joining. Otherwise, he was admonished, "you will burn like this card." He was then instructed about various formalities of the LCN such as how to introduce a member to one of a different family. If the person to be introduced was a made guy he was to be introduced as "a friend of ours." If he was not he was "a friend of mine." Then all those assembled, and it seemed like all the made members were present, lined up to give the famous Italian kiss on both cheeks to the new member. It had all the grandeur of a marriage—which, I guess, is what it was. Even with all the kissing.

None of that was done when Tony got made, however. Oh, there were present many of the other three hundred made guys in Chicago. And he was formally introduced to them and it was made known that, with Philly as his sponsor, he was now made. He was now a member of the select circle. A soldier, as the LCN denominated their lowest rank. A great honor for anybody with Tony's background.

As Tony's sponsor, Philly was on the spot. If Tony went bad in any respect, it would be Philly's ass. In fact, in view of

Philly's role in the mob as its hitter, he would be given the contract to whack Tony. If Philly was still alive then.

Although Tony didn't know it then, he had hitched himself to a fast horse. The fastest horse in the paddock, although few realized that in 1963. I sure didn't.

I spent considerable time in the late Fifties and very early Sixties watching Philly. I had some run-ins with him, some personal confrontations—the government's heavy, as he had put it, versus the mob's heavy. But I never had the intelligence in those days to ever suspect that Milwaukee Phil had what it took to become the boss. Sure, he did his jobs well, handled his contracts with ability. But that meant, most of all, that he had the brawn. I did not perceive in those days that he also had the brains. But then I was just a young kid of thirty-three with only a few years under my belt as a specialist on organized crime investigations. In retrospect, all the agents on the Top Hoodlum Program, not just in Chicago but throughout the Bureau, were still wet behind the ears. We were catching up fast now, thanks to Little Al, the mike at mob headquarters which was our only bug then—the only one in the country, in fact—but we were still youngsters in terms of coming to grips with the crime syndicates.

Shortly after Tony began easing away from Mad Sam, but while he was still working for him on a part-time basis, there occurred a rash of gangland slayings in Chicago. I was in constant touch with my informants, with our hidden mikes in mob headquarters and meeting places, and with my fellow agents on C-1. One of these agents in particular had the most suspicions. Duncan Everette was my age, with my experience in the Bureau, but he was a recent arrival on C-1. When Bobby Kennedy had become Attorney General in 1961 he had instructed J. Edgar Hoover to beef up his investigations of organized crime. Hoover had initially assigned ten of us to the Program in Chicago, but then it dwindled to five and we were assigned other investigations besides organized crime. Hence my assignment to the Artie Adler obstruction of justice investigation. Now, however, under RFK's instructions we beefed up the squad, which was renamed the Criminal Intelligence Program, from five agents to seventy! One of the newcomers was Duncan Everette and he was made the case agent on the young Tony Spilotro, who, at the time, was not considered to be a major force in the Chicago mob. But more and more the very capable Dunc Everette began to develop some very interesting information about his subject. He suspected Tony of being very much involved, along with Philly Alderisio and Chuckie Nicoletti, in the murders that were occurring in Chicago.

The first one occurred on February 21, 1963. Ben Lewis was a black alderman representing the 24th Ward on the west side, just south of Tony's stomping ground. On that date his body, shot in the head, was discovered in his headquarters at 3604 W. Roosevelt Road. The 24th Ward in Chicago had long been under the domain of the Outfit, but when the neighborhood turned black, Lewis was elected notwithstanding the efforts of the mob. In an attempt to intimidate Lewis so that he would do their bidding, the mob put extreme pressure on him. It was our perception that they were getting their way but then we learned that although Lewis was allowing the mob their "offices," their wire rooms, their gambling joints and their bookmaking establishments, he was demanding a big piece of the pie, a piece bigger than the Outfit was willing to give him. One thing led to another and when Lewis refused to back off since he was, after all, the alderman, the mob finally made the decision to use on him what I call, euphemistically, the ultimate discipline. According to Dunc, a finger pointed to the Alderisio-Nicoletti hit crew of which Tony was now a major player.

Then Irving Vine was slain. Vine was a bookmaker operating out of the Del Prado Hotel on the mid-south side. He was one of Chicago's most prominent bookmakers, known to many of the gamblers in the city. He had been married to Betty Jeanne Neibert, called Jeanne, who was a cocktail waitress in the Loop. Murray "The Camel" Humphreys fell in love with Jeanne. Although she was about half his age, he divorced Billie, his first wife of about forty years, and married Jeanne. He furnished two lovely homes for her, one on the 51st floor of Marina City—where we installed a bug before they even moved in—and another at 210 Keystone Boulevard in Key Biscayne, Florida, right on Biscayne Bay. It was not a marriage made in heaven. I recall coming to work one morning and playing the tape from what the mike, which we code-named Plumb, had picked up the night before. It seemed that Hump and Jeanne had been out drinking the night before. They returned to their condo and engaged in a loud argument. It got most vociferous. In fact, according to what I heard, Jeanne made every effort to throw her old man, literally, out the window. Over the 51st floor balcony.

Soon Hump got into some difficulty with the IRS. He tried to explain his style of living—two very expensive homes for instance—by claiming to the IRS that Jeanne had money stashed away and she was the source of the wealth. I was developing a net worth and expenditures case on Hump, even though that was the domain of the IRS, not the FBI. But Hump was my subject, I had the assignment card on him, and I was out to get him in any legal way I could.

Irving Vine became a prime target. If he would testify that Jeanne had no money when she left him to marry Hump, it would go a long way toward debunking Hump's story and helping to send him to prison for the second time in his life. Finally, Vine caved in. He would testify. But Hump learned of his cooperation.

On May 6, 1963 a maid at the Del Prado entered his room to clean up as was her daily custom. But Room 507 that day contained a surprise for her. A shock. Because there was Irving Vine's body with his legs taped together, his hands tied behind his back and a bed sheet over his head. He had been strangled. It was an obvious gangland killing and I felt sure I knew the motive.

I sat down with Hump, as I had done many times, and discussed the killing with him. Obviously, I got no response of any positive nature. Hump claimed he had never met Vine. Maybe not. I never believed he had actually carried out the killing himself. That was not his function then. He had

killed—a lot—on his way up while working for Al Capone
and Frank Nitti in the Twenties and Thirties, but by 1963 he
was well beyond that. What I believed he had done was take
his problem to San Giancana, the Outfit boss in 1963. Sam
would have sanctioned the hit of Irving Vine and assigned it
to the crew whose function it was to perform such heavy
work: Alderisio and Nicoletti at the helm, with Spilotro carrying the spear.

Then, in June 1963, Kenny Gordon was killed. Kenny was
a Top Jewel Thief, one of Chicago's very best. I know why he
was killed, but am not free to make it public even at this late
date. Let's just say he was not my informant. On June 7,
Kenny became trunk music. He was then forty-one, at the
peak of his career. He was found shot in the head in an auto-
mobile at 3006 Waterloo Court at three-thirty in the morning.
It was clearly a mob hit and again it seemed likely that the
Alderisio-Nicoletti crew, including Tony, had done the job.

Soon afterward, in June 1963, we decided to make the FBI's
presence more directly known to the man who was the Outfit
boss in Chicago—Sam Giancana. During my years with the
Bureau, I guess I had some fifty personal confrontations with
Giancana. The first time I met him was at O'Hare Airport in
1961, as he was arriving from Phoenix with his mistress, the
lovely Phyllis McGuire of the singing group the McGuire Sis-
ters. We got into a shouting match that day and I wound up
calling a hundred airline passengers over to our little tête-à-tête
and yelling to them that this guy was "Sam Giancana, this
slime, the boss of the underworld here in Chicago, this scum!
You people are lucky, you're passing through Chicago. We
have to live with this jerk!" Nobody, I guess, had ever talked
that way to Sam Giancana, the successor to Al Capone as the
absolute boss of the Chicago LCN. He was infuriated. He
pushed his nose right up into my chest. "Roemer," he shouted,
"you lit a fire tonight that will never go out. We'll get you if
it's the last thing we ever do!"

In 1963 we initiated the lock-step surveillance program. For
six weeks during that summer, I stayed a half-step behind
Giancana and a half-step to his left, shadowing his every

move. The primary rationale for such close surveillance was that it prevented him from meeting with his associates. We had many more sweet words for each other.

You recall that when Sam set up his ambush for me at Rudy's apartment he told me that Tony Spilotro and Leo Foreman were with him. I knew neither at the time, had never heard of them. But that morning C-1 had opened 92 case files on each. We learned that Leo Foreman was another of Sam's juice collectors, a pal of Tony's. Foreman was unusual because he was a Jew, one of the very few involved in such activity. He was into a lot of things in addition. He was a bondsman, just as Tony was, thanks to the auspices of Sam and Judge Richard Austin, who served as Tony's reference when he filled out his application to become a bondsman.

Let me deviate from my story here to tell you about Judge Austin. In the early Fifties, Austin had been an assistant state's attorney, a local prosecutor. A complaint had been made by a mid-level hoodlum that the Chicago police officers assigned to Scotland Yard, the detail designated to investigate the Outfit, had harassed this mobster and had brutalized him in their headquarters on Canalport on the near north side. Austin ran with the complaint. He indicted Joe Morris, the commander of Scotland Yard, Bill Duffy, then just an officer, and a couple of other police officers assigned to Scotland Yard. The trial got very bitter. In fact, while Austin was delivering his final argument, his summation to the jury, somebody in the audience arose and hit him with a stink bomb! Years later, in 1965, Sam Giancana filed a similar complaint against me and my fellow C-1 agents. In federal court. Who do you think the judge was? Right. Richard Austin. In whose favor do you think Judge Austin, in his supreme wisdom, ruled? Right. For Sam Giancana. The same Richard Austin who supplied a favorable reference to Tony Spilotro when Tony applied for a license as a bail bondsman in Chicago.

To return to my story, Leo Foreman was some piece of work. Not only a bondsman but a real estate salesman, an insurance salesman—and a thug working for Mad Sam. But Leo

got on Sam's wrong side. Sam went to Leo's office one morning in November 1963 and began to harangue him. Leo was
nobody's patsy. Even Uncle Sam, as DeStefano insisted that
his underlings call him, didn't intimidate him on this occasion.
He threw Sam out of his office! Wow! But it was just about
Leo's last mistake.

Sam hurried back to Sayre Avenue. He hastily summoned
Tony, Sam's kid brother, Mario, and another of his enforcers,
Chuckie Crimaldi. They plotted to set Leo up.

Tony and Chuckie contacted Leo. They told him that Sam
wanted to meet with him, that Sam was sorry that he had
caused Leo to flare up and that he needed to apologize to Leo
so that they could continue their good working arrangement.
Leo fell for it.

He was lured to the home of Mario DeStefano in Cicero.
They told him Sam would arrive soon. They enjoyed some
coffee and genial conversation. Then Tony excused himself.
He wanted to see Mario's basement. Leo had no desire to see
the basements of any of the DeStefanos. But when Mario informed him that Tony had gone to see the basement because
Mario had recently built a bomb shelter therein, Leo succumbed to his curiosity. Mario and Chuckie showed him the
way down the stairs, following him. When Leo arrived at the
foot of the stairs, there was our friend, Tony. They quickly
grabbed Leo. His screams in the soundproofed basement
would go no further. Now they awaited the arrival of Mad
Sam. But just to take their kicks, they beat Leo a little. To
have him subdued when Sam arrived to apply the coup de
grace. I don't know exactly when, before the appearance of
Sam, or after, but they cut some flesh out of his body, they
beat him with a hammer on his kneecaps, they beat him with
their fists on his head, ribs and crotch and they reduced him
to a blubbering incompetent. I do know that when Mad Sam
arrived he brought with him his infamous ice pick. Oh, how he
loved it! Twenty times he applied that ice pick to the body of
Leo Foreman. As only the master could do. Now Leo was
screaming, "Kill me, Unc, kill me! Please get it over with!
Kill me, Unc!" Finally, Sam did. He pulled out his pistol and

finally ended the life of Leo Foreman. "Throw me out of his office, will he!"

Leo's body was trunk music thereafter—found like so many other bodies were found after the mob had finished with them.

7 Tony Tracks Me and We Track Him

My first contact with Tony Spilotro occurred at this time. I was exercising regularly at the Austin YMCA on Central Avenue on the far west side, not all that far from Tony's boyhood residence. FBI agents were encouraged in the latter stages of J. Edgar Hoover's reign to work out three times a week and were allowed to do so on Bureau time. So it became my regular routine to work out at the Austin YMCA from about nine-thirty to ten-thirty every other morning or so.

I knew that the mob was aware of my routine. How could they not be when Johnny "Bananas" DiBiase, an Outfit member, and some of his people worked out there almost as regularly as I did. He and I both played a great deal of handball in those days and we frequently played in adjoining courts— there were only three of them. We nodded to each other but never talked. However, I knew that he knew who I was because one time when I had a sit-down with Lenny Patrick over a personal problem he was having involving one of his daughters, he initiated the conversation by letting me know that he knew I worked out "every day" at the Austin YMCA.

One day as I came out of the YMCA in late morning I noticed a man sitting in a green Oldsmobile 98 about three-quarters of a block north of where I had parked my Bureau car on Central Avenue. I was always alert for a tail. I never wanted to be followed by the mob for any reason but on this occasion I was on my way to have lunch with my best CTE, a highly placed informant in the Outfit who at the time was supplying me with intimate details of mob activity. I certainly did not want to be observed in his presence—not for my sake, of course, but for his. Any mobster seen talking cordially to me would have a hard time explaining to the mob what that was all about. Especially with his head in a vise or his body impaled on a meat hook. That would be no fun and I took every precaution to prevent such an occurence.

So when I exited the YMCA, I took every precaution from the moment I left the building. Under these circumstances I had no trouble spotting the guy in the green Olds.

Sure enough, when I got into my car and U-turned to go south on Central Avenue back toward the Eisenhower Expressway, so did the guy in the Olds. He was good; he waited until I was about four blocks on my way before he moved, but since I was watching for him he was easy to spot.

This was the first time I was to be tailed from the Austin YMCA. However, quite naturally I had anticipated there might be times when this would happen and I had prepared for it. Located adjacent to the Eisenhower, just north of it and just west of Central Avenue, is Columbus Park. I knew it well because Columbus Park is where Sam Giancana occasionally was chauffeured by his driver-bodyguard-appointment secretary, Butch Blasi, to meet with politicians under his control, on his pad, corrupted. Giancana met with his associates at his headquarters in the Armory Lounge, which he had bugged, but he didn't want politicians coming there since it would be a dead giveaway if they were observed doing so by us. Learning of Sam's fondness for Columbus Park, I had scouted its every nook and cranny and had surveilled Giancana on several occasions when he met with a couple of crooked judges and, on one occasion, with a police captain.

I allowed the guy in the Olds to keep close to me when I turned into Columbus Park. I parked in the lot, observing that he had me in sight but not letting him know I was aware of his presence, and walked into the park. I felt that the guy would almost *have* to follow me on foot. There were only two reasons for him to be following me. One, he wanted to see what I was doing. The mob by this time knew I was developing informants inside. After all, most of the mobsters I made approaches to declined my advance and hurried to inform their superiors of my contact. They sure didn't want to wind up on a meat hook like Action Jackson. Had he quickly notified the mob of my approach to him, Action might still be alive. The other reason for the man to stay with me was that he might be assigned to hit me. What better place to do so than in the woods? So I felt he had to follow me on foot if he was to accomplish either purpose. My advantage was that I knew the park, I had planned for just this contingency, I knew just what I was going to do.

I walked as far into the park as I could. When I got to the most heavily wooded area I hid behind an oak tree and pulled my gun. I did nothing to alert the guy that I was aware of his presence but I assumed that he must be following me a hundred yards or so away. Sure enough, within two minutes I heard his footsteps. He had obviously lost sight of me but knew I had come this way. When he came parallel to me, about twenty feet west, I made my presence known.

I pointed my gun at him and called out, "Looking for me, pal?"

The guy was startled. For a moment he said nothing. Then he snarled, "Just taking a walk. Ain't this a public park?"

I took a good look at the guy. He had on a fedora of the style so popular with the mob at that time. Sam Giancana had taken to wearing this headwear and it seemed most of his minions followed his example. Actually, it was a tip-off. Although many men in those days wore hats—as did all FBI agents under Hoover—those fedoras with short brims were pretty good indicators that a guy we suspected of being a mobster was just that. This guy's was gray. He also wore a gray sweater without a tie underneath, gray slacks and black loafers. All in all, he was a pretty dapper dresser. He was short, very short, but to me he seemed wound tight. Muscular. Not in any way a wimp, but quite the opposite. Nevertheless, I didn't consider him dangerous because of any physical ability since by then I had found out that hardly any mobsters were what you would call great physical specimens. With very few exceptions they were not the kind of people who would take you on, *mano a mano*, look you in the eye and then do their work. The heavy work of a mobster is done on the sneak, when he can come up behind you, unawares, and shoot you in the back of the head or stick a shiv in your back. This was not the wild west where a man would be challenged to a gunfight and the fastest gun would win. There is no honor involved in a mob hit.

I didn't expect that this guy had intended to confront me face-to-face and give me a chance to defend myself—if, in fact, it was his intention to do me harm. Still, I wasn't about to take any chances. It's vital to take control from the start.

I pulled my credentials, showing my photo and my identification as an FBI agent. I very seldom carried my badge unless I knew I'd be talking to an illiterate who could not understand the credentials. Although the guy knew who I was, it was necessary to identify myself officially if I was to demand that he identify himself. What I was hoping for was that the man was armed and that I could then make a citizen's arrest for unlawful possession of a firearm (that not being a federal crime) and haul him into the Austin District police headquarters—for embarrassment, if for nothing else, because it would probably turn out that the gun was registered to him legally.

I was now within two feet of the guy. "Show me something. Who are you?"

"None of your fucking business!" was his sharp reply.

"It is my fucking business, slimeball. I just showed you my credentials. I'm an FBI agent."

"I don't give a shit who you are, asshole, you don't have the right to question me unless you get a warrant."

The guy was well aware of his legal rights. He had a point. But I had not gone this far to be put off now.

"Listen, scum, I don't see a lawyer in the woods here. I'm going to find out who you are and why you're following me before we leave here. One way or another. It's up to you."

I had found out something in my many confrontations with

mobsters. If you got down to their level and called them obscene names, especially the eleven- and twelve-letter names, it didn't seem to faze them. But if you called them slime and scum it seemed to get to them.

The guy didn't say a word at this point. I was six-one and 215 pounds. This guy wasn't even five-six, maybe 135 pounds, a lightweight, maybe 147, a welterweight. But certainly no heavyweight. He was about thirty-five years old, just a few years younger than I was. We were alone in the woods. I had my gun on him. What chance did he have? I had demonstrated to him that I was in good shape; hadn't I just come from my regular workout? But he still held out. It was obvious that I was going to have to take him by force and find his driver's license.

But when I made my move to do so, the guy backed off. I pointed my gun at his head, ready to resist if he went to grab it. FBI agents are taught at the FBI Academy in Quantico, Virginia, never to put a gun up close enough where it can be grabbed and taken. I didn't put it that close. Actually, in view of my physical superiority, or my *perceived* physical advantage, my gun was now a handicap. I wasn't about to use it—I sure couldn't shoot an unarmed person who was committing no crime—and if I put it back in my holster and then got into a wrestling match with the guy he might grab it from me. But I decided putting it back was my best choice. Then I grabbed him by his shirt.

"Listen, scum, I'm gonna find out who you are or we don't leave here. You follow *me*, you take the consequences."

One of my real problems as an FBI agent was to *sound* tough. I looked tough, I guess, and I felt I was. But it has always been my nature not to act tough, it doesn't come easy to me. I'm more of a soft-spoken, easy-natured guy than I am a loudmouth. I was always a little uncomfortable in situations like I was in now. Not because I feared much, but because to be effective I had to put on an act—the act of being a tough guy. I probably never would have made a good cop. Cops have to act tough much of the time. FBI agents get into more sophisticated situations, we don't get down in the muck with offenders nearly as often, due to the different nature of our jobs.

The guy was smart. He kept his mouth shut. But he showed no sign of submitting to my demand. I pulled him up on his toes and looked down on him, almost face-to-face. I grabbed his left arm, which could have been a mistake because it left his strong arm, his right, free. I twisted the arm behind him, forcing my weight onto him. I don't believe he really tried, at that point, to resist. I think he realized it would be futile. He could see and feel my bulk, he probably knew my background as a college boxing champ since most hoods did. I quickly found his wallet. I pulled it out and let the guy go.

In the wallet was his driver's license and some other identification. Anthony John Spilotro. With an address on Maple Avenue in Oak Park, a western suburb. So this was Tony Spilotro! I should have guessed. Now I took a real good look at him. He did look vaguely familiar. Hadn't I seen him somewhere before? Then it hit me. This is the guy I occasionally saw outside the house of Sam DeStefano when I visited there.

I threw the wallet and the driver's license on the ground at Tony's feet.

"So you're Tony Spilotro!" I hissed.

"Yeah," was all he said.

"You were with that slime, DeStefano, at Rudy's house," I said.

"I don't know what you're talking about," Spilotro stated.

"I think you do, Tony."

"I don't even know *who* you're talking about!" Tony spat.

"Ha. I hear you're with Philly now. 'Made.' "

"Who's Philly? What's 'made'?" Spilotro said.

"What was your purpose in tailing me today, Tony?" I asked.

"Who's following you? I'm just taking a walk in the park!"

"Yeah, and I'm here picking daisies. You think I believe that?" I asked.

"I don't give a fuck what you believe!"

I knew it would serve no purpose, but I then gave Tony some earnest advice. "Tony, get out before you get in too deep. You're still a young guy. You've got a bondsman's license. Get legit. That business you're in is no good. You'll wind up in prison or dead. We'll get you or your own people will. You can't win. Years ago, before we got involved, you could. Now you can't. Look at Giancana, Battaglia, Ricca, Infelice, all the guys. They all wind up in prison now. Be smart."

"Yeah, like you, asshole. I see how you live. I seen your house. Big shot! Live in a little dump out there by the steel mills. Big fucking deal. I should be like you, huh?" Tony had a way, I found, of getting under a guy's skin. In view of the problems Jeannie had had with phone calls and the times they followed my children and then came to my house, I was a little sensitive about mob guys talking about seeing my house. Now I began to loose my cool, much as I had with Giancana at O'Hare. I grabbed him once more.

"Listen, punk," I shouted, very loud even though I had my face up tight against his. "If I *ever* see you around my house, I'm coming after you! You understand that! I tried to give you a little advice, I see that was a waste of time. You want to run with those guys, be my guest. But now we've met, Spilotro, I'm not going to forget you! You're on my list now, right up there with Giancana and your pal, Alderisio. I gave you a chance, like I do everybody, but you don't want to listen!"

"Fuck you, asshole!" That was Tony's rejoinder.

At that I pushed him. I didn't strike him. He stumbled back, almost fell. He stared at me. If looks could kill I wouldn't be here to tell the story.

It was then that I coined the name, part of it anyway, that would thereafter stick with him.

"Pissant!" is all I said. "Go!"

Whenever I would talk to my pals in the press afterwards about Tony Spilotro I would refer to him as "that pissant." Sandy Smith of the *Tribune* and Art Petacque of the *Sun-Times* and later John O'Brien of the *Trib* began to use the name "The Ant" when they wrote about Tony. I guess Pissant in those days was not proper for the public press. Soon it became Tony's featured press nickname. Tony "The Ant" Spilotro.

Tony went. I followed him by about twenty feet. He got into his Olds and drove away. I got into my Bureau car and took off on my routine, my meet with my CTE. The first thing I queried him about was his knowledge of Tony Spilotro. Tony wasn't assigned to me, I wasn't the case agent on his investigation, but now he would become a guy in whom I would be very interested. Whenever I talked to one of my informants I would bring up Tony. Then I would go back and sit down with Duncan Everette, the agent who did have the assignment on Tony. I'd fill him in on what I had heard and I'd ask him about what he was learning of Tony.

I mentioned my incident to Dunc and my partners but hardly anybody else. Certainly not in my report. I knew a few agents in other offices who had been transferred for what the Bureau perceived to be their own good when they got too close to a mobster or vice versa. It was for the same reason that I never made a written report of the problems I had with them calling Jeannie and coming to my home. I made it known to my colleagues but I never wanted to go on record with it or take it to the front office. I was in my office of preference, Chicago, close to South Bend, my home town, ninety miles away. I was on the elite squad, C-1, perhaps the most reputable squad in the entire FBI, doing precisely the work I wanted to do. The challenge was just what I was looking for when I joined the FBI. I didn't want to jeopardize all that. Besides, it would sound a little whiny to complain of these guys harassing me. Furthermore, I didn't want my superiors to learn that the mob knew enough of my habits to pick me up and tail me. The Bureau might well decide, even if they didn't transfer me, to assign me to another squad, checking on the background of government applicants perhaps. I sure didn't want that. I was right where I wanted to be.

8 A Violent Decade

There was a slight lull before Al Romano was murdered on March 6, 1964. Romano was the son of Louis Romano, a close pal of Al Capone. He was shot to death in an alley behind 4137 Grenshaw Street. Romano was, among other things, a drug dealer. At the time, that was a real no-no in the Outfit. As long as Tony Accardo was alive and functioning as the *consiglieri*, the real "Man" in the Outfit, the Chicago family of La Cosa Nostra did not allow its members to deal drugs. Although there is some doubt whether Al Romano was actually a made guy, he came from a long line of Outfit people. The mob could not allow anyone to peddle drugs in view of their prohibition against it. So the crew of Alderisio-Nicoletti was assigned the job.

During these years, Dunc learned that Tony's main concession from the Outfit, the one that gave him a fine income, was his "office," his bookmaking establishment. Tony was given a very nice territory on the northwest side of Chicago where a dozen or so bookmakers were under his dominion. In those days, as now, bookmaking was the most lucrative source of income for the Outfit, although at that time their income from Las Vegas rivaled it. There were hundreds of bookmakers in the area controlled by the Chicago mob—from Kankakee on the south to the Wisconsin line on the north and from Lake Michigan on the east out past Aurora on the west. And, of course, the mobs adjacent to them were under the control of Chicago; the Outfit got a big slice of what they were doing.

After twenty arrests for investigation (mopery), for resisting such arrests, for possession of burglary tools, for investigation of robbery and for investigation of burglary, Tony's arrest record under Chicago Police Department IR (Identification Record) Number 13146 showed a big move up.

Tony had been sent to Miami in 1964, shortly after he had joined Alderisio and been made, to work with Frank "Lefty" Rosenthal, a big man in sports betting in south Florida and other areas of the south. Rosenthal was convicted in the Sixties for fixing sporting events such as football and basketball games. His sports betting operation in Florida was one of the largest in the country. Miami is open territory for La Cosa Nostra. Any family can set up down there without any need for permission from any other. Chicago had sent Rosenthal to Miami to conduct its operations there. They sent Tony to assist Lefty, though Tony was always ready to fly back to Chicago or be sent anywhere Alderisio and Nicoletti needed some help with the heavy work.

In 1964, Ralph Hill, my old partner, had requested a transfer to Miami, his home town. Due to his outstanding record in Chicago on C-1, Ralph's request was granted. He soon became the supervisor of the organized crime squad in Miami and the head of its criminal intelligence program. So when Duncan Everette learned that Tony was now in Miami, he quickly telephoned Ralph to let him know. Ralph assigned one of his men to Tony, Weldon Merry as I recall, a fine agent. Merry soon discovered just what Tony was doing down there and alerted the Dade County Sheriff's Office. On May 17, 1984, they went out to talk to Tony, to "roust" him, as they call it. Tony gave them some of the same kind of lip that he gave me. Their authority is such that you don't do that with them. They grabbed him, placed him under arrest for resisting and threw him in the pokey. Now he got his first conviction. He was fined two hundred dollars and spent ninety days in the Dade County Jail in Miami. The conviction was for disorderly conduct as well as resisting arrest. Tony, obviously, was not an immediate success down south.

* * *

On August 31, 1964, one of the major hits in the history of Chicago took place. Guy Mendola was a Top Jewel Thief, one of the major targets of C-2. He was also a bank robber. And an informant for C-2. He robbed a bank with several partners, but within days C-2 solved the case. Thanks to Mendola. But Willie "Potatoes" Daddano was, in those days, the liaison between the Outfit and burglars. No made guy was allowed by the Chicago Outfit to engage in such silly stuff as bank robberies or burglaries and none did. But as a "street tax" any thief or robber who operated in Chicago or from Chicago had to pay a percentage of each score to the Outfit. Daddano was the guy who made sure the mob was not cheated, that the street tax was paid.

Now, probably due to the swiftness with which the FBI had solved the bank robbery, Daddano had his suspicions. He called Dick Cain, whose real name was Ricardo Scalzitti. At the time Dick was the Chief Investigator for the Cook County State's Attorney. But he was also a made guy, a member of the Chicago Outfit assigned to infiltrate law enforcement, first as a member of the Chicago PD and then as a top official of the Cook County Sheriff's Office. He would later become Sam Giancana's closest confidant and associate. He would later become one of my closest friends, a double agent inside the mob keeping me advised of the activity of the members of the Outfit in Chicago and in Las Vegas. I'm getting ahead of my story but he was murdered on December 20, 1973 when two guys, one of them possibly Spilotro and the other probably Joey Lombardo, put a shotgun under his chin at Rose's Sandwich Shop and blew his brains out the top of his head. Rose's Sandwich Shop was then located at Grand and Ogdon Avenues, the same intersection where Patsy Spilotro opened his restaurant so many years earlier.

But to get back to my story, Daddano called Cain since Cain was an accomplished polygraph operator. Daddano wanted all members of the bank robbery gang put on the lie box. Cain was vacationing in Paris at the time so he instructed his underling in the Sheriff's Office, Bill Witsman, to do the job. Witsman fingered Mendola.

The job was assigned to the Alderisio-Nicoletti crew once more. Guy Mendola was killed by shotgun blasts as he parked his car in the garage of his home.

In 1965 the major killing was that of Manny Skar. This one had more than just a suspicion that Tony Spilotro was involved. Skar was a very prominent restauranteur in Chicago. He owned the Sahara on Mannheim Road. He was attacked in the entrance to his residence, a condo at 3800 Lake Shore Drive, by two guys. Shot. I don't know that we ever fully developed a motive for the killing but we assumed it was a mob hit and that it therefore would be assigned to the Alderisio-Nicoletti crew. Then, years later, when a pal of Tony Spilotro would tell us that it was, indeed, Tony who bragged about being the shooter, we knew that our assumption was correct. Tony was never prosecuted for that crime, however.

There's a funny story relating to Skar. Every August during the early Sixties, the College All-Stars played the NFL champions from the previous year at Soldier Field. One day we got a tip that some of the top mobsters from New York were in for the game and that they were staying at the Sahara, Manny Skar's joint. This was right up my partner's alley. Ralph Hill and Johnny Bassett, two of the very best if not *the* best FBI agents of all time, hustled out to the Sahara to locate the mobsters. They spent the night there, casing the dining area and the bar. The next morning I was not available to assist them, but early that afternoon I was summoned into the office of Vince Inserra, the fine supervisor of C-1.

"Bill," he told me, "Ralph and John just called. They have identified those guys out at the Sahara as definitely New York mobsters but haven't pinned down exactly who they are. The mobsters are heading to the Grant Park marina where Manny Skar keeps a yacht, the *Sahara*. Why don't you hustle over there and take a look at these guys and see if you can identify them. Ralph says they're all swarthy, Italian-looking guys but he can't make them except he says they are definitely hoods."

So I hustled over to the yacht club, and quickly spotted the *Sahara*. There on the bow were several guys. I walked by, trying to be inconspicuous but at the same time attempting to get a look at the hoods. As I did, a loud voice from the *Sahara* called out: "Hey, Zip!" Now Zip has been my nickname since eighth grade, but was especially common when I was boxing at Notre Dame. I turned and quickly recognized the caller. He was Russ "Jake" Skall, a former Notre Dame football player and boxer, an old pal. There at his side were the supposed hoods: Alex Karras, the All-Pro football player and, as I recall, Ara Parseghian, then the Northwestern football coach. Ara and I would later become friends when he became the ND coach. Those were the "swarthy, Italian-looking guys" identified by Ralph Hill. Since Ralph was always big on sticking needles in guys, ribbing them, I had a lot of ammunition now to get him back!

Later that year Angelo Boscarino went down. His throat had been cut and he had stab wounds and bruises throughout his body. He was a well-known thief, had participated in the hijacking of $380,000 worth of silver bullion. He had held out on the mob, cheated on his street tax.

In 1966 Van Corbin got it. His real name was Sam Panveno. He had been the contractor who built the new home of Tony Accardo in River Forest. Two guys were seen shooting him with .38s equipped with silencers, outside the Country Club Motel at 8303 North Avenue in Melrose Park, a western suburb of Chicago. He was hiding out there with his wife and kids. Apparently, Accardo was not satisfied with his work. The job had been assigned to Alderisio and Nicoletti, of course.

By 1967 Tony was back in Chicago, full time, attending to his "office." On October 7 of that year he was arrested by Bob Fuesel, then the top agent on the Intelligence Unit of the Internal Revenue Service in Chicago, a good friend of mine and currently the Executive Director of the Chicago Crime Commission. Tony was arrested for violation of the law requiring that a federal wagering stamp be purchased by anyone engaged in illegal gambling. His arrest took place at his residence at 1102 Maple Avenue in Oak Park. The agent broke in Tony's front door to collar him. He had not paid the fifty dollars needed to purchase a wagering stamp before accepting bets, a federal crime. The arrest was one of five made that day in three Chicago locations and in Oak Park and Skokie, Chicago suburbs. The United States Attorney at the time, Ed Hanrahan, announced that the most significant of the arrests was that of Tony Spilotro, who had been identified by the Illinois Crime Investigating Commission as a "mob loan shark." He was subsequently fined but did not serve any time for this violation.

In 1967, the big hit was the job on Arthur "Boodie" Cowan, a major Chicago bookmaker who made the mistake of holding out on the street tax. He left home at eight-thirty in the evening, telling his wife he had a meeting on the south side. His car was first noticed at eight-thirty the next morning in front of 418 South Kilpatrick. The Chicago PD was notified that day. When they broke into the trunk of his car they found his body inside. Another example of trunk music. Cowan had been shot behind the left ear with a .32.

9 Arrests

Finally, we were able to "pinch" Philly Alderisio. Philly's "work," as they called it, would bring him to the apex of the mob. When the Top Hoodlum Program started in 1957, Sam Giancana had just succeeded Tony Accardo as the "boss," but by 1969, Felix "Milwaukee Phil" Alderisio had ascended to the throne. He didn't hold the job very long.

It was at this time that we pinched him. I participated in his arrest, on Sunday morning, July 27, at his home at 505 Berkley in Riverside, a western suburb of Chicago. In fact, I would be criticized by the Special Agent in Charge of the Chicago office of the FBI, Marlin Johnson, for allowing myself to be photographed while hauling Philly to the Chicago PD's lockup at 1121 South State Street, police headquarters. The Marshall's lockup in the Federal Building was closed on Sunday and we had to haul Philly to the Chicago police lockup. Someone had alerted a photographer for the *Chicago Sun-Times* to our arrival in the back alley and Johnny Bassett, Denny Shanahan and I were pictured on the front page of the *Sun-Times* the next day, leading Alderisio into the back door of police headquarters. If every mobster in Chicago hadn't known me before by sight, they would after that day. That didn't bother me one bit—I was always vain enough to want my enemies to know their nemesis—but Mr. Johnson felt that was not the way I should be conducting my business. It was not the first time Marlin had me on the carpet but it would be about the last before he retired in 1970.

Philly and I had a brief but stormy clash as we hauled him from his home and took him downtown by Bureau car. I was in the back seat with him, on his right. He was most upset this Sunday morning and in no mood to be jostled by "the G's heavy," not him, the mob's heavy. He loudly complained about my "bad-mouthing him all over Chicago" and went into a tirade about my telling Accardo he had double-crossed him. I didn't get into it much. No sense kicking a guy when he's down. He was fair game when he was on his game but now he was a wounded tiger. I shut him up by telling him "I wouldn't be saying these things if they weren't absolutely true. And if I were you I wouldn't worry now about what Roemer might be spreading around town about you. You now got a lot more to worry about than that!" He was pretty much silent the rest of the ride. He had begun to contemplate what might now happen to him, now that he had been pinched.

Actually, what we got him for was pretty minor. It was for conspiracy to defraud a bank, the Parkway Bank in Harwood Heights, of the paltry sum (to him) of some $79,000, a violation of the Federal Reserve Act. But it would be enough to rid us of Philly for the rest of his life. He would die in prison. Not a pretty place or a pretty way to go. But I didn't shed tears for him.

Tony was back in the hands of the law on September 12, 1969. Circuit Court Judge Lee had signed a search warrant for Tony's bookmaking establishment. When the officers of the Chicago PD's Vice Control Division Gambling Unit under the direction of Sergeant James Brady arrived at Tony's office, they found the front door locked. Looking in, they saw Spilotro and his crew run from their desks and throw their records into a bucket of water, kept in the office just for that purpose. Their records, like all those in mob handbooks, were kept on water soluble paper and dissolved immediately in water. Only then were the officers able to gain entrance. They immediately placed Spilotro and five of his crew, including Matt Raimondi, a well-known bookie, under arrest and then conducted their search. They found some betting records, sports schedules and a supply of soluble paper. While there the phone rang constantly and was answered by the police officers, who found that the callers wanted to place bets on football games, college and pro. Tony was charged with the violation of "keeper of bets."

In the Sixties Tony also came to the attention of Charley Siragusa. Charley was a most aggressive, highly vocal former Treasury Department, Federal Bureau of Narcotics, agent who in the Sixties was the director of the Illinois Crime Investigating Committee, a creature of the Illinois state legislature. Charley held hearings in Chicago on the loan-sharking business and hauled many such people before his committee for public hearings. One of the loan sharks he spotlighted the most was Tony. Tony snarled his way through the hearings, refusing to answer questions by resorting to the Fifth Amendment. However, the hearings did bring him to the attention of the general public in Chicago since they were televised and reported heavily on the radio and in the print press.

Tony had been unmasked. He was becoming known to the local media. No one believed that he was now a real top hoodlum, but we were all beginning to come to the realization that he was somebody, somebody who should be given a lot of investigative attention. I know that some of the best agents on C-1, such as Lenny Wolf and Hal Johnson, although burdened with other assignments of their own, pitched in and assisted Dunc with his investigation of Spilotro. We devoted considerable attention to Tony as the Sixties wound down.

Due to the combined efforts of the above three agents, working in close harmony with the Justice Department's Organized Crime Strike Force, Tony was indicted by a federal grand jury on May 20, 1970. The charge against Tony was that he had falsified information on a loan application when he bought the Oak Park duplex in which he now lived. The investigation was commenced by the Bureau based on the assumption that he would not want to reveal the real source of his income when he made the application for his mortgage. It was found that he obtained the mortgage from the Uptown Federal Savings and Loan Association on April 5, 1969. On the application he falsely claimed that he earned $150 a week working at the Illinois Concrete Construction Corporation at 6230 West Addison. The investigation determined that this information was false and that Tony had intimidated the president of Illinois Concrete Construction to verify his employment. Art Petacque, the ace crime reporter for the *Chicago Sun-Times*, identified Tony in his story of the indictment as "mob whiz kid Anthony Spilotro, 31, who federal agents contend is a specialist on the invasion of legitimate business by the syndicate and a stand-in for jailed high-ranking gangster Felix Alderisio."

Also in 1970, Tony was arrested once more on gambling charges. This time he was not present when the cops arrived but entered while the raid on the apartment of one of his cohorts, Mike Segreti, was in progress. Tony was not only arrested for bookmaking but on charges of aggravated battery and resisting arrest when he slugged one of the arresting officers while trying to escape. On this occasion the *Chicago Tribune* described Tony as "the reputed heir apparent and the

protégé of Felix 'Milwaukee Phil' Alderisio" as boss of the
Chicago mob.

Tony served no time in prison on any of these charges.

There were several other gangland slayings in the late Sixties and then one last one before Tony would go on to bigger
and better things.

Mario Sprovieri was a well-known Chicago burglar, a top
target of C-2. In 1965 he had been charged with murder. But
on September 28, 1970, in a vacant store on West Huron being
used as a social club, he was killed by five bullets to the head.
Duncan Everette believed that Spilotro was "good" for that job
also.

Dunc believed that Tony was responsible for one more job
before he left Chicago, but I'm not sure about that. I wasn't
sure because at the time it took place Tony would have been
out of town—or at least he was gone from Chicago around
that time. Obviously, he could have stopped in for the day and
flown back out. The killing would become another of the classic mob hits and Dunc may have been on to something as he
usually was when it involved Tony. It was known as the "kill
from the grave."

It seems that in the Sixties, Philly Alderisio had a mistress
named Nan with whom he was madly in love. He went away
to prison, but before he died, according to one of my sources,
Gerardo Denono, he gave the order. Nan had been fooling
around with Sam "Sambo" Cesario while Alderisio was in
prison, dying. Cesario, a made guy, should have known better.
At least he should have waited until Philly expired.

On October 19, 1971, Sambo, then fifty-three, was sitting
out in front of his building at 1071 West Polk in the Patch, on
a lawn chair, with his wife. Two masked gunmen approached.
Holding the wife and a friend at bay with their guns, they beat
Sambo. "This will teach you to fuck around with Philly's
girl," they shouted. Then they shot and killed him.

I wondered what Sambo's wife thought about that, her husband being killed because he was screwing another woman. I
wonder if she cried at his funeral. Sambo had been an impor-

tant "made" guy, in charge of the Maxwell Street area for the mob. But he had violated the oath of *omerta*, he had coveted another member's girl.

Dunc believed that Tony was one of the two gunmen who killed Sambo because it would be expected that, in loyalty to his old boss, his sponsor in the mob, and with his expertise as a killer, he would be the logical guy. I really couldn't disagree with his theory. But we never got any evidence to substantiate Tony's involvement.

PART TWO

1971 to 1982
THE RISE

10 Las Vegas

As the Seventies opened, Las Vegas was in full swing. Nevada had legalized all forms of gambling in 1931. At the same time the state passed a law that allowed divorces with just a six week residency requirement. Thousands and thousands of women flocked to Nevada to shed their husbands. Some men came also to rid themselves of their wives. They created an instant pool of gamblers at the slots and tables.

Casinos were erected in many areas of the state, particularly in Reno, but also in downtown Las Vegas, Carson City and at Lake Tahoe. By the beginning of World War II, there were some very nice gambling casinos in the state, particularly Harold's Club in Reno and the El Rancho and Harrah's Club in Las Vegas.

World War II, however, brought an influx of servicemen throughout the state and demonstrated the potential gambling presented. The servicemen flocked to the casinos and gambled millions, even on just a twenty-one dollars a month salary.

Then came the big breakthrough. Benny "Bugsy" Siegel was dispatched to Las Vegas in 1943 by his fellow New York mobsters, Frank "The Prime Minister of Organized Crime" Costello and Meyer "The Chairman of the Board" Lansky. He was sent to run the mob's wire services in Las Vegas, Los Angeles and other parts of Nevada and California. While in Vegas he recognized the potential. During the war the rapid growth in revenue from gambling became apparent to him. At the time Las Vegas may have been a hick town of just thirteen thousand people, but fifteen casinos attracted the servicemen and many other visitors.

By Christmas 1946, Bugsy had completed most of the Flamingo, the first really gaudy hotel on Las Vegas Boulevard, then known as Highway 91, also known as The Gay White Way. But Bugsy was already in trouble. First, the Flamingo did not do well. It ran into a string of bad luck, losing money. It closed. Then Costello and Lansky, meeting in Havana, Cuba, with dozens of leaders of La Cosa Nostra from all over the country under cover of a show put on by Frank Sinatra, reported that Bugsy, with help from his mistress, Virginia Hill, was skimming money. Not just from the tables and slots but from funds set aside for the construction of the casino. Virginia was moving the money to Switzerland for deposit in a secret bank account in Zurich. The mob bosses at first decided to clip Bugsy but eventually decided to give him another chance.

But the next summer, at the home on Linden Drive in Beverly Hills that Bugsy and Virginia shared, the deed was done. A rifle shot fired through his front window and into his right eye did the job.

The mob replaced him with Gus Greenbaum but soon soured on him also. They killed him—and his wife, Bess— again not in Vegas, where the players might be scared off, but this time in Phoenix. Only then did the Flamingo fulfill all the dreams Bugsy had. From then on it was a big money-maker for the mob.

Gross annual revenues of the casinos soon hit $32 million. With a newly enacted 2 percent tax, it became a nice gift for the taxpayers of Nevada.

When the Chicago family of La Cosa Nostra saw what their brethren were about to accomplish in Las Vegas, they recognized the potential and stepped right in.

Al Capone had sent an emissary to the west to represent the Chicago mob in Los Angeles, to capture for Chicago whatever might be gained from that territory. This *representato* was known as Johnny Roselli, but that was not his real name.

Years later I would investigate his background and establish that he was in the United States illegally, that his real name was Felipe Sacco, that he had been born in Sicily and was fleeing crimes there when he landed in Boston and assumed the false identity of somebody called John Roselli, sometimes spelling his name Rosselli. When Capone was sent away in the early thirties, his successor, Frank "The Enforcer" Nitti, kept Roselli in the west to oversee Chicago's interests there. In 1943, Nitti was indicted with Roselli and other top echelon leaders of the Chicago mob in "The Hollywood Extortion Case" for extorting a couple of million dollars from all the Hollywood movie studios of the day. Nitti would commit suicide before trial but Roselli and the others would be convicted.

Roselli got out of prison after only three years, in a large scandal, thanks to Tom Clark, the Attorney General in the Truman administration, soon to be rewarded for his parole of Roselli and the other Chicago mob leaders by being appointed by Truman to the Supreme Court. Roselli got back out west in 1946, just in time to follow Bugsy to Las Vegas. He could oversee the control by Chicago of all mob activity from Chicago to the Pacific Ocean.

Through this control it was natural for Chicago to develop a quick understanding of what the New York mob in the person of Bugsy Siegel was attempting out west, in Vegas. They gave firm instructions to Roselli to expand his interest to the desert, to Highway 91. They even sent Murray "The Camel" Humphreys out there to guide Roselli. Hump had been designated "Public Enemy Number One" by the Chicago Crime Commission in 1931 when Capone had been convicted. He was the brains of the Chicago Outfit. New York may have gotten the jump on Chicago, even in Chicago's own domain, but Chicago was just a step behind. It wouldn't be long before they took over the construction of the Stardust, just north and across the street from the Flamingo.

In 1948 Meyer Lansky and his brother, Jake, opened another nice casino on the Strip, way up on the north end, the Thunderbird.

In 1949 a significant development occurred, although it wasn't evident at that time just what it would mean to Las Vegas and other Nevada casinos. The International Brotherhood of Teamsters initiated their Central States Pension Fund. In years to come it would lend millions to high-risk Nevada hotels and casinos.

That same year Moe Dalitz would arrive with his partners in the Mayfield Road Gang from Cleveland to finish construction of the luxurious Desert Inn, also located on the north end of the Strip, but about halfway between the El Rancho and the Flamingo. The Mayfield Road Gang owned 74 percent of the Desert Inn.

In 1950 the Kefauver Committee of Congress arrived in Las Vegas to hold hearings. During the hearings they focused the country's attention on our biggest gangsters—Costello, Lansky, Accardo, Ricca and Mickey Cohan of Los Angeles to name just some of the mobsters featured.

In 1952, Doc Stacher, the New York mobster, had arrived in town and opened the Sands, just south of the Desert Inn.

Sidney R. Korshak was also in Las Vegas in the mid-Fifties. Sid was the Chicago mob lawyer who was sent to the west to handle legal affairs—and some others—for the Chicago mob. He was the agent-attorney for some of the big performers and made sure they did their best for the mob. I recall Murray Humphreys, in front of our mike, telling Gussie Alex, who normally handled the liaison for the mob with Korshak, how he, Hump, had reamed Korshak out when he put Dinah Shore, one of Sid's clients, at a hotel other than one of the mob's. Hump told Gussie on that occasion that he had informed Korshak in no uncertain terms that he was "our man, we raised you, you drop everything when we call." Korshak not only represented the Chicago Outfit in Vegas, but in Hollywood where he was a close pal of movie moguls like Lew Wasserman, one of the biggest in Hollywood. I had several meetings with Sid and he was a slippery guy to deal with.

In 1955 the Strip really began to fill up with the opening of the Riviera, the Dunes and the Royal Nevada.

That was also the year Nevada attempted to close the barn

door after the cows had escaped. They created the Gaming Control Board to investigate the background of gaming executives and require them to be licensed if they were found fit. It was a great idea. They should have thought of it in 1931. Like New Jersey did when they first legalized gambling in Atlantic City in the late Seventies.

The biggest year ever, perhaps, for the Chicago mob in Las Vegas was 1955. A Los Angeles gambler, Tony Cornero, had begun construction of the Stardust. As it neared completion he died. The Chicago mob moved in behind their front, Jake "The Barber" Factor, the brother of Max Factor of cosmetics fame. The Outfit had now established a toehold in Vegas, just north of midway on the Strip, to compete with the New York mobs.

In 1957 the Tropicana opened, way south on the Strip, close to the airport, which would eventually be named McCarran International Airport for the U. S. Senator who represented gaming interests in Las Vegas. I have a story about Senator Pat McCarran. In 1949–50 I was the vice president of the University of Notre Dame Student Law Association, the Chairman of the Law Ball, the chairman-moderator of the Natural Law Debate Society, a member of Blue Circle, Notre Dame's only honorary society, and the first four-time university boxing champion. As such I was one of the few invited to dinner with Senator McCarran when he came to address the school. Over dinner, I and another law association officer mentioned to the senator that we might be interested in joining the FBI upon graduation from law school. He cordially invited us to use him as a reference when we applied. My fellow law school association officer did. I didn't. He had at least as many qualifications as I had, but was rejected. Later, I realized that his use of Senator Pat McCarran as a reference probably is what did him in. I found out that J. Edgar Hoover did not consider Pat McCarran an ideal sponsor, to say the least. The director felt that Senator McCarran had been corrupted by the ambience of Las Vegas, perhaps not personally but just by the mere fact that he represented a class of citizens who did not meet Mr. Hoover's accepted standards.

The Top Hoodlum Program would soon have a devastating effect on Las Vegas, but in 1957 Las Vegas wasn't even a field office of the FBI. It was what is called a resident agency and it reported to FBI headquarters in Salt Lake City, many miles away. Mr. Hoover found little to investigate when he did not feel he had jurisdiction over organized crime. But then came the Apalachin meeting and, suddenly, Las Vegas became a headquarters city for the FBI and scores and scores of agents were assigned there. The whole situation for the mobs in Las Vegas began to change.

In fact, an incident involving Las Vegas was one of the reasons for the sit-down in Apalachin. Frank Costello was shot in the vestibule of his luxury apartment building at 115 Central Park West in New York City. When police came to his aid they found a piece of paper in his pocket. It was the financial record, what is called the gross, for the Tropicana, which had opened the previous day in 1957. The figure was $851,284. Not bad for one night. It was in the handwriting of Lou Lederer. Lou had been close to most top hoodlums in Chicago, an occasional visitor to Little Al. He was the Outfit's foremost gambling advisor although he himself was never considered by us to be one of them. In fact, in later years he would become a close friend of mine. A real gentleman, a Jew who had converted to Catholicism. But he was also the front for Costello in the Trop.

Gaming revenues in 1957 hit $132 million, $100 million dollars more than when Bugsy opened the Flamingo.

In 1958 the Chicago mob leased the operations of the Stardust to the United Hotels Corporation. That was the Mayfield Road Gang of Cleveland, Moe Dalitz and his partners. Chicago's Johnny Drew was still in control at the Stardust, however. The next year Dalitz would be granted a $1 million loan for the Stardust from the Central States Pension Fund of the Teamsters.

It was also the year Governor Grant Sawyer ordered the Gaming Control Board to keep organized crime out of the casinos. Big words, little real action.

Years after Roselli returned to his functions in the west, particularly in Las Vegas, the Chicago mob determined that he needed help. It was now the mid-Sixties, and Sam Giancana reached into his organization to pluck a likely guy to send to Vegas. The man Giancana picked at this time was Marshall Caifano, or John Marshall, the man whose wife, Darlene, Giancana had taken such a fancy to.

In 1960, the great Convention Center opened, which would bring the largest conventions to Las Vegas forever after, and Dalitz got another loan from the Teamsters. This one to refinance three hotels he was running: the Stardust, the Desert Inn and the Fremont, a big hotel downtown on Fremont Street, downtown being known in Vegas as "Glitter Gulch" in contrast to "The Strip," south of downtown. Another loan would come in 1962. Soon Dalitz would lead the drive for contributions to build Guardian Angel Catholic Cathedral, just off the Strip behind the Desert Inn, with its copper roof reflecting the neon lights of the nearby Stardust. When in Vegas I make a visit to Guardian Angel every day, but I am never inspired there. I look at the mosaic in the sanctuary depicting the Risen Christ and it reminds me of a disco dancer, not a holy figure. What would you expect from Dalitz? But perhaps I am being too hard on him. Soon his fellow citizens would name Dalitz "Humanitarian of the Year." Such was the ambience of Las Vegas.

But 1962 would be remembered also for something else, something which—in retrospect although it was far from evident then—would be the beginning of the end for the mobs. Howard Hughes came to town! When he did, Nevada law prohibited private enterprise from ownership of hotel-casinos if you can believe that. The mob was OK. Sheraton or Marriott or Ritz Carlton or Ramada was not! The recluse used the considerable talents of his top aide, my friend Bob Matheu, to purchase some of the best hotels in Vegas, and let me tell you, Bob would run them honestly. And most efficiently. Bob had been a key FBI agent in Washington and then was the "cut out" the CIA used when they wanted Fidel Castro assassinated. They had Matheu approach Johnny Roselli with the plan. Roselli put him in touch with Sam Giancana, Roselli's boss, and a meeting was arranged at the Fontainbleu in Miami Beach with Santo Trafficante, the mob boss in Tampa. Trafficante had the wherewithal to do the job in Havana where he had spent so much time. When the mobs had several major hotel-casinos there, they had bribed President Fulgencio Batista to allow them the privilege of ownership. Now Bob Matheu represented Howard Hughes well in Las Vegas and soon Hughes would own the Desert Inn, the Frontier, the Sands, the Castaways and the Landmark, all nice hotels. Bob made sure they were run aboveboard, conforming to all laws. No skimming for the mob. His success for Hughes would lead other public companies to buy hotel-casinos in Vegas, and that process eventually would lead to the ruin of the mobs. But that would be a while yet.

The year 1963 was another high point for law enforcement in Las Vegas, more specifically for gaming enforcement. We listened in Chicago to "Mo," the mike hidden in the special headquarters of the Chicago mob, as Sam Giancana talked about his hidden ownership in the Cal-Neva Lodge on Crystal Bay on the north shore of Lake Tahoe. This is what we thought to be the case, at least. The official "licensee" there, the owner, was Frank Sinatra. We had learned a great deal by 1963 about the close association between Giancana and Sinatra. We perceived from what we heard that Sinatra had been "brought up" by the mob in New Jersey, which owned the night spots on the Jersey Turnpike where Frank got his start. We learned that Sinatra was first a close pal of Joe Fischetti, the Chicago mobster, and his brothers, Rocco and Charley, all of whom were cousins of Al Capone. Sinatra was also close to some other people in the New York and Chicago mobs. He was the guy who touted Judy Campbell Exner on Giancana and John Kennedy. As we know, Judy was bedding with both when one was leader of the underworld and the other leader of the free world. To be precise, I guess, Sinatra touted Judy to Johnny Roselli who then touted her to Giancana while Sinatra was recommending her to Kennedy. We learned of the liaison when we checked Roselli's phone calls in Los Angeles. They led us to Judy, then to Sam, then to JFK. J. Edgar Hoover, as we all know by now, spoiled Kennedy's fun when he advised him at lunch one day that we in the FBI were alert to his playmate and her visits to the Oval Office.

You will recall that in the summer of 1963 we lock-stepped Giancana. But Judge Richard Austin ruled that Sam was right when he complained that we were violating his civil rights by such a tight surveillance. Giancana slipped free from his six-week ordeal and skipped off to Sinatra's Cal-Neva to be with his paramour, Phyllis McGuire. However, we tracked Giancana down and alerted the head of the Nevada Gaming Control Commission to the presence of Giancana at the Cal-Neva. Giancana was in the Black Book—he was one of the dozen or so people excluded from any Nevada casino. When the commission representative called Sinatra, the licensee, to inquire whether Giancana was at the Cal-Neva, Sinatra lost his temper. He cursed the man, who was recording the conversation. Charges were brought against Sinatra and he lost his license.

That year, 1963, was a bad one for Sinatra for other reasons. It was the same year that his son, Frank, Jr., was kidnapped from Lake Tahoe for a demand of $240,000 in ransom. The FBI in Las Vegas, Los Angeles and San Francisco got on the case, kidnapping being a federal crime. My pal, Curt Lynum, the SAC in San Francisco, took charge of the case. They solved it and apprehended the kidnappers.

In 1964, Doc Stacher, the New York mobster who owned the Sands, pleaded guilty to two tax counts and took voluntary exile to Israel. Jimmy Hoffa, whose Teamsters pension fund had meant so much to the mob in Vegas, was convicted for manipulating the fund. Loans for Caesars Palace, not yet completed, began the following year. Eventually the Central States Pension Fund of the Teamsters would put over $20 million into Caesars.

Eventually, the enforcement arm of the Gaming Control Board began to hear some rumors. Just who is this John Marshall? They sat down with their counterparts in the Las Vegas Field Division of the FBI and received an earful. A supervisory agent named Tommy Parker called in Mike Simon, the former Chicago agent who had been sent out to Vegas permanently once we realized that the Chicago mob was rapidly supplanting New York as the prime mob in the casinos. Mike gave the GCB the rundown on who John Marshall really was.

We were getting to know just about everything the Outfit was involved in in Vegas, thanks to our bugs in Chicago—Little Al, Plumb and Mo. Also by this time Marshall Rutland and I had led our sound men into the Democratic Headquarters of the First Ward in Chicago's Loop, on LaSalle Street right across the street from City Hall. We called our bug there "Shade." Although Las Vegas wasn't the prime subject of most of the conversations picked up by Shade, we did get some further information on the mob involvement in Vegas. So we were able to feed Mike Simon out in the Vegas FBI enough to bring him up to speed. The combination of our information with his own investigations out there resulted in a thick dossier on John Marshall.

By that time the GCB had compiled its first "Black Book," which listed a dozen or so of the top gangsters in Las Vegas. By law in Nevada, anyone listed in the Black Book must be excluded from every casino. Violations result in severe sanctions, even loss of a casino's license to operate.

Did the publication of the Black Book slow Caifano down? Hell no! Disregarding the instructions of The Man, Caifano decided to make the Black Book an issue. Nobody could keep him out of the casinos! What was the use of being in Las Vegas if you couldn't go into a casino? That's like being a Bear fan in Chicago but being kept out of Soldier Field!

So Caifano challenged the GCB. He frequented the casinos. Made a big point of it in fact. Eager to get credit for doing its job, the GCB surveilled Caifano one night, caught him in a casino, and brought him to the attention of the management!

Wow, did that get the attention of Joe Batters back in Chicago. The Outfit's fronts there might now well lose their licenses to operate. All that work putting them in place, keeping them out of harm's way by not allowing them to come to the attention of the GCB and all the effort in allowing them to learn their trade, might now be down the drain. All because that lousy Caifano can't keep his head down!

Worse to come. Against the advice of Accardo, but still with Giancana as his mentor and supporter, Caifano decided to take the GCB to court. Make a big issue of the Black Book and its constitutionality. Wow! Talk about high profile.

Now Accardo decided enough was enough. But as long as Giancana was the boss he chose not to cross him. He talked to Sam but Giancana was adamant. He had promised Caifano this spot and he was a man of his word.

That year Sam Giancana left the scene, not for good, but for a while. After he took us to court and won, we took him to court and won. We did something never before done, anywhere. We took the Fifth from him, his right not to incriminate himself. Even though he was given complete immunity from any prosecution for any crime, state or federal, he would not answer questions. If he lied, we could get him for perjury. If he told the truth, his associates would get him. He went to jail for contempt of the grand jury in Chicago, a case I was very much involved in. A case that gave me great happiness. When Sam got out of jail in 1966, he abdicated and with my pal Dick Cain he roamed the world for eight years, setting up gambling enterprises in the Caribbean and even bribing the Shah of Iran, in Tehran. There he used the services of another of my pals, Lou Lederer, as his casino manager.

That was also the year Paul Laxalt would become governor of Nevada. He would repeal the law against public corporations owning casinos, an issue when Hughes moved into Nevada in 1962. He was held up until Laxalt became governor. I would get to know Laxalt well after I retired and was retained by the *Sacramento Bee*, a newspaper sued for libel after it had reported his involvement as the owner of the Ormsby House Hotel and Casino in Carson City. It was my job to prove the accuracy of what they wrote about Senator Laxalt, Ronald Reagan's closest friend. In short, the *Bee* reported that after Laxalt had retired as governor of Nevada but before he was elected to the United States Senate, he built the Ormsby House, very arguably the most luxurious hotel-casino in Carson City, the state's capital. Then, the *Bee* continued, he got into financial trouble and in order to secure additional financing went to Chicago where the mob may have used its influence. The result, as reported in the *Bee*, was that Laxalt agreed to place one of their men into a strategic position in the Ormsby House. Then the man skimmed for the benefit of the mob. It was my job to document what was written by the *Bee*. We succeeded in that we never had to change a comma in the story or print a retraction or an apology. I later discussed the case with Senator Laxalt in Washington at the wedding of my nephew, Congressman Tim Roemer, Democrat of Indiana, to Sally Johnston, the daughter of Senator Bennett Johnston of Louisiana. Laxalt is a personable guy whose judgment, in my estimation, was faulty when he operated the Ormsby House.

In 1966 Jimmy Hoffa went on trial for jury tampering and lost control of the Teamsters pension fund. It didn't much matter to the Chicago mob; their man, Allen Dorfman, was now firmly entrenched and doing their bidding.

That year the FBI in Las Vegas, in the person of such good agents as Warren Salisbury, Tommy Parker, Mike Simon, Al Zimmerman, Frank Cornett and Chuck Thomas, presented information of skimming at the Riviera to the federal grand jury and obtained indictments.

In 1968 Howard Hughes attempted to buy the Stardust, which would have given the Chicago mob a big profit, but the Securities and Exchange Commission blocked the sale, citing the monopoly Hughes was amassing in Vegas. He now had the Landmark, the Sands, the Desert Inn, the Frontier and the Castaways. Three of these were among the best hotel-casinos in Vegas.

There is no doubt that Las Vegas was changing.

11 Tony Arrives

Leave it to Tony "The Ant." When he decided to make his move, he would do so with a splash. He would file a lawsuit against the federal government!

Tony would even make the announcement in the daily newspapers. He filed the suit, he stated, due to "continued harassment by federal law enforcement agencies," and said that as a result of their treatment of him he would move from Chicago.

What caused the suit and the announcement, at least as the final straw, was the fact that when the moving van arrived at his home at 1102 South Maple Avenue in Oak Park on May 6, 1971, to pack his household goods and cart them off to a place then unspecified, the IRS waited until everything was packed into the van before seizing it to satisfy a $19,759 tax bill against him! Imagine the scene. Tony and Nancy assist the movers all day, hauling their refrigerator, stove, television sets, bed frames and mattresses, dressers, chairs, tables and other furniture out of the home and into the van. Meanwhile the IRS is waiting down the street. Finally, late in the afternoon as the van is fully loaded and ready to take off, the IRS swoops down and confiscates it! Enough to make most people weep. Nancy did. Tony got into a shouting match with the IRS agents.

"You fucking guys! You got no business doing this. I never heard of such a thing," he shouted.

"If you have a lawyer, call him and ask if what we show you is a court order to do just what we're doing," he was told by the lead IRS agent.

"I don't give a fuck! This is the gestapo! You can't just take away all the furniture I have in the world! Who gives you the right to do that?"

The IRS was adamant. They had the authority and they exercised it. What the IRS showed Tony was that they had filed a lien for the $19,759 in wagering taxes against him based on the arrest the police had made years earlier. Judge Louis J. Garrippo, one of the very best Chicago judges, had honestly suppressed the evidence against Tony and he was acquitted, but the lien was authorized by a federal judge.

Spilotro would subsequently ask Judge Frank McGarr in federal court to dismiss the lien against him and return the confiscated goods, but Judge McGarr was never "on the pad" of the Chicago mob and he refused. Tony's suit was eventually dismissed by Judge McGarr.

So it was that Tony fled from Chicago. Fled is the wrong word. That's what we thought in May. But it wasn't long before Duncan Everette got the word from Mike Simon. Simon, the transplanted FBI agent in Las Vegas who had been one of us on C-1, found Tony in Las Vegas. After Philly Alderisio was sent to prison he was succeeded by Jackie Cerone. Jackie was called "The Lackey" by the Chicago media due to his close association with his mentor, Tony Accardo, "The Big Tuna." But Jackie was never anybody's lackey. I got to know him well through the years as a result of several direct contacts, several eavesdroppings on his conversations furnished by Mo and Little Al, and information supplied by a couple of my CTEs who had dealings with him. He has always been one of the sharpest of all Chicago mobsters. Tough and savvy, articulate, well-read, and well-versed in all functions of a mob leader. He killed, he ran gambling, he corrupted, and his job description filled the bill for the spot to which he was elevated. He was a worthy successor to Al Capone.

However, he didn't last long. A fine agent on C-1, Paul Frankfurt, developed one of Jackie's underlings, Lou Bombacino, as a CTE. Several of us spent weeks guarding and debriefing Lou at a safe house on a farm near Elgin, a town some thirty to forty miles west of Chicago. Lou became a great favorite of ours. He was a man with courage. He got up on the witness stand, stared the killer, Cerone, in the eye and testified against him. He not only put Cerone away but three of his top guys as well: Donald "The Wizard of Odds" Angelini, Dominic "Large" Cortina and Frank Aurelli.

With our dispatch of Cerone, the mob was now hurting for good leadership. What they did was bring Tony Accardo back! We had believed that we were diminishing the able leaders of the Chicago LCN, but here they were, bringing their best boss in history back. Accardo had been the *consiglieri* ever since he had stepped aside to give Sam Giancana the power in 1957, but he had been spending most of his time at his condo on Roadrunner Drive in Palm Springs, California, except on the infrequent occasions when the Outfit needed him. Now they insisted, in this emergency, that he come back. But Tony insisted he get help at the top. He mandated that my first target, Gus Alex, be elevated into the top leadership and that Joey Aiuppa be delegated to run the day-to-day activity of the mob.

One of the first things the Accardo, Alex and Aiuppa leadership did was to recognize the problem in Las Vegas. They found that the protégé of Sam Giancana, Marshall Caifano, was not handling his duties well and that Johnny Roselli, also out there now, was not much help either. They decided they needed a better hand at the helm as their *representato* overseeing their interests in Las Vegas as their enforcer.

The *representato* of the Chicago crime syndicate has little to do with developing and maintaining the skim, the sine qua non for the mob's being in Vegas—or Tahoe or Reno or Laughlin or Sparks or any other of the Nevada gaming hot spots. But when problems arise with those minions of the Chicago mob who are delegated to flow the skim, then the Chicago rep steps in. He is the enforcer.

The new leadership of the Outfit decided to bring Caifano home and to leave Roselli in place but to downsize his responsibilities. Caifano and Roselli were each having problems with the law at that time—Caifano had been indicted for extorting an Indiana businessman, Ray Ryan, and Roselli had been indicted in California for cheating Hollywood movie moguls and others in Beverly Hills. No wonder Accardo et al felt that they weren't minding the shop in Las Vegas where their sole job, in the opinion of Accardo, was to enforce Outfit edicts.

Becoming the Chicago Outfit's man in Las Vegas, their top man, was quite a move up for Tony Spilotro. I recall well that when Dunc advised me of his call from Mike Simon in Las Vegas telling him about Tony's physical presence out there I was surprised. Then I touched base with my CTEs. Sure enough, Tony had been given the spot representing Chicago in Vegas, making him one of the most important mobsters in the Outfit. He was still just a soldier, but perhaps now their most important soldier, more important, probably, than three or four of the six or seven capos. Certainly the amount of money being produced from the Outfit's interests in the casinos in Las Vegas was more than any of the Chicago capos were bringing in. Just on the basis of money, it can readily be seen just how Tony's importance had escalated.

As I thought about it, I reflected on his rise. The pissant had become a tiger in mob affairs. I realized, however, that my perspective would always be biased due to my initial perceptions of the guy. I suppose the Outfit had another handle on Tony. They viewed him in relation to his peers. In retrospect, if I had then compared him to his competition, to the other up-and-coming young studs in the Chicago mob, I would have given him a higher grade. I would have realized that in his make-up he had all the qualifications the mob looked for. He was still just a young guy, now thirty-three, but look at what he had already accomplished in the affairs of the mob. He had been involved in the heaviest of the mob's heavy work, he had run their life-blood, a gambling operation in a prime district of Chicago, and he had been involved in the corruption of the police officers who were mandated to bust his operation. All in all, he had accomplished in just several short years what most of his fellow soldiers would never accomplish. In now looking back, therefore, I realize that at that stage of his career Tony Spilotro was well qualified to assume the duties the Outfit thrust upon him.

12 The Casinos

Unless you've spent some time in Las Vegas or studied its brief but hectic history, it can be difficult to distinguish the various casinos. Make no mistake about it, however, each is unique. Certainly Tony, in his new position, wouldn't be paying the same attention to every one of them.

Let me give you a brief description of the hotel-casinos that had been mobbed-up by the time that Tony arrived.

The Flamingo. It opened the day after Christmas in 1946. Bugsy Siegel operated it until he was killed by his pals in the New York mob in July 1947 and then others ran it in his place. However, in 1971 it was purchased by the Hilton Hotel Corporation. Except for a flap Hilton had with the New Jersey Casino Control Commission, the counterpart of the Nevada Gaming Control Board, over a consulting contract Hilton had with Sidney R. Korshak which kept Hilton from obtaining a gaming license in Atlantic City, Hilton has run a clean operation.

The Stardust. The flagship hotel-casino of the Chicago mob from the time it opened through 1971. First Johnny Drew was the casino manager, even after Moe Dalitz and his Mayfield Road Gang from Cleveland also became involved in its operation. Then it was sold to Parvin-Dohrman, a furniture company owned by Del Coleman, who shouldn't have been proud of his associations in Chicago. Lefty Rosenthal would arrive shortly before 1971 and, officially the entertainment director, run things for Chicago. Allen Glick would be the front, the licensee. He was also fronting for the Chicago Outfit. Carl Thomas, the master of Las Vegas skim, would later testify that

$400,000 a month would be skimmed from the Stardust and given to Rosenthal for the boys in Chicago. That amount did not include the skim from the crap tables, blackjack, keno, roulette or poker. These yielded a vast additional skim.

The Tropicana. Frank Costello was the man behind the Trop. Lou Lederer was his front there, Lou being very close to many Chicago mobsters and their gaming guru. When Giancana anticipated opening a large gambling operation in the Dominican Republic in 1963, he sent Lederer with Leslie Kruse, another gaming expert, to scout the situation and do a feasibility study. It was this situation which caused us to lockstep Giancana in the summer of 1963 to prevent him from keeping his intended meeting with Porfirio Rubirosa, the playboy Dominican ambassador who Giancana intended to influence to allow the Outfit to move into the Dominican Republic. The Trop would later be put in the hands of the Civella family of the LCN in Kansas City.

The Aladdin. In the Sixties it was the Detroit and St. Louis families of the LCN who controlled this hotel located between the MGM Grand and Bally's.

The Dunes. After it opened in 1955 it was owned for years by Major Riddle, closely associated with the Chicago Outfit, and by Morris Shenker, an attorney who represented mobsters in St. Louis and Kansas City. Raymond Patriarca, the boss of the New England family of the LCN, also had a piece of the Dunes.

The Sands. This hotel and casino was owned by New York mobster Doc Stacher when it opened. It became the home of The Rat Pack, Frank Sinatra's groupies. Sinatra had a piece of the ownership in the early Sixties and then in 1967 Howard Hughes bought it and it went legit.

The Desert Inn. When it opened in 1950 it was Moe Dalitz and his Mayfield Road Gang from Cleveland who owned it. These owners included Morris Kleinman, Sam Tucker and Lou Rothkopf, partners of Dalitz for years in Cleveland and Las Vegas. I recall well when Little Al informed us that Dalitz and Kleinman were in Chicago in January 1961 to negotiate a new deal with Murray Humphreys and Sam Giancana to give the

Chicago Outfit a bigger piece of the pie in Las Vegas including hidden "points," as they called them, in the Desert Inn and the Riviera.

Actually, I had a small hand in disclosing that the Desert Inn was one of the casinos in Vegas skimmed by the Chicago mob. A very small hand. In 1966 Philly Alderisio was appealing his conviction with Willie "Ice Pick" Alderman and Ruby Kolod for extorting a Denver businessman named Robert Sunshine. Philly's appeal, filed by his attorney Thomas Wadden of the law firm of Edward Bennett Williams, an owner of the Washington Redskins, attempted to show that a hidden mike at the Desert Inn was the source of some of the evidence we used in the extortion trial of Alderisio and Alderman. The problem was, for Alderisio, that if full disclosure of the bug at the Desert Inn was made during the appeal it would show the extent of the skim from the Desert Inn. That, of course, the mob did not want because that information showed that some quarter of a million dollars *a month* was being skimmed from the Desert Inn and the Stardust and being delivered to Sam Giancana in Chicago. Notwithstanding orders from Giancana not to bring the Desert Inn bug into play, Alderisio, knowing he would never survive a lengthy sentence for the extortion as well as his sentence from the bank fraud in Chicago, disobeyed Giancana's orders.

As a result, some of us from Chicago were subpoenaed by the defense to appear before the Court of Appeals and testify that we did not use any evidence from our mikes in Chicago as evidence against Alderisio. In June 1966 we went to Denver, and Gus Kempff, a fine C-1 agent who had Alderisio assigned to him, was selected from among us to testify. But it was a nice vacation for us in Denver and I was united with two of my former partners in Chicago, Ralph Hill and Marshall Rutland, for several pleasurable days there. Ralph and Maz had taken promotions in view of their great success on C-1. I never accepted a promotion in the Bureau, or any of several other offers of employment, because I never grew up. I enjoyed just what I was doing, performing in my own mind as the nemesis of the Chicago mob, and didn't want to sit behind a desk vicariously living the life of what my agents were accomplishing.

Following the hearing the court ruled against Alderisio and his conviction stood.

The Riviera. In the Sixties it was licensed to owners Ross Miller and Bernie Nemerov. Miller had been a bookmaker in Chicago and was closely associated with the mob. His son is the governor of Nevada today. Nemerov would later go to the Ormsby House when Paul Laxalt left the governor's office and opened it before he became a U.S. Senator. Allegedly he did so as part of a deal with Chicago to oversee the skim so that it could flow appropriately to the Outfit. Executives of the Riviera were indicted for skimming in 1967.

There would be other hotels mobbed-up, or at least with problems indicating mob control, after 1971. They would include the Fremont, Circus-Circus, the Hacienda and the Sundance. All of the hotels mentioned above are free of mob influence today and other major hotels such as the Golden Nugget, the Mirage, Excalibur, the MGM Grand, Treasure Island and the Luxor have never been thought to be under any organized crime influence.

13 VEGMON

I had gotten my feet wet with the investigation of mob activity in Las Vegas in many ways by 1971. First of all, I monitored the conversations of the top mobsters in Chicago about their holdings in Las Vegas. Then I was assigned two case files entitled Skimming Activities—Nevada Casinos, and Nevada Gambling Industry, which meant that everything any agent in Chicago developed concerning organized crime activity in Nevada was to be routed to me for perusal for any logical leads, either in Chicago or Nevada, and then to be reported to our Las Vegas field office. I was, therefore, in almost continuous contact, by phone and letters, with our agents in Las Vegas, especially Mike Simon, who was assigned to the organized crime squad there and handled most of the investigation there involving the Chicago Outfit. Mike had assigned to him most of the Chicago hoods in Vegas.

In addition to these activities, I was assigned in the mid-Sixties to a major investigation that we coordinated with field offices throughout the country. We code-named it VEGMON, for Vegas Money. We set it up after the Las Vegas office placed bugs in the executive offices of several of the mobbed-up casinos including the Fremont. On that bug we got precise information on how the fronts for the mobs throughout the country were moving the skim, the money they were stealing when it left the tables and slots and before it could be officially counted and recorded in the counting rooms.

Here is how it is done: At any casino there are stickmen at the crap tables and dealers at the blackjack and poker tables. Then, above them in the hierarchy, are floormen. Floormen monitor the dealers and stickmen. Above them are pit bosses, monitoring the dealers, stickmen and floormen. Above them is the shift manager, the overseer of the day, graveyard and night shifts, the three eight-hour shifts around the clock in a Las Vegas casino, which never closes down. (Atlantic City casinos don't operate twenty-four hours a day.) Above all of these is the casino manager.

Any of these employees can be involved in the skim. Obviously, the higher up the more important to the skim. Under each table is a "drop-box." Any bill of $100 or more is recorded as it's dropped into the drop-box, which has two keys. One key is used to dislodge the box from underneath the table and another to open it. The dealer can skim because he can palm any bill under $100 since it is not recorded. But that's kid stuff, nice for him but not adding up to much. But when you get to the floorman, to the pit boss, to the shift manager and to the casino manager, then you can open up the flood-gates of skim. Usually, a security officer is on the skim since he accompanies the drop-box to the counting room.

The "eye in the sky," the opening in the ceiling where a camera is aimed at each table and each slot machine, is designed to catch any skimming activity. On one of my visits to Las Vegas, Warren Salisbury, a former Las Vegas agent then in charge of security at Caesars Palace, gave me a tour of the entire security operation at Caesars, from the "eye in the sky" to the counting room. He gave me an insider's tour of how he guarded against skimming. Several top ex-FBI agents have been employed at Caesars Palace to protect against skimming and other problems. They keep the Palace well protected.

In the Sixties, however, other casinos were being heavily skimmed. Bobby Kennedy projected in the early to mid-Sixties that $10 million a year was being skimmed from Nevada gaming casinos. I don't feel that was any exaggeration.

That is what led us to set up Operation VEGMON. The bug at the Fremont would eventually be discovered and would lead to a lawsuit by the licensee there, Eddy Levinson, but before it was found we learned that the boys in Vegas were using a woman, an unlikely conduit in those days especially, to move their skim. It was taken from Vegas to those mobsters around the country who had the hidden "points" in the casinos that were mobbed-up, entitling them to the skim. Ida was the wife of Irving "Niggy" Devine, the owner of the New York Meat Company, which supplied meat to the casinos, a very nice concession. In return for it, apparently, he offered his wife as the skim courier.

Ida would travel every couple of weeks, always by train. We never knew why. Perhaps she was afraid of planes. But probably because her suitcases were so heavy.

Chicago, of course, was always on her itinerary. She would come into Union Station and be met by either Mike Brodkin or George Bieber of the prominent Chicago law firm of Bieber and Brodkin. One of them would then escort her to the Ambassador East Hotel, a very nice hotel located at State and Goethe near the near north side, on Chicago's Gold Coast.

There the prominent Chicago attorney would take the cut of the skim designated for the Chicago Outfit from Ida. She would ordinarily remain at the hotel overnight and then be escorted back to Union or Northwestern Station. Ida would then travel to New York, Miami, Philadelphia, Hot Springs, Detroit, St. Louis, Cleveland and/or Boston, wherever there were mobs who deserved a piece of the pie. She was ordinarily met by people like Bieber and Brodkin, who would mask the operation with their respectability and then subsequently make the drop to their mobster clients. Talk about legal ethics!

I can't recall that we ever busted this operation. Not in Chicago at least. It gave us great intelligence, but the U.S. Attorney's office never used the results of VEGMON to prosecute any mobster. Not that I recall.

14 Triumphs and Defeats

When Tony arrived in Las Vegas to take up his duties for the Chicago mob, he settled in at Circus-Circus, the nice casino located midway on the Strip, set back a little toward I-15. Circus-Circus, in 1971, was the one hotel catering to families, a trend which today is much more pronounced.

Tony set up his operation in the gift shop at Circus-Circus. He bought that concession for $70,000 and operated there under the name of Anthony Stuart, Stuart being his wife Nancy's maiden name.

Circus-Circus had then, and still maintains today, a circus atmosphere. High-wire acts, animals, clowns, that sort of thing, were frequently on display, intentionally appealing to kids. The idea was to lure their parents into the hotel—and then, of course, into the casino. And the rooms were moderately priced, about the lowest of the nice Strip hotels.

Circus-Circus, then and now, caters to the low rollers. It was then what is known as a "grind joint." It grinded the gamblers in and grinded them out. Much like the Stardust, not far south of it on the same side of the Strip. The high rollers, those who gambled for high stakes, frequented the Desert Inn or the Riviera, across the Strip from Circus-Circus.

Circus-Circus today is a clean operation. But in 1971 it was owned by Jay Sarno, who had purchased it with a $43 million loan from—who else?—the Central States Pension Fund of the Teamsters Union. In 1972 Sarno would become the target of a major investigation into possible kickbacks on the loan. Sarno had been an executive of Caesars Palace who moved over to Circus-Circus, building it with the $43 million loan. In those days a guy didn't get a loan from the Teamsters pension fund without some very nice connections. And he didn't open up his hotel to the Chicago mob's rep in Vegas if he doesn't owe the Outfit something. Sarno obviously did.

It was a very nice deal for Tony. The gift shop at Circus-Circus did a very nice business, located as it was in this busy family hotel in the heart of the Strip. But that was not the primary reason for its success. It served as a place where Tony could be reached, as his "message drop" and his meeting place. Frequently during the day and night his phone in the gift shop rang and pages for him under the name of Anthony Stuart rang out throughout the hotel.

Shortly after Tony arrived in Las Vegas, however, he got down to some business that had been left unhandled by Marshall Caifano and Johnny Roselli. An investigator for the Las Vegas Police Department, not yet merged with the Clark County Sheriff's office to form Metro, said it best. "We've had at least five unsolved shylock murders since that guy got here," he announced.

The beaten and tortured bodies of five victims, some of them casino employees, were found in the desert near Las Vegas, the investigator told the *Chicago Sun-Times*. He added that although Tony had set up a legitimate business at Circus-

Circus, "You'd have to be retarded to think that guy was out here to sell gifts." Pretty well put.

Tony was having nothing but trouble since he arrived in town. First he was put under immediate surveillance by Mike Simon and his pals in the FBI. Then, in June, soon after he arrived, he was seized by the Clark County Sheriff's Office. He had registered as a felon soon after he arrived, as required by Nevada law. So Tony couldn't be rousted on that. But the Sheriff's Office found a way. The charges were vagrancy and loitering. Even though he was grabbed in his brand-new chocolate brown 1971 Lincoln Continental Mark IV!

Clark County detectives found that Spilotro did not have what the Nevada law calls "visible means of support." Tony scoffed at that. "I can buy every guy in this station house ten times over," he snarled at the detectives as he ripped bills from his pocket to pay the $250 bond. "And this is just my walking-around money!" he shouted. "How can I be a vagrant?"

Tony had a point. Later the charges would be dropped before trial. But the authorities had made a point. They demonstrated to him that they knew he had arrived. And that they would take no guff from him. Mike Simon would make sure that even though the federal authorities had nothing on Tony— yet—the local authorities would be kept informed on his activities so that they could bring whatever charges came within their jurisdiction. Tony was off to a rough start.

Then the investigation looking into kickbacks on the Circus-Circus loan heated up again in 1972. It was being directed by the Federal Organized Crime Strike Force headquartered in Los Angeles, which covered Las Vegas. The attorneys there, especially Dick Crane, were being assisted by Jack Barron, the supervisor of the organized crime squad of the FBI in LA, and his men Dick Richards, Skeet Daugherty, Dick Cromwell and Al Husted. For the first time the name of Joseph Lombardo surfaced in this investigation. We would learn a lot more about this mobster from Chicago as the years went by, but now we might have been put off by his media moniker, "The Clown." We would find, for one thing, that he was no clown.

Also figuring in the investigation was another name we had become familiar with, Allen M. Dorfman. Dorfman, then forty-nine, was the son of Paul "Red" Dorfman. Red had been the guy who brought Jimmy Hoffa to the attention of Murray Humphreys with the caveat that he could "control" him if Hump would lend the support of the Chicago mob to the ambitions of Hoffa in the Teamsters Union at a time when Jimmy was just an ambitious young Detroit local union leader. Hump and his pals then arranged for the advancement of Hoffa and when they got him in place as the Teamsters president they had their own guy in the spot. I vividly recall Hump saying on Little Al: "Jimmy is one of the very best guys I've ever known. When we ask for something he just goes boom, boom, boom!" One of the first things they asked was for Jimmy to put Allen Dorfman into the key spot where he could do the Chicago mob's business with the Central States Pension Fund. From then on, numerous high-risk loans were made to Las Vegas hotel-casinos, many of them to guys like Jay Sarno.

Speaking of Hoffa, he had been paroled in December 1970 from his prison sentences for jury tampering and for diverting pension funds for his own use. We learned that the Chicago mob did nothing to help him gain his parole from Richard Nixon's administration—they had no clout there—or to assist him in his plans to resume the presidency of the Teamsters. The Outfit, and other interested mobs in New York and New Jersey, had replaced the guy who went "boom, boom, boom" for them, with Frank Fitzsimmons. If Hoffa acceded to *most* every wish of the mob, Fitz acceded to *every* one. Jimmy would say no once in a while, he was a tough guy. Fitz never said no—not to the mob. So the mob had no desire to bring Hoffa back to replace Fitz. When Jimmy continued to act tough, he was taken out. In July 1975 his body was thrown into a vat of boiling zinc in a fender factory in Detroit. Not in New York Giants Stadium at the Meadowlands in New Jersey as some have it.

It wouldn't be long, however, before Tony would be in even bigger trouble. Back in Chicago. In September 1972 he was indicted back home. The case would make headlines in Chicago because the indictments included Mad Sam and Sam's brother, Mario. It was for the murder of Leo Foreman!

It seems that Johnny Bassett, my partner in the FBI, and as fine an agent as there ever was, had been talking to Chuckie Crimaldi. You'll remember that Chuckie was with Tony, Sam and Mario when they tortured and killed Leo Foreman in the basement of Mario's home in Cicero. Now Johnny loosened him up and then turned him over to the Cook County State's Attorney's office where a few former agents like Ross Spencer, my old supervisor, and John Glenville, another fine ex-Bureau agent, had gone after they retired from the FBI. The trio was indicted in Chicago and Tony waived extradition from Las Vegas and was taken into custody at the Cook County Jail. He remained there for weeks while his attorney argued that a recent ruling of the U.S. Supreme Court made murder a bondable charge because the Supreme Court had eliminated the death penalty. But then Judge Howard Babcock ruled that Illinois law clearly stipulated that bond can be denied in cases where the sentence might be life, so Tony stagnated in the hellhole which is the Cook County Jail. Sam argued that "this is a nine-year-old case built of straw," but to no avail. The "Foreman Three," as the press called them, remained incarcerated.

The trial was set for May 1973. It would be heard at the Civic Center, now the Daley Center, in the Loop, before Judge Robert A. Meier III. Chuckie Crimaldi became a star witness in the galaxy of mobsters who have "flipped," come over to our side. He was expected to be a fine witness, to describe for the jury the murder of Leo Foreman. DeStefano put on a real show at pretrial. He acted as his own attorney, with help from attorney Bob McDonald, now married to the Mafia Princess, Antoinette Giancana. Tony was most fearful that the antics of Mad Sam would prejudice the jury.

After the pre-trial, it happened. Mad Sam, Mario and Tony realized that without Chuckie Crimaldi the case against them for the murder of Leo Foreman would collapse. It all hinged on his courtroom testimony.

One fine day Tony and Mario, delegated by Sam to locate

where the state was hiding Chuckie, happily announced to Sam that they had located him! Now they planned to take him out.

The trio devised a devious plan. Mad Sam was insane with the anticipation. Tony and Mario had come up with a fool-proof plan. They told Sam they had found that Chuckie was being hidden by the police at a house near Lake Geneva, many miles northwest of Chicago. They then came back to Sam and told him they had been able to bribe the guards and that they would be able to walk into the house on any upcoming Saturday morning when the particular guards who had been bribed would be on duty. The deed could be done that Saturday if Sam was ready. Was he ready? He was ready!

That Saturday Sam was out in his garage, eager to go. Mario and Tony arrived as scheduled. Sam was beside himself. Not only would he save himself from going to jail for what would probably be the rest of his life, but he would teach a lesson to the man who had betrayed him, Crimaldi. Oh, how sweet it would be! Mario approached Sam first, Tony a couple of steps to the rear. As they got within several feet, Sam's brother suddenly stepped aside. Tony, who had been carrying a shotgun behind his back, stepped forward. He leveled the shotgun at Mad Sam and pulled one trigger of the double barrel. He then pulled the other. At such short range, Tony couldn't miss. The first blast tore Sam's right arm off. The other hit him full in the chest. He was dead before he hit the ground. Mad Sam had been rendered docile. He would torture and kill no more.

More to the point, he would not prejudice the trial of Mario and Tony. Sam had been representing himself, as per usual, in his bombastic style alienating judge and jury and making a circus of the pre-trial motions. No judge or juror could be influenced—by bribe, previous corruption or intimidation—to acquit the defendants under those conditions. The trial had become such a media carnival that no one would bring himself to withstand the furor that would be created by an acquittal. But, really, only because Mad Sam was the center of the prosecution. His kid brother, Mario, was a media nonentity. Tony, although known to the press and the public somewhat by this time, was nowhere near the celebrity that Mad Sam had become. Eliminate Sam from the trial and it would fade onto the inside pages, below the fold, and no longer be the lead item on the nightly television broadcasts. This, then, became the strategy of Tony and Mario.

It worked. Sure enough, not long into the trial, on May 22, 1973, Judge Meier called State's Attorney Bernie Carey into his chambers for a private conference. Bernie was one of the very best State's Attorneys in the history of Cook County. He had been an FBI agent, was a neighbor of mine in South Holland and had been a frequent companion of mine on our trips from South Holland to the FBI office in the Loop. I don't mind telling you I felt very free to confide in him now that he had left the Bureau and was the top prosecutor in the Chicago area. Besides, we were both protégés of the same man. The most respected public official I have ever known, Dick Ogilvie, gave Bernie his start. He offered both of us top positions in his administrations as he progressed from Cook County Sheriff to President of the Cook County Board (tantamount to being the mayor of Cook County, which includes Chicago) and then to governor of the state of Illinois. Bernie accepted.

Judge Meier told Bernie he suspected jury tampering. As a result of the meeting the courtroom was cleared of spectators for the rest of the trial. Even the media was excluded from the courtroom.

As I say, Chuckie Crimaldi was an excellent witness. He had made up his mind to go all out, he said, after he was accosted by Mad Sam in an elevator in the Federal Building while under the protection of the police. There Sam snarled at him something about fish, which indicated to Chuckie that Sam was going to feed him to the fishes. Chuckie sat eyeball to eyeball with Tony and Mario at the defense table. He never blinked. Frank Whalen, Tony's lawyer, couldn't shake him on cross-examination.

We all thought it was a dead bang case. Chuckie's testimony was well supported by other evidence, including chips of paint on Foreman's body that an expert witness testified were identical with chips of paint taken by the police from Mario's basement.

We were wrong. Although the jury brought back a verdict of guilty for Mario, Tony was acquitted. He was declared innocent of participation in the heinous murder of Leo Foreman! Tony had skated.

I was there that day. When the verdict was announced, Tony raised his arms in triumph. Then he looked at the group of law enforcement people I was a part of. He had a big grin of scorn on his face. His eyes focused for a moment on me. As he exited the courtroom, now a free man, I stepped into the aisle. "You're still just a pissant, Tony. We'll get you yet," I said, very softly but forcibly.

"Fuck you!" Tony smiled.

It was not the best day of my life. I had nothing to do with the prosecution of his trial. Charley Siragusa, the Executive Director of the Illinois Crime Investigating Committee, and Bernie Carey were the ones who deserved the credit for bringing the case. They were even more downcast than I was. But I wondered just how such a miscarriage of justice could come about. Had Judge Meier's suspicions been correct? Could there have been jury tampering? I believed then, and I believe now, that that is just about the only answer.

Mario DeStefano, a defendant in the same trial, was found guilty and sentenced to an appropriate period of time for his deed. It would be years before he would go to jail due to a lengthy appeal process. He has since died of natural causes and is no longer around to spread his brand of evil.

Tony, however, had won another round, he had walked. Now he would return to Las Vegas in triumph. The Enforcer!

15 Tony's Domain

As Tony returned to his new home on Sahara Avenue in Las Vegas in fine spirits, he was elevated to a special place of honor back in Chicago. The Intelligence Unit of the Chicago Police Department published their own Black Book, although they didn't call it that, which they distributed to all Chicago police officers. It was an encyclopedia of the top mobsters in Chicago, showing their latest photos, descriptions, home addresses, addresses of their hang-outs, associates, cars, license numbers, criminal background and *modus operandi*. Heading the list, of course, were the mob bosses of the era, Accardo, Alex and Aiuppa. But up high on the list was the name of Tony Spilotro.

The book was copied after what we called The LCN Index. Every field office of the FBI had such a listing, including not only each member of La Cosa Nostra and their close associates in their own territory, but a listing with photos of every such guy in every other field office. We had started it in the late Fifties and kept it current. It was of immeasurable use not only for tracking local mobsters, but for when we were asked to surveil or investigate a mobster of some other LCN family. If we got a phone call from the Milwaukee FBI office that Frank Balistrieri, the boss there, was coming into Chicago, or maybe Pete Licavoli from Detroit, we had his picture and description right at hand. Or if we called our New York office to tell them that Sam Giancana or Tony Accardo was being tailed into their city, then they had a photo and background of those guys. And that happened frequently, especially in the case of Giancana who traveled a great deal, to be with his love, Phyllis McGuire, who entertained all over the world. We got a great photo of the pair in London.

In June 1973, Tony would step into the limelight once more, in association with two men who would later figure prominently in his life. It was learned that he was jetting around the country with Irv Weiner, a bail bondsman closely associated with many Chicago made guys but who was not one himself, and Allen Dorfman. Dorfman had purchased a twin-engine Gulfstream jet from Frank Sinatra with $2,978,670 borrowed from the Central States Pension Fund—where else?

It was disclosed that Dorfman, then in the toughest federal prison of them all at Marion, Illinois, had been the beneficiary of glowing letters of recommendation from two prominent judges in Chicago, one of them the Chief Judge of the Criminal Courts, Joseph A. Power. That was a surprise to me. I always had considered Power to be a top guy. The other judge did not surprise me at all. He was Circuit Court Judge Daniel J. Covelli.

I knew his career had been enhanced through his association with Pat Marcy, the power broker in the regular Democratic organization of the First Ward of Chicago, who carried the orders of his superiors in the Chicago Outfit to those politicians, cops, judges and labor leaders who were "on the pad" of the Outfit. More than a handful of judges in Cook County held their positions because they were "Pat's guys," put on the bench by Pat after he received the go-ahead from Hump, Gussie, Joe Batters, Giancana or other top mob bosses. The hidden mike we had placed in Marcy's office in the First Ward across the street from City Hall had given us volumes of information about the people who were "Pat's guys." This bug, "Shade" as we code-named it, also furnished us with reams of information regarding the fixes Pat arranged but, unfortunately, it was not in place when Tony went on trial for the Foreman murder. Years later, after I left the FBI, the Chicago Office developed the Greylord cases and the Gambat cases. Dozens of Chicago area judges were convicted of corruption in the Eighties and Nineties in those cases, many of them sponsored by the First Ward. Marcy himself was indicted in the Gambat case but was severed from the trial in early 1993 when he suffered a heart attack. A few weeks later he died. I had had several confrontations with Marcy and wish he could have lived to finish his trial.

When Tony went to Las Vegas he brought along some people from Chicago to assist him. One of them was Herbie Blitzstein. "Fat Herbie, the Fat Hebe," as he was ungraciously called by many in law enforcement, was a six foot, three-hundred-pound muscle guy. At that time he sported a goatee and mustache, dressed flamboyantly and tooled around the town in a 1973 white Cadillac Eldorado. No shrinking violet, Fat Herbie had been one of the guys we tailed in the very early days of the Top Hoodlum Program. He lived at 6720 North Damen on the far northwest side with his third wife, but he spent a great deal of his time at the Tradewinds. Herbie had been a close associate of Boodie Cowan, who had been bumped off in a killing for which Tony was a prime suspect. He also had been close to Henry Kushner, another mob bookie. When we sent Kushner away, Herbie took over his clientele, just as he had Boodie Cowan's. Now Tony decided he needed some help in Vegas, not inside the casinos but outside. To help him enforce "the law."

Another guy Tony brought with him to Vegas was Joey Hansen. Tony and Joey had dropped out of Steinmetz High School about the same time and had partnered in burglaries and robberies when Tony was a top moper. But Tony didn't put Joey in Vegas; he stationed Joey in Los Angeles, actually in Marina del Rey on the ocean. This was a clear indication of the extent of Tony's new responsibilities and domain. The Outfit in Chicago rules everything in organized crime west of Chicago, with the exception of Arizona, which for some reason is open territory. Any mob can function in Phoenix or Tucson without permission from any other, just like Miami. Las Vegas and Atlantic City were open until the mid-Seventies, when the ruling body of the LCN, "The Commission," gave Las Vegas to Chicago in exchange for allowing the eastern mobs to have Atlantic City shortly after the referendum of New Jersey vot-

ers made gaming legal in Atlantic City. Hansen would thereafter handle the affairs of the Chicago mob, working closely
with the "Mickey Mouse Mafia," the family of La Cosa
Nostra which operates in southern California under the orders
of the Outfit.

Another guy Tony kept with him was Chris Petti, also a pal
of Tony's in Chicago. Like Hansen, Petti could not be
made—he was not Italian, he was Greek. But Tony trusted
him and therefore gave him the responsibility for San Diego.
The FBI was in good shape in San Diego because we had
Bomp there. Frank Bompensiro was the acting boss of the
LCN in San Diego, a made guy of the Los Angeles family
who they detailed to watch over their interests in San Diego.
But we had one fine agent in San Diego, Jack Armstrong. He
had "turned" Bomp. Everything the mob in southern California was doing we knew about. I recall eagerly waiting on
more than one occasion for the latest 209, the informant report, from Jack on Bomp's latest info. But one day in the Seventies, Bomp was in a phone booth making a call. He knew he
could not trust the phone in his home. Somebody walked up
to him and did it to him with the weapon of choice when it
can be done close up—a .22 with a silencer. After that, we
were no longer able to keep so intimately informed of Tony's
activities in the Southland.

Another guy was Paulie Schiro. Tony put Paulie in
Scottsdale to oversee the open territory of Arizona. I've been
to Paulie's house but could not find him at home. It was Paulie's reputation that whenever Tony needed help on a hit, anywhere, he called on Paulie.

There would be others added as the years went by, but two
more were noteworthy. Frank Cullotta had grown up with
Tony. In fact, before they were ten they had fought with each
other over territory, a corner on the west side where each
thought he should have the right to shine shoes. Probably the
last time Tony ever did an honest day's work. Frank Cullotta
and Tony became very close boyhood friends. They formed
the K-Knights Gang during their early teen years. They became inseparable. Then they joined together as thieves, fre-

quently working together mugging, shoplifting and stealing. Cullotta would have his own problems and his own accomplishments, but Tony would upstage him. Cullotta never joined Mad Sam or Philly, but now when Tony got his own "regime," as it is called when a guy gets a crew, gets a territory, he added Frank Cullotta to it. Tony Spilotro brought Cullotta to Las Vegas and gave him responsibility to assist him when he had problems with any recalcitrant Mr. Insides.

Another guy he would add to his stable was Sal Romano. Sal had been associated with Tony in some scores during their early years on the west side. He was never made, but he had demonstrated to Tony during their work together that he could handle himself. Tony could use Sal Romano in Las Vegas.

We can't talk about associates of Tony without mentioning one other guy, the most important man in Tony's life. His capo.

In Chicago there are generally about a half-dozen capos in the Outfit. Captains. "Crew chiefs." In mob parlance each capo has a crew, usually a dozen or so soldiers who do the work of a particular capo. Usually operating their offices, or their juice business. This is the usual work of the Chicago mob. I have often testified that gambling is the lifeblood of any organized crime family. And that "juice," loan sharking, is concomitant with gambling—the two prime sources of income to any family of La Cosa Nostra.

But Tony's capo had two responsibilities: one was to oversee Tony's activity in Las Vegas, the other was to oversee Allen Dorfman's activity regarding the Central States Pension Fund of the Teamsters. Because that pension fund was the bank of the Chicago mob—and to a great extent that of the New York, New Jersey and Detroit families of the LCN as well, these were two great responsibilities. Two great resources of the Chicago Outfit. The Chicago mob spent a great deal of time and effort making sure they had control of Las Vegas and of the Teamsters pension fund.

Tony's capo was Joey Lombardo, the guy the papers call "The Clown." As I write this he has recently been released from prison and many in Chicago law enforcement and in the media believe he will be the next boss of the Chicago mob. I don't. I agree he is the best man for the job; he has done it all. But he is on parole. Any violation will send him back to prison to complete his term, period. The FBI and every other law enforcement agency in Chicago is watching Joey. Association with mobsters is grounds for repeal of the parole, and Joey is nobody's clown. He's not an Accardo or a Humphreys or an Alex or a Cerone in intelligence and personality, but an intelligent guy. Nobody to underestimate. Joe Lombardo, as we say in FBI parlance, is one "sharp cookie."

I remember Joey well. One day my partner at the time, Johnny Bassett, and I were sent out to arrest him. We arrived at his house in the 2200 block of West Ohio, where he still lives, and pounded on his door at about six in the morning, under the impression that we would collar him before he got up. But he was already gone according to his comely wife. We pushed our way into his house and discovered she was not lying to us. We decided we would remain in his house, awaiting his return, surreptitiously, not having any better leads to find him. It became early afternoon. Lombardo's wife approached us as we sat in her living room. "Do you fellows like Italian?" she asked. (I sure do—it's my favorite food.) Would you believe that while we were waiting there to arrest her husband, Mrs. Lombardo fixed us a wonderful Italian meal? I'll admit I didn't accept her offer of coffee, remembering the pretty wife of another mobster, but Johnny did. And he told me it was great.

Joey finally showed up about six in the evening. We pounced on him as soon as he opened the door, knowing that it is a gray area as to whether we had the authority to invade his private premises like that. He was naturally irate. He yelled at the top of his lungs at his wife, demanding to know why she had allowed us to stay. I didn't have the heart to let him know she not only let us stay, she fixed us a scrumptious meal to make us feel at home. I kind of hate to tell this story now, bringing it to Joey's attention for the first time, but I hope enough years have passed so that Joey won't take offense at his wife's hospitality to us. Joey must realize by now what a gem of a wife he has, after all these years that she has stuck by him.

Such was the guy the Outfit designated as Tony's capo, his immediate boss. In all his days in Las Vegas, Tony responded to the orders of Joey Lombardo. Tony would never be anything but a soldier in the Chicago family of La Cosa Nostra. A most important soldier, obviously, responsible as he was for Nevada, the most important operation they had. Their enforcer.

Speaking of Nevada, let me say this. We often overlook the other gaming hot spots in Nevada. We refer to Las Vegas like that's where all the action is. It surely is not. It is the largest gaming location but there are others that rival it. And Tony had responsibility for all of them.

In recent years, Laughlin has flourished. It is located just across the Colorado River from Arizona, closest to the source of its largest clientele in California. It's close to Bullhead City, Lake Havasu and Yuma, and is not all that far from Phoenix and Tucson. There are a dozen very nice hotel-casinos in Laughlin, all along the Colorado. It is to Las Vegas as Branson is to Nashville: nice entertainment, nice ambience, not as sophisticated. Laughlin gets good entertainment, though not always the big stars like Wayne Newton, Sinatra and Minnelli. Nevertheless, the gross from Laughlin has increased each year during the Eighties and Nineties and it has become a favorite for thousands of players.

Reno is another hot gambling spot. "The Biggest Little Town in the Country" was established as a gambling mecca long before 1946, when Bugsy made Las Vegas its bigger brother. It was strong before Bugsy and it is still strong. There are dozens of very nice hotel-casinos up north in Nevada and it is a very nice town to visit. I enjoy the Bally Grand, which once had the largest casino floor in the world. I've stayed there a half dozen times and I always enjoy it.

There are other nice spots in Nevada, like Sparks, where the large Nugget hotel-casino is located. And Carson City, where I spent so much time looking into the Ormsby House, down from the State House and the Nevada Supreme Court on the main drag.

But my favorite place in all of Nevada is Lake Tahoe. The four major hotel-casinos on the south shore all rival anything in Vegas. The Cal-Neva, Sinatra's old joint, is on the north shore, on Crystal Bay, on the state line between California and Nevada, hence its name. It was the place Sam Giancana had a hidden interest in and the hotel Sinatra lost his license over when he welcomed Giancana there in violation of the Black Book rule.

So when I saw that Tony Spilotro was sent out west to enforce mob rule in Las Vegas, I mean a lot more than that. Not only Las Vegas, but Reno, Laughlin, Sparks, Lake Tahoe and all the other operations west of Chicago that the Outfit might have an interest in—or might envision having an interest in. At the age of thirty-four, Tony was stationed in Vegas to oversee *all* the activity of the Chicago mob in the west. California, Arizona, Colorado, wherever the Outfit had interests, all were overseen by "Tough Tony," as he was now sometimes being called, Tony Spilotro. The Enforcer.

16 Tony Wins Big

Tough Tony just couldn't stay out of trouble. On February 18, 1974, just months after he had skated on the Leo Foreman murder, he was indicted once more and hauled back to Chicago to make bond. The case made the front pages of all four Chicago daily newspapers and was at the time the lead item on the television and radio news.

Indicted with Tony was his capo, Joey Lombardo. I recall a

newspaper photo of the two of them, head to head, signing papers to make bond.

Also indicted was Allen Dorfman, who had just been released from prison in December after being convicted for taking a kickback for a loan from his Central States Pension Fund, and Irv Weiner, the bail bondsman.

A fifth guy indicted was someone I never met but for whom I was always on the lookout, Don DeAngelis. He was the electronics expert of the mob. He came to our attention when he was caught by the Chicago PD on a boat off Navy Pier attempting to bug the nearby headquarters of the Intelligence Unit of the Chicago PD, the unit responsible for the CPD's investigation of organized crime. We also learned that DeAngelis had developed a scanner which could pick up our radio broadcasts. For instance, if we had a surveillance on anyone, say Sam Giancana, DeAngelis would be listening to our car/radio transmissions. If we called Giancana by name or transmitted that "he's leaving his house at the corner of Wenonah and Fillmore, going to head toward Harlem," DeAngelis was primed to realize that Wenonah and Fillmore was the corner on which Giancana's house in Oak Park was located. Giancana made his business to stop at a pay phone on the street and call DeAngelis soon after he took off on his daily rounds. If DeAngelis had positive information for him, Giancana thereby knew we were on him. If not, then Giancana knew he was free that day to go about his mob business, at least at that time. So we were interested in nailing DeAngelis. It was good to get him indicted and, hopefully, on his way to the slammer.

The indictment was the work of IRS agents and U.S. Postal Service inspectors. We at the FBI worked with them on the case, but the credit should rightfully go to them. The prosecution would be handled by the staff of Jim Thompson who would use it, if successful, to further his political career. Indeed, Thompson later served as governor of Illinois.

It charged that the defendants defrauded the Teamsters Central States Pension Fund of $1.4 million. A loan in that amount had been made from the pension fund for a plastics company, since defunct, in Deming, New Mexico. The indictment charged that most of the money thereby obtained was not used for the company, the American Pail Company, but instead was "siphoned off and diverted for the personal benefit of those involved in the scheme." In fact, it would later be charged that some of the money thus diverted was used by defendant Anthony John Spilotro to purchase his gift shop, Anthony Stuart, Ltd., in the Circus-Circus Hotel. The offenses charged came within the jurisdiction of the federal courts because the mails and interstate phone service were used in furtherance of the scam.

The vast bulk of the information on which the indictment was based came from Daniel Seifert, a typical American citizen. Maybe not all that typical, though, when you think about it. He had great courage. He came forward after being contacted by state investigators and the IRS and the postal authorities.

Seifert, age twenty-four, was formerly the president of the International Fiber Glass Company in Elk Grove Village, a western suburb of Chicago. He told the investigators:

"I used to have a fiber glass business and I lost it. I took a job as a carpenter's helper. In 1967, I was working at the home of Mr. Weiner and he heard me talking about all the money that could be made in the fiber glass business. A few days later, Mr. Weiner contacted me and asked me to tell him more about the prospects of this business. I told him then about how well I had done in 1965 and how, with the right kind of location and financing, a thriving business could be started."

Seifert went on to say that he guessed that "Mr. Weiner must have been impressed because Mr. Weiner asked me to meet with him to pick out a good location for such a business. We started the new business with $10,000 of which I put up $3,333, Mr. Weiner put up $3,333 and a man named Felix Alderisio put up the final third."

Seifert advised that he had no idea who Felix Alderisio might have been until a customer picked up a copy of *Life* magazine that identified Philly as a well-known mobster. The customer then stopped doing business with Seifert's company.

Nonetheless, at the time, Dan Seifert thought he was running a legitimate business. Instead, the proceeds of a loan to the company from the Central States Pension Fund of the Teamsters, arranged by Alderisio through Allen Dorfman, his pal, were siphoned off, thereby defrauding the pension fund.

After the bond was placed, Tony returned to Las Vegas. But soon another problem reared its ugly head. If Tony thought that by physically being in another state he would be out of sight and mind of law enforcement in Chicago, he had another thing coming. Art Nasser was an Appeals Attorney for the IRS in Chicago. He got involved with John D'Arco, the corrupt alderman and Democratic Ward Committeeman of the First Ward. I ran into Nasser one day while he was with the IRS, dining with D'Arco.

Afterwards I told Nasser through a mutual friend that he had some lousy friends and that if anything further came to my attention I'd have to take a good look at him. Shortly thereafter we arrested Nasser and some of his associates. When I brought in one of Nasser's friends to the FBI office, I ran into Nasser as he sat waiting to be fingerprinted and mugged. He gave me a wry smile. "I should have listened to your advice," he said. I just nodded. Actually, Art is a nice guy and a sharp attorney. He just used some poor judgment when he was young. My most recent encounter with him was on November 15, 1993 when I chatted with him during a break in the trial of Sam Carlisi, the Chicago mob boss, in federal court in Chicago. Carlisi had been indicted under RICO for running a gambling operation called "The Sam Carlisi Street Crew," and Nasser was one of the attorneys who defended him in this trial. Nasser has come a long way from his days working for the government to his current work against it.

IRS agents seized a typewriter in Nasser's law office during an investigation of an income tax return Tony Spilotro had filed. The agents felt that it was a fraudulent return and they wanted to ascertain whether it had been typed at Nasser's office. IRS believed that Spilotro filed a false return when he claimed employment from Gaylur Mercantile Corp., a company connected with American Pail, the Deming, New Mexico company. The president of Gaylur was then Harold Lurie, who all the while was cooperating with C-1 agents John Roberts, Denny Shanahan and Christie Malone. Lurie denied, privately at the time, that Spilotro was employed by Gaylur.

Before the "Teamster Fraud" case could come to trial, Tony again hit the headlines in Chicago. The media there just couldn't get him out of their heads. Sam Giancana had been slain by his own people and the media went on a feeding frenzy as to who might succeed him. Tony was mentioned as a prime candidate. Actually, the media was misinformed about Giancana's position with the Outfit. At the time of his death Giancana had been out of the mob leadership since he got out of jail in 1966. He had voluntarily exiled himself for eight years, traveling around the world with my informant, double agent Dick Cain, who kept me advised of all the contacts they were making, setting up a worldwide gambling operation. Finally, however, we prevailed upon the Mexican government to throw Giancana out of Mexico in 1974. When he returned via O'Hare to Chicago, I was there to greet him. He blamed me for his problems, but it was one of our few confrontations that was not hostile. He apologized to me for making it personal and told me I would now find he was into nothing in Chicago. About a year later he was dead. He refused to cut the Outfit in on what he had developed during the eight years of his exile, saying that it was his personal business, not mob business. Tony Accardo didn't agree with that. Accardo had chopped many in his day—what was one more? One evening in the summer of 1975, Sam was in the basement of his home at 1147 South Wenonah in Oak Park. Somebody he trusted came down to see him. Pow. Multiple shots with the same type of weapon that killed Bomp in the phone booth in San Diego. A .22 with a silencer.

So now the great buzz in the media those days was which "young Turk" would succeed Sam, even though Sam had been out since 1966. It was a real non-story, but it was the talk of the media in 1975.

Who else but Tony Spilotro could succeed Sam Giancana in

1975? One article in the evening *Daily News* described him as "ruthless." The *Daily News* was right. The reporter further identified him as "having many of the traits of Giancana." He went on to say that "Spilotro learned how to turn a fast buck, using terrorist methods, as a protégé of Felix (Milwaukee Phil) Alderisio, a long time mob terrorist." Right again. The article went on to identify one other prospective successor to Giancana. He was James "Turk" Torello, the capo in charge of the west side of Chicago, another tough guy, another real killer. The article cautioned that "Spilotro and Torello could become rivals if a power struggle [were to develop] among the mob's younger faction."

I am frequently questioned on talk shows about the possibility of a power struggle in the Chicago crime syndicate and the possibility that a young Turk might gun his way into power. Some even refer to the "time when Giancana overthrew Accardo." Listen—Giancana never overthrew Accardo. Accardo had had enough. Enough power, enough money, enough headaches. He wanted out. The Outfit let him go *only* if he would agree to stay on as *consiglieri*. There was no revolt. The Chicago family of La Cosa Nostra is the most monolithic, disciplined, united family of the LCN in the country. Succession comes only after deliberation by the leadership. It does not come from any dissident faction. There simply is none. Never really has been.

None of this attention did Spilotro any good. When the media promotes a mobster into celebrity status, it goads law enforcement to go after him. After all, if you take down a top moper, fine, well and good. If you take down a Top Jewel Thief, hey, that's a good job, fellas. But if you take down an upper-echelon member of the Chicago crime syndicate you deserve a merit raise in salary, maybe even a promotion.

Naturally, therefore, any law enforcement agency will devote its manpower to the top mobsters, not to the low-ranking officers. Get the boss, the underboss, the *consiglieri* and the capos. Devote lesser attention to the soldiers and the mob associates, as non-members but "connected" hoods are designated.

* * *

The almost indispensable witness in the Teamster pension fund case against Spilotro, Lombardo, Dorfman, Weiner, DeAngelis and two others was still Danny Seifert, now twenty-nine, the president of the company in Chicago which was utilized to divert much of the money from the fund.

Three months before the trial was to begin, in September 1974, Seifert, his wife and four-year-old son were in their factory in suburban Chicago. It was a Friday morning. Four men entered the building. They were masked and Dan knew they were up to no good. To protect himself and his family he ran, separated himself from them. But the men caught him. They blasted him in the face with a shotgun. While on the ground and in full view of his wife, one of the men stepped up to Seifert and, according to Mrs. Seifert, "blew his head off" with a shotgun. It's hard to understand how we can have such people in our society, but we sure do. Spilotro and Lombardo were generally suspected of being two of the four gunmen. It figures. Both had performed similar acts and it was in their best interest to kill the prime witness against them.

When the government still went ahead with the trial they had just one witness left. Harold Lurie. Lurie was not a Seifert. He was nervous and unsteady. I would say cowardly, but maybe that's unfair—after all, he took the stand. But his testimony was shaky. Harold sat on the stand with Spilotro staring at him intently. He sweated, he whimpered. He was anything but a good witness. Before the case went to the jury Tony was dropped from it. In April 1975 Lombardo, Dorfman and the others were acquitted. Tony had skated again!

The problems with Harold Lurie were typical. Many times a witness will tell a good story while being debriefed and it looks like he will stand up under cross-examination. Therefore, based to a large extent on the assessment of his ability to convince a jury he is telling the truth and that the truth will be instrumental in convicting the defendant, the prosecution goes ahead. Most of the time the witness holds up. But sometimes his poor performance dooms the case. Shanahan, Roberts and Malone, ably assisted by another C-1 agent of great ability,

Gus Kempff, did all they could to develop and maintain Lurie as a CTE. He was great when he could relate his information in private as an informant, but not in public as a witness, in front of the people he was accusing. The agents couldn't hold his hand while he was on the stand. He collapsed up there and the case fell apart. Double-jeopardy set in and Spilotro, Lombardo and the others could not be retried. It hurt.

More and more now, back in Las Vegas, the heat was on Tony. The Gaming Control Board pressured Jay Sarno at Circus-Circus to throw Tony "Stuart" out of the gift shop where he was then making his headquarters. They only succeeded when Sarno sold Circus-Circus in late 1974 to a group of buyers from Reno. So Tony was forced to sell his concession. It wasn't so bad. He'd paid $70,000 for it but sold it for $700,000. One of the buyers felt sure the gift shop was worth a lot less than $700,000. But when Spilotro appeared and demanded the full amount, the group immediately caved in. They had read all about him in the *Las Vegas Review-Journal* and the *Las Vegas Sun*. "We didn't want any trouble with that guy," the group decided.

Smart choice. And they weren't alone.

17 Lefty

The guy Tony had to work with most closely in Vegas was his old friend, Frank "Lefty" Rosenthal. Lefty was the hidden boss of the Stardust, Chicago's flagship hotel-casino. It was a major hotel, almost in the middle of the Strip, in a most strategic location. It really was a gold mine for Chicago. It had some luxury suites but it mainly catered to low rollers. Out back it had a long string of what looked like Motel 6 one-room cabins. Further out, a big lot for RVs and vans and trailers.

The owner of record during these years was Allen Glick. Glick was a young San Diego businessman who had gone to school with one of the sons of Frank Balistrieri, the LCN boss in Milwaukee, Milwaukee being subservient to the Chicago LCN. The son recommended Glick to his dad, his dad contacted Chicago and suddenly Allen Glick was the ostensible owner of a multimillion-dollar property. Due to his clean record, he was quickly granted a gaming license by the Gaming Control Board and things looked rosy for him.

Lefty Rosenthal was sent to Vegas to control Glick and to make sure the skim was huge and that it got to Chicago.

Let's take a look at Rosenthal's background. He came out of the same west side neighborhood of Chicago as Tony, ten years earlier. He started out working in hot dog stands that were also book joints. He served in the Army, but the year I first met him, 1961, was the year he bribed players in the Oregon-Michigan football game and later took the Fifth.

That year I infiltrated a large bookmaker office in Chicago headed by Donald "The Wizard of Odds" Angelini, several years before he became a capo. Donald is a very personable guy, with a nice appearance, trim build and white hair. He's educated, articulate and was never hostile to me in some fifty times we have talked. I posed as a degenerate sports bettor. The Cincinnati Reds were not figured to win the National League pennant that year. Their odds, especially in the early to mid-season, were very good. Donald knew I was an FBI agent—I made no bones about that—but I pretended, while betting with Bureau money, to be a degenerate bettor. It worked out a lot better than I had any reason to believe. I bet on the Reds and as the season went by Donald thought I was the luckiest guy in the world. Later he seemed to concede that I knew what I was doing. He came to me one day in August as I sat talking to one of his clerks, who just happened to be young Lefty Rosenthal, getting his start in the gambling business.

"Bill," I remember him saying, "I was talking to Mike

Brodkin, our lawyer, today. We both know Bobby Kennedy has just had those three federal gambling laws passed giving the federal government jurisdiction over local gambling for the first time and giving you guys the whip. Mike doesn't think it's very wise to let you bet into us anymore. In fact, he thinks maybe you knew about these laws and you have been setting up for the time they would be passed. All in all, Bill, I think it best if you stopped coming around. Here's what we owe you, your figure" [as they called the amount of a player's wins and losses]. "Thanks a lot."

I arrested Donald twice in the years to come, not that I enjoyed it. He is now spending the rest of his life in federal prison after a conviction in early 1993 in San Diego for attempting to infiltrate the Rincon Indian Reservation so that he could skim it for the Chicago mob. Too bad.

Lefty went on to bigger and better things from the days when I knew him. He was banned by South Florida officials from the race tracks there, then he was convicted in 1962 for bribing an NYU basketball player and fined $6,000. Then he was sent by the Outfit to do their business in sports gambling, his field of expertise. That's where Tony joined up with him. In the late Sixties he was reassigned to Las Vegas where he had the Rose Bowl Race and Sports Book, a betting establishment independent of any hotel.

In 1970 he was indicted with Jerome Zarowitz, a prominent Las Vegas hotel executive associated with Caesars Palace, and Elliot Paul Price, who had been perhaps New England's best known bookmaker before he relocated to Vegas. I recall looking into his affairs when I discovered he was a pal of Gussie Alex, my first target under the Top Hoodlum Program, a guy Gussie laid bets off to when Gussie had the Loop for the Outfit. The arrests were for Interstate Transmission of Wagering Information, one of the laws passed under the aegis of Bobby Kennedy in 1961 to which Donald Angelini had referred. The arrests of Rosenthal et al were made as part of a nationwide raid. Rosenthal was arrested during a raid on his Rose Bowl betting establishment. Warrants were also served at Caesars Palace, where in Zarowitz's safety-deposit box $1 million in

$100 bills was discovered. All charges were subsequently dismissed.

Following his arrest, Rosenthal moved into the Stardust. In 1971 he was called back to Chicago, summoned to a meeting with Tony Accardo, Gus Alex and Joey Aiuppa. It was Accardo who did most of the talking. He said something like this:

"Lefty, we're giving you a big step up. As you know, we got the Stardust out there. The skim from there has been very good. We've had Johnny Drew there since we opened it. Now we find we need somebody else there to make sure the skim comes good. So we're gonna give you that responsibility. You will be our man inside the casino. You run things. Everybody reports to you and you report to us. It's your ass if things don't go well, nobody else's. Now we are also sending another guy to help you out there. Not inside the Stardust or the Desert Inn or the Fremont or the Riviera, the other joints we skim, but to do what has to be done to keep the guys inside those places in line. You know the kid, he was with you in Florida. Spilotro. You know Vegas. Help him get his feet on the ground there. But keep him quiet. You have trouble with anybody out there, go to him, let him handle the heavy stuff out there. You keep your nose clean. You and Spilotro work together. Close. You inside, him outside."

And so Lefty moved into the Stardust. First ostensibly as a floorman, overseeing the dealers and stickmen. But a floorman must be licensed by GCB, the Gaming Control Board. In view of Lefty's arrests in Florida, he was refused a license. It didn't make much difference, the Outfit just moved him into public relations at the Stardust, a position which did not require a license because employees in public relations were not directly involved with gaming. Lefty's function for the Outfit didn't require any work in public relations or anything else. Just the skim and that was sub rosa.

In 1974, the Argent Corporation had taken over the Stardust as the front for the Chicago mob and Allen Glick had become the executive in charge, what is called the licensee. Lefty became the Executive Casino Coordinator then. On the surface he reported to Glick, but he and Glick knew who was the real boss.

In 1975, Lefty became Executive Consultant and Director of Nevada Operations for Argent. Again, just a cover for his real position as overseer of Chicago's interests.

In 1979 the GCB and the FBI discovered a tremendous slot skim at the Stardust. The Bureau and the GCB had been working together and had placed undercover agents inside the Stardust. Lefty was held responsible by his bosses in Chicago, but was left in charge. Now, however, he was forced out of the Stardust by the GCB and became a columnist for the Valley *Times*, a community newspaper in Vegas.

When the charges based on the slot skim were overturned, Lefty returned to the Stardust as the Food and Beverage Director, another position that did not require a license.

In 1978, Lefty would become the Director of Entertainment at the Stardust.

Lefty had traveled a road paved with controversy and dispute. I guess you might say Lefty was representative of Las Vegas. He fit in well in the ambience there. You might even say he was a good partner for Tony. But that marriage was not made in heaven.

18 The Alibi

In 1975, Allen Glick, then running Argent Corporation, the holding company for the Stardust, the Hacienda, the Fremont and the Marina, was having a problem. In addition to the big money he had gotten from the Central States Pension Fund of the Teamsters he had also gotten a big hunk from a prosperous real estate owner in southern California. Glick had gotten almost $2 million from her. Not much when compared to the $62.75 million loan he had gotten from the mob's bank, the Teamsters pension fund, but nothing to sneeze at, either. It was to him some walking-around money. But now Glick was having some difficulty with Tamara Rand, although I was never clear on the gist of the problem. I knew that she had signed a contract with the Hacienda to receive $100,000 a year as a consultant and that she had been in Vegas meeting with Glick over the problem in 1975.

The way the FBI in Vegas figured it, Glick went to Lefty with his problem with Rand. Lefty took it right where he had been instructed to take such problems. To Tony.

The deed was soon accomplished. With the weapon of choice once more, a high standard .22 with a silencer. To the head. A lot like the method involved in the Giancana killing the same year. Tamara Rand had been causing Allen Glick problems. Therefore she had been causing the Outfit problems. She had to go, and she did. In San Diego where she lived.

Actually, it is very unusual that the Chicago mob would hit a woman. Chopping a woman is not an ordinary practice for them, but this case was very irregular. The Outfit decided that Tamara Rand should be killed because she had operated in a man's world, or so they perceived. She was not protected as somebody's wife or girlfriend. She had gotten involved in their operation in Las Vegas with their prime front, Glick, and now it mattered little what her gender was. She had done her deed, now they did theirs. It was as simple as that.

Mike Simon and his fellow agents felt sure they knew who was responsible. So did Jack Armstrong and his fellow agents in San Diego. But they could never develop the evidence to show that "the Little Guy," as they called him, was personally responsible. It seemed obvious but Tony had covered his tracks well.

I'm not sure it was on this occasion, but to the best of my recollection it was the Tamara Rand situation over which Duncan Everette got himself in trouble.

Dunc had some conversations with Tony when Tony would make him on a surveillance. Tony was very friendly with

Dunc. And, in turn, Dunc displayed a friendly attitude when talking to Tony. To outsiders it might seem somewhat out of line for an FBI agent to be friendly with his adversary, his target. Not really. We are all taught first of all to obey all the rules of civil rights, to conduct ourselves as gentlemen even when up against our subjects. But even more important, all agents of organized crime investigations are judged by our informants. If Tony Spilotro could be influenced by any means to provide information of value to the investigation of organized crime it would well be worth being nice to the guy, no matter what Dunc might think about him personally.

It worked for me on several occasions. I always treated my targets as they treated me. If they snarled at me like Giancana I sometimes lost my cool and retaliated in kind. But if they treated me with respect I reciprocated. Murray "The Camel" Humphreys was a typical example. I ran into him during my investigations of him on several occasions. He treated me with respect. He and I negotiated the "family pact," where we stayed away from the families of the mob and they stayed away from our families. Yet, I single-handedly built the case against him in 1965 which resulted in his arrest. That same night he died of a heart attack. I didn't rejoice over his death, quite to the contrary, but my point is that an FBI agent can be friendly and respectful of his foe, but at the same time do his utmost to put him away.

In any event, Dunc and Tony, although adversaries, were not bitter toward each other. Dunc badly wanted to develop Tony as a CTE, but he couldn't do it by fighting with the guy.

However, in this instance Dunc went a little too far, was a little too friendly. And Tony sucked him in. Or so it appeared. Tony still spent a great deal of time in his Maple Avenue home in Chicago, mostly tending to his business in Vegas, conferring with Joey Lombardo and his other bosses. When Tony was in town, Dunc would learn about it from the sources on Tony he had developed. He would then put Tony under physical surveillance. Tony would sometimes spot Dunc and they would talk.

Tony invited Dunc to visit him in Las Vegas. He would

have Dunc comped at the Desert Inn and Dunc would have a good time at no expense. Dunc had made a big mistake. Not by accepting Tony's invitation, because he was hopeful that it would lead to a relationship with Tony that would be beneficial to our investigative interests. But Dunc didn't discuss it with Vinnie Inserra, his supervisor, or with any of the rest of us. He decided to take Tony up on his offer and fly out to Vegas on his own time, on a weekend.

The only problem was that on that weekend Tony was off to San Diego, probably to kill Tamara Rand. He met with Dunc when Dunc arrived in Vegas, helped him get settled, excused himself for several hours while Dunc napped after his flight, and then spent the rest of the weekend with Dunc. He never furnished Dunc with anything helpful concerning any investigation and Dunc flew back to Chicago on Sunday evening, having had a good time but not accomplishing his real purpose. He had tried to flip Tony, but you don't win every inning of every game.

While investigating the murder of Tamara Rand, the San Diego PD quite naturally determined that Tony was the prime suspect. They asked the San Diego field office of the Bureau for help. The San Diego office asked the Las Vegas office to interview Tony to determine his whereabouts on the day in question. They eventually brought Tony in for an interview. He had an alibi. A pretty good alibi. He disclosed that he had spent the weekend with Dunc!

The Special Agent in Charge of the Las Vegas Office called the SAC in Chicago. Dunc was brought in. Was this true? Dunc explained his legitimate reason for his trip. He explained that he hadn't sought authority for the trip and had made it at his own expense because it was a shot in the dark—he knew the odds of developing Tony as an informant were low but he had wanted to give it his best shot. He felt he should be commended for his effort. I sympathized with him. Knowing Dunc as I did, I accepted his story that it was not a comped time in Vegas that he was seeking but the accomplishment of his goal to turn Tony. However, the SAC did not see it that way. Dunc received a letter of censure and a suspension for a couple of weeks, as I recall.

More important than that, however, Tony skated on the Tamara Rand killing. Typical Tony. He had led Dunc into a trap and used the overeager agent to set up his alibi. Needless to say, Tony was never arrested for the murder.

The entire episode led me to desire all the more to get the guy. To bring him down would be a major accomplishment, in my opinion. I could just see him out there where he was the cock of the walk, gloating over what he had done.

19 Face-to-Face Encounters

When Duncan Everette returned to Chicago from his not-too-successful trip to Las Vegas, he and I sat down. He told me everything that had happened. I fully understood what he had tried to do. On paper it might appear to have been foolish. But the best agents are those who don't always go by the book. Had it worked he would have been a hero, bringing Tony over. It didn't and now he was severely second-guessed. I decided to do something about it. Not much, but something.

Three days before Dick Cain was brutally murdered we had sat down for the last time, after scores of such meetings when he reported to me in his role as a double agent. He told me that Tony returned to Chicago frequently to report to his capo, Joey Lombardo, and that when he was in Chicago he frequented Ragtime, a nondescript bar located near his Chicago home in Oak Park.

Knowing this information, I sat down with one of my CTEs who was high up in the Outfit and in a position to know when Tony would be coming back to report to his capo. I asked him to call me immediately when he learned that Tony was in town. Sure enough, my CTE reached out for me within three weeks. And I headed for Ragtime that night. And the next night when I didn't find Tony there the first time.

Tony was seated at a table with several of his Chicago playmates. I walked up to him. I could see he recognized me immediately, just as I expected he would after our meeting in Columbus Park and our brief encounter following his trial in the Foreman murder case.

"Feeling pretty good about yourself, I see," I opened.

Tony was. He was flying high at this time. His capo had congratulated him on his achievements in Las Vegas and, of course, he had skated on the Foreman killing and the Tamara Rand murder—along with others. And he had had a few drinks. Besides, he was a big man with this crowd. He couldn't look weak in this company.

"Well, well, well, lookee see who's here!" I recall him saying. "Fellas, this is Roemer. But I'm sure you don't know who Roemer is! He's the flunky with the FBI. Goes around throwing his weight around, scaring women and children!"

Now I began to get my ire up a little. I replied in kind.

"Look who's talking, guys," I flashed. "This is the guy who *kills* women and children!"

Now it was Tony who bristled.

"Fuckin' lie!" he shouted, as he rose now for the first time since I had entered. But then he sat down immediately. He had pushed up close to me and realized the disparity in our sizes.

"Tell Danny Seifert that, Pissant!"

"Nobody killed his wife and kids!" Tony responded.

"But you killed him right in front of them. Takes a lot of guts, guys," I said as I turned to Tony's companions at his table, "to be one of four guys who walk in on a lone guy, just a private citizen, unarmed, unexpected, walk in with shotguns, and gun him down. Don't get on the wrong side of this man, guys, you might be next. You don't know what Pissant here might do next!"

Tony was really mad now.

"I want to talk to you, Tony, privately. Want to step outside?"

"Hell no, I don't want to go anyplace with you, Roemer!" Tony said.

"I didn't think so. This guy isn't much for one-on-one, face-to-face," I told his pals.

Tony turned red. This was not exactly his idea of a victory party. He was at Ragtime, with all his pals, picking up the tabs, feeling very good about himself, the king of his neighborhood, the big man on the campus. Now some big guy walks in and starts tearing his image down. And believe me, image means a great deal to a mobster. They've all seen the *Godfather* series many times. Mario Puzo did a great job of capturing the ambience of the mob. And most of them try to live up to those characters. Just as they try to imitate the character in *Wiseguy* which Nick Pileggi wrote so well and turned into the movie *Good Fellas*. Don't think many, many mobsters haven't gone to school on the people in Puzo and Pileggi's books. Sad, but true. Now here was Tony Spilotro trying to capture that persona and some asshole walks in and shoots him down—or does a good job trying. He couldn't take it. Not under those circumstances.

"Fuck you, Roemer," he shouted.

"You ain't gonna fuck me, Pissant. Not like you did Duncan Everette. You think you're a fuckin' wise guy, Pissant. Let me tell you what I came here to tell you. You ain't gonna get away with it. We might not get you for the San Diego thing, we might not get you for a lot of things. But we'll get you. This latest act of yours isn't going to go unpunished, Spilotro. You're on top of our list now, Pissant, and we're gonna get you for something, sooner or later, and by God we're gonna make it as soon as we can!"

I was finished, I had done what I had come to do, but I didn't rush out. I stood over Tony, glaring at him.

Tony didn't say a word. But he didn't flinch either. He glared back. Then he whispered, "Fuck you, Roemer! Go throw your best shot!"

Slowly I turned. I gave him one last shot of my hardest look and then smiled. I looked at the guys at his table and widened my smile. All of them, and everybody else in the joint, had taken this in. In silence. They heard it all, much to Tony's dismay. He had not exactly won this exchange. I slowly turned with my head high, began to leave the bar. I reached over, grabbed a handful of peanuts and walked out the door.

But I wasn't finished yet.

Very early the next morning, I drove over to 1300 Lake Shore Drive, the high-rise apartment building overlooking the lake, where Gus Alex lived in his condo. Gussie and I knew each other well. He was my first target, almost twenty years earlier. We have never been friendly. He repeatedly kept me at arm's length when I attempted to turn him. I had tried several times and we knew each other by sight and name.

Gus Alex was then the leader of the "connection guys." We called them the corruption squad because corruption is what they do. Every mob needs public officials in their hip pocket. Judges, cops, labor leaders, all kinds of people who can grant them favorable treatment from their position of power. The Outfit has done an outstanding job in this regard and Gussie has been a prime mover in the connection guys for decades. First under his mentor, Jack "Greasy Thumb" Guzik, and then under Murray Humphreys. When Hump died in 1965 Gussie took over. He would remain the top man in the connection guys until he went to prison in 1992, when Lenny Patrick flipped and testified against him.

From sad experience I knew that Gussie, or Slim as I called him, since that was his code-name in the Outfit and I wanted him to know I knew it, would not let me into his apartment. There was no sense trying that, no sense even knocking on his door. Nor would I be successful if I waited for him in the lobby. I knew the doorman was on his pad, and would alert Gussie to my presence.

I did what I had done scores of times. I parked my Bureau car on a side street and kept the building under observation. I knew Gussie's Mercedes well and I watched for it. Finally, about eight-thirty, I spotted him coming out. Gussie has always been most conscientious. He had made me the very first time I ever tried to fisur him, and now as he drove up to the top of the ramp, he looked. All around. To see if he could spot me or any other law enforcement officer who might want to tail him this day. But I'd been through this drill many times with Gussie. I made sure he didn't make me, and when eventually he pulled away, slowly, watching through his rearview mirror, I made my move. I sped to him, intercepted him after a couple of blocks and cut him off.

I jumped out of my car. Gussie was astonished. I believe he thought he was going to be arrested.

"Slim!" I shouted. "I got something I want to discuss with you. Just give me a minute."

Gussie looked. Then slowly rolled down his window. We were on Lake Shore Drive, in the height of the morning rush hour. Cars were whizzing around us at fifty miles an hour. But I was on the inside of the inside lane.

"Slim," I told him, "I want to tell you something. Your guy, Spilotro. He jackpotted one of our best agents. Out in Vegas. Used him for a phony alibi that he didn't do that job in San Diego. You understand what I'm saying, you're aware of that?"

Alex didn't say a word. But he nodded.

"I just want to tell you, here and now, Gus, that that ain't done! You understand me?" Gussie kept looking into his rearview mirror as cars slammed to a halt just feet from the rear of his car and then honked as the drivers swore at us. We were impeding the rush hour. And risking Gussie's prize Mercedes, to say nothing of his life. He was distracted. But I made sure he understood what I was saying. I was yelling and pronouncing my words very clearly, talking very slowly, giving great emphasis to each word.

"You understand that, don't you, Slim? You don't put an FBI agent in the jackpot! You do and you got some *real* enemies! You understand what I'm telling you, Slim?"

Gussie still didn't say anything. But he nodded, looked at me and then back quickly into his rearview mirror as another car skidded to a halt just a couple of feet behind him.

"You don't do what Spilotro did!" I made that clear once

again. "If you do, Gussie, not only does the FBI get pissed at *you* but at the whole Outfit!"

Gussie was highly nervous by now, but not because of my remarks. The commotion we had caused on Lake Shore Drive made him fearful for his life. He nodded once more.

"We're coming after him, Gus, but we're coming after all of you for allowing an asshole like him to do what he did! You got me on that, Slim?"

Gussie finally spoke. "Yeah, I got that, Roemer. Now can I go?"

"Be sure you understand, Slim. And get it to your pals. Make sure Joe knows," I said, referring to the Man, Tony Accardo, aka Joe Batters.

"Yeah, yeah," Gussie said. "Now let's get out of here."

I nodded and then slowly walked to my car, parked somewhat sideways in front of him. Just then I heard a siren. It was the cops. A big, burly one yelled at me. "Get that fucking car out of there! You want to kill somebody!"

I got it out of there. I guess, in retrospect, I could have waited and followed Gussie until he exited Lake Shore Drive, stopping somewhere a lot less busy. But I wouldn't have made the impression on Gussie that I did. I bet you that right now, sitting in his prison cell, Gus Alex remembers that morning. And what was done and said. Alex has always been a highly nervous guy, very unusual for a mobster, especially for a killer like he has been. But maybe that is what shot his nerves. I'd like to think it was the pressure I put on him, but probably not. *I* was never successful in putting him away. That happened long after I had retired.

The reason I had picked Gus Alex is that he was the leader of the connection guys. He would be listened to when he spread my message. And I knew he would realize that no mob should do anything to increase the intensity with which the FBI goes after them. I had heard Hump deliver that message several times to his people in front of Little Al. I knew that was the gospel of the connection guys. I knew Gussie followed in the footsteps of Hump. So I knew he would complain to Tony Accardo. I could have done to Accardo as I had done in the past but I had learned that he was at his other residence, his condo on Roadrunner Drive in Palm Springs. I needed a top guy who was in Chicago where I could find him—and hopefully get his attention. I believe I did.

20 ## The Gold Rush

When Tony sold his gift shop concession at Circus-Circus, he moved over to the Dunes. The Dunes, now torn down, was then a very nice hotel-casino located on the busiest corner of the Strip, across from Caesars Palace on the north, kitty-corner from the nice little Barbary Coast with The Flamingo next to it, and across the street from what was then the MGM and is now Bally's Grand.

Tony set up his new headquarters in the poker room at the Dunes, which was then operated by Major Riddle, a Chicagoan with some associations there, and by Morris Shenker, an attorney who represented mobsters in St. Louis and Kansas City. Now, however, the FBI had the hots, as it were, for Tony. Mike Simon got the word to the GCB, and they put all kinds of pressure on Riddle and Shenker. Even called them in to show cause why they shouldn't lose their license for allowing this known hood to make a home in their hotel-casino. We made sure GCB was aware and would question Riddle about the numerous poker games he played with the *representato* of the Chicago family of the LCN. Although it was well known that Tony was cheating Riddle for tens of thousands, Riddle, while acknowledging he frequently played with Tony, denied that he had lost that much to him. However, the mere fact that he not only allowed Tony in the casino but admitted actually playing with him there was a violation of the Black Book.

Shenker also admitted knowing that Tony frequented his casino but insisted that he didn't know Tony was in the Black Book or that he held a position with the Outfit. Both were severely admonished by the GCB and instructed to keep Tony out of the Dunes on penalty of loss of license.

Tony solved that problem by moving his brother, John, into his place, to maintain the poker room as his message drop. The only difference was that John Spilotro now took his calls and forwarded them to Tony. That was just another way to skin a cat.

Soon, however, Tony found that the arrangement with John was not convenient enough. He went to see two old pals. One was Lefty Rosenthal. The other was a guy from New York I would get to know later, along with his most attractive wife, Emily. His name is Joey Razzano, aka Joe Rossano. He had been a nightclub owner in Queens, New York, where he had some pals who were "wise guys." They helped him move to Las Vegas and become a shift manager of the Hacienda casino, where I got to know him. The Hacienda was part of Argent Corporation, part of the Chicago Outfit set-up. Now it is owned by Paul Lowden, also the owner of the Sahara, who was at the Tropicana when it was mobbed-up and heavily skimmed by the Kansas City mob for Chicago.

Rosenthal and his wife, Geri, and Joe and Emily Razzano were members of the Las Vegas Country Club, a very exclusive walled-in residential and recreational facility located a long stone's throw from the Strip. As I would find out, it was very difficult to penetrate the security at the Country Club because of the walls and the guarded gate. You had to exhibit your credentials and then everybody in the place was alerted to your presence, including one of the club founders and builders, the venerable Moe Dalitz.

Lefty and Joey went to bat for Tony, and sponsored him for membership, but in June 1976 the Country Club turned down his application. Dalitz even instructed the club employees to quit their almost constant paging of Spilotro when he dined and golfed at the club as the frequent guest of Lefty and Joey.

Then somebody from Chicago talked to Moe Dalitz. Suddenly, the vote of the membership committee was overturned. Tony was accepted as a member in good standing of the Las Vegas Country Club, the most exclusive in town. He now hob-nobbed with the leading citizens of Nevada, he played poker and gin rummy with the best of them. Nancy learned how to play tennis and spent much of her time with the circle of friends she made at the club. And now Tony headquartered himself in the club card room and the dining room, and the club rang out once again with his numerous pages.

Then Tony moved into something else, something which would come back to haunt him from two sides. He made one huge mistake.

Tony opened Gold Rush, Ltd., in late 1976, in a building one block off the Strip. On the first floor was a jewelry store and on the second floor he had a virtual electronics factory. He alarmed the front door and hired a private security firm to monitor the building at all times. They also constantly swept the building for bugs. Upstairs he installed five radio scanners, just as he had been taught to do by Ron DeAngelis, his old co-defendant in the case involving the American Pail Company of Deming, New Mexico. In fact, he brought Ron out to install the scanners and other electronic equipment. Ron put in scanners with crystals so that one picked up the FBI car radio transmissions, one the police department's intelligence unit, one the sheriff's intelligence unit, one the GCB's radio transmissions and one the IRS intelligence unit's transmissions. Tony had law enforcement in the area well covered! He also set up a radio transmitter of his own so that he could talk to his outside associates.

Tony stationed his brother, John, and "Fat Herbie" Blitzstein to run the store. That's where I first met John. At the time, John was the first of Tony's five brothers to join him in his mob activities. Vincent and Pat never did, but Victor and Michael would. Victor would later be nabbed in the Chicago FBI's "Operation Safebet," John would be nabbed doing Tony's business in Las Vegas and the youngest brother, Michael, would operate one of the mob's favorite hangouts in Chicago, Hoagy's.

Having the hots for Tony after the Duncan Everette incident, the FBI focused on his operation at Gold Rush. We would later charge in affidavits that the Gold Rush was "a veritable warehouse of stolen jewelry" and that 70 percent of the jewelry there arrived after being stolen from locations all across the country.

Let me give you an example. Shortly after I retired, I was retained by Fireman's Fund Insurance Company to investigate the theft of many thousands of dollars worth of jewelry and furs from a wealthy lady who was a guest of the famous Camelback Inn in Scottsdale. The theft had been fully investigated by the Phoenix PD and another private investigative firm but the insurance company wanted me to go up and take a look prior to paying the claim. I did. I could do no more than the investigators had already done. But I had one ace in the hole. Geraldo Denono.

Gerry is one in a million—among other things, he was one of the top burglars in the history of the world. He was also a good friend. Still is. I gave him a call and then went to see him in prison where he is incarcerated for three murders for the mob, one in Las Vegas and two in Florida. He solved the theft for me. He got one of his pals to go to Las Vegas. There he found the jewelry and furs. It was easy. Most of the top thieves in the country, especially in the western part of the country, fenced their jewels and furs at Gold Rush.

Ordinarily, of course, I don't identify my informants. Except in rare instances like the case of Dick Cain, who wanted to be credited with being a double agent inside the mob if anything ever happened to him. In the case of Denono, I have gone to bat publicly as a sponsor for his parole. He has served about twenty years for his crimes. In view of the way we let murderers out these days in a lot less time than that and in view of his cooperation not only with me on several cases but with several other law enforcement people, I believe he has done his penance.

Denono, of course, is the source of the famous Denono Diary. He is some piece of work. He first came to our attention when he was arrested for bank robbery. One day he drove some mob guys from Las Vegas, where he was living, to La Costa, in Carlsbad, just north of San Diego. He dropped them off and then went off to get some lunch. He noticed the local bank there. It looked like a soft touch. He had nothing better to do for an hour or so. So he robbed the bank, and our agent in Carlsbad, Wayne Wickizer, nabbed him. Wayne also is a sponsor of Denono on his application for parole.

Gerry had something to bargain with, however. A few months prior to the bank robbery, he had traveled on mob business to contact Carlos Marcello, the mob boss in New Orleans, about a plan to build a hospital with Teamster financing, of course. Marcello put him up for the night at the home of an associate. While drinking with the associate, Gerry watched him put the plans for the hospital in a wall safe behind a painting in the living room. In the middle of the night, Denono got up and penetrated the wall safe. He thought it would probably have some cash and jewelry—something of value. It did. Serendipitously, it contained a ledger of the skim in Las Vegas!

Gerry didn't know what it was but thought it might be something he could blackmail Marcello with. So he grabbed it and quickly headed back to Las Vegas. On the way he stopped and examined the document. Wow! It was a detailed summary, obviously prepared by some hood for Marcello, who, as we knew from VEGMON, was one of the recipients of the skim. I recall that when Gerry presented it to the FBI in Vegas as leverage for leniency, it was sent to me in Chicago for analysis. It was also sent to FBIHQ in Washington. I interpreted it as possibly being authentic since it was obviously prepared by somebody who had an intimate knowledge of the mobbed-up hotel-casinos in Vegas, how the skim worked and who had the hidden points to make them eligible for receipt of the skim, and how much. I believe the Bureau was officially a little more skeptical about it than I was, but certainly nobody could point at anything in the ledger that marked it as a fake.

However, the ledger was never used, to my knowledge, as evidence in any prosecution. It was utilized for our intelligence purposes and we pursued the investigative leads it presented.

I still have a copy of it in my possession, given to me by a contact of Denono's with his sanction. The contact has the original in a safety deposit box in a bank in a large western city.

Gerry Denono is also a painter. I have several of his paintings, all done while in prison. One is in the style of a Rockwell painting showing a guy, who looks a heck of a lot like me, on a mule with the *Chicago Sun-Times* in his pocket, looking out over the cactus desert thumbing through a booklet entitled "OC." He sent it to me when I was transferred out of Chicago the next year. One of these days those paintings will be collector's items!

But back to the Gold Rush. Spilotro organized a group of some forty burglars and fanned them out to burglarize some of his fellow Las Vegas Country Club members and some of the best jewelry stores all over Nevada—and California, Utah and Arizona.

Now this was a real no-no. He was prohibited by rules of the Chicago family of La Cosa Nostra from engaging in such petty activity! But, apparently, he felt that as far geographically as he was from Chicago, he could get away with it.

What he also did was corrupt members of the Clark County Sheriff's Organized Crime Unit, at least three officers and maybe even the sheriff himself. One was Detective Joseph Blasko, a key member of that unit. Not only did Blasko furnish Tony with reports of his own unit but also with our reports. Reports which were disseminated to the Sheriff's office through official channels. Then Blasko served as a lookout—in his squad car, yet—while Tony's guys, now called the Hole-in-the-Wall Gang, were ripping off their victims. He sat in a squad car communicating with Tony's guys at Gold Rush while the burglaries were in progress and reported any law enforcement activity. He also furnished Tony with information on the identity of informants and undercover agents working for the FBI and the local police units. A real nice guy! Blasko was later convicted on racketeering and obstruction of justice charges. He is now out and the last I heard he was working as a bartender in a Vegas topless joint. Good spot for him!

Another member of the organized crime unit of the Sheriff's office in Clark County, Sergeant Phil Leone, was indicted on bribery charges in 1980. But charges were dismissed due to his ill health. FBI search warrants would also disclose that one-time Deputy Chief Gene Clark, of the Las Vegas Police Department, had accepted a $181,000 loan from Allen Glick, Chicago's man in the Argent Corporation. No charges have ever been brought against Clark, who was head of the OC unit of the LVPD. Maybe Glick just wanted to do Captain Clark a personal favor with no strings attached. Maybe.

21 King of Vegas

I'm not going to tell you that the decision to intensify the investigation of Spilotro was made solely by those of us in the FBI who respected Duncan Everette and who had, therefore, pleaded to right the wrong Tony had inflicted on him. I'll just let you use your imagination. Let's just say we are a closely knit organization and we fight to protect our own.

In any event, we put a full-court press on Tony. Mainly, of course, in Las Vegas where he spent most of his time, although his orders were coming from Chicago.

But were they? That is the way it was supposed to be. But Tony was now off on his own. No way did Tony Accardo want him devoting his time to the Hole-in-the-Wall Gang. That wasn't accepted procedure in the Chicago LCN.

We assigned some fifteen agents to investigate Tony and his pals, particularly brother John and Fat Herbie Blitzstein, but also long-time associates Frank Cullotta and Sal Romano who were an important part of the gang.

The IRS came in also. They even made an attempt to turn Spilotro's maid, Lessie Taylor. She declined the honor.

After about six months of tough legwork, the Las Vegas field office was ready. We helped, a lot, with electronic surveillance information. And some other field offices like San Francisco and San Diego chipped in. They had Jimmy "The Weasel" Fratianno and Frank Bompensiero, "Bomp," working for them. Jimmy had been turned by agent Jim Ahearn in San Francisco and, as we know, Bomp was turned by Jack Armstrong in San Diego.

After gathering the information from all sources, the Vegas FBI agents put together an affidavit. Now, in order to obtain a court order for a legal elsur, the results of which are admissible in a court of law against the subject of the eavesdropping or wiretap under Title III of the Safe Streets and Organized Crime Act of 1968, there has to be probable cause. It is sent out in an affidavit which is then presented to a federal court with the appropriate jurisdiction, in this case the U.S. District Court covering Las Vegas. We call such an elsur a Title III.

In March 1978, the affidavit was presented to a federal judge and he granted the Title III. Hidden microphones, much like those we had placed in Chicago—Little Al, Shade, Mo and Plumb—were then placed inside Gold Rush and the apartment of Fat Herbie Blitzstein.

It wasn't long after the Title IIIs went in that we struck gold at the Gold Rush. Everything Tony was doing was fed to the Vegas FBI office. Did he act as the *representato* of the Chicago mob, the Mr. Outside in Vegas? He sure did. Was he leading the Hole-in-the-Wall Gang? He sure was. Was he a juice guy, plying his trade as he had learned it from Mad Sam? He sure was. Was he conferring with Lefty Rosenthal and with Allen Glick? He sure was. He even ordered who was to be employed at the Stardust when a pal of his was fired. One time when he talked to a delinquent juice victim he threatened to "put you in the ground!" "Put you in the ground!" Oh, my—remember those words!

The FBI learned all kinds of things from the elsur, the Title III electronic surveillance. Tony coached witnesses in grand jury proceedings in San Francisco and San Diego. One guy came to thank him for the preferential treatment he had received in the federal prison at Leavenworth. Top Jewel Thieves came from all over the country to fence their stolen loot at Gold Rush, Ltd. Tony discussed many public officials and politicians who seemed to be on the pad.

At that time Barbara McNair was a well-known entertainer, a singer. Her career was on the rise. Rick Manzie, a small-time moper on Rush Street, was put with her by the Chicago mob which had an interest in her career. Soon McNair and Manzie married, but Manzie, who was a heroin addict, introduced Barbara to the drug, and before too long the pair was arrested in her dressing room for possession. It made all the papers. Her career started down the tubes. Manzie was held responsible for the problem by his capo in Chicago. The Title III seemed to indicate, though not directly, that Tony was given the job to take Manzie out of the picture. In December 1975 Manzie was killed in Las Vegas with a .22 pistol, fired at close range. Tony was never charged, however, because the Title III didn't state precisely that he had killed Manzie. Nevertheless, as far as I was concerned, Tony Spilotro had a piece of McNair, he put his piece to Manzie's head and he got a piece of him. Period.

Another hot voice picked up on the mike was that of Detective Blasko, information about grand jury proceedings, personalities in the Sheriff's Office and who they were assigned to investigate and, lo and behold, even details of the investigation Blasko was pretending to conduct on Tony's juice clientele. Blasko's voice even came in on the mike. "They're tailing Tony!" he would report. Or "You're all clear!" Even the voices of the FBI dispatcher and agents came over the mike—from their car radios as they went about their FBI business. Blasko, a big, powerful weight lifter, had once beaten a Vegas cabdriver to death although he was never charged with the killing. He dressed like a hood, with black shirts and white ties. He looked more like a goodfella, a wise guy, than Tony did. One time his voice was picked up at Gold Rush saying about a federal witness, "He ought to be dead." The FBI did not have to wonder about who's side Blasko was on.

After the Title III had been in operation almost three months, some three hundred tapes with more then eight thousand conversations had been monitored. It was deemed to be more than enough.

I was very much aware of what Vegas was doing. It was a transitional time for me. Having spent twenty-four years in the Chicago office, I asked for a transfer. I wanted to work in Tucson on legendary mob boss Joe Bonanno. Plus Jeannie and I had fallen in love with the place and wanted to be near our son Bill, a sportscaster there. I got the transfer. In May 1978 I was assigned to Tucson. The next month, the FBI in Vegas made a move.

A search warrant was prepared and presented to the U.S. Magistrate in Las Vegas, Joseph Ward. He authorized it. More than one hundred FBI agents, many from out of town, were assigned to search the persons, homes, offices and cars of Tony and his pals, several dozen of them, including Cullotta, Romano, Fat Herbie and brother John. In John's home almost $200,000 in cash was found under the cushions of his living room sofa. The search of Tony's home on Sahara Avenue was not as productive, but electronic devices, $6,000 in bills, financial records and other not-so-important material was found. Ominously, however, there was one further piece of paper found. A report of a private investigator detailing Lefty Rosenthal's daily habits. Obviously done at the request of Tony. Why would Tony want knowledge of what Lefty was doing day and night? Lefty, his old pal from Chicago, Miami and now Las Vegas? The agents noted the report, didn't attach a lot of significance to it and mostly ignored it. After all, they knew it was Tony's job for the Outfit to be Mr. Outside to Lefty's Mr. Inside. It didn't raise a lot of suspicion.

However, what they found when they searched the Gold Rush premises did cause suspicion. A lot. For good reason. The agents confiscated almost four thousand pieces of jewelry and nearly $40,000 in cash. Also some "markers," IOUs, from the casinos adding up to some $74,000.

Tony, Blasko, John and Fat Herbie were indicted on racketeering charges. I was elated. That will teach you, Tony, I thought. I told you. We put one hundred agents on you, fifteen full time. Talk about full-court presses. And we got you. That'll show you and your pals in Chicago and in Vegas. You can't beat the FBI!

Or can you? Pride goeth before the fall! It took four years, but in the end a United States Magistrate in Vegas ruled that the search was beyond the limit prescribed by the search warrant! Nothing seized could be used as evidence against Tony! The big grin on my face fell into a scowl. Tony had won another round. The FBI might not be so smart after all. I was glad I was not at Ragtime when Tony next returned to Chicago. I'm sure he paid for all the drinks in the house, as usual, with a big smile on his face. Tony was still the king of the hill. Moe Dalitz might be the Godfather of Las Vegas, but no one was telling that to Tony.

22 A Final Confrontation

When I heard about the ruling of the magistrate in Las Vegas wiping out the evidence against Tony and his pals, I got to thinking.

Then I received a report from the Vegas field division of the FBI. It read: "Spilotro is an extremely trusted soldier in the LCN. He performs important responsibilities on behalf of the Chicago family. Spilotro has often been mentioned as a potential successor to the leadership presently headed by Joseph Aiuppa. On March 16, 1978 Spilotro met alone with Aiuppa in a Palm Springs restaurant for approximately two hours. Spilotro's name has surfaced in investigations into numerous unsolved gangland slayings. Spilotro continues his close dealings with known criminal figures in Illinois, Nevada and California. Substantial information strongly indicates that Spilotro was dispatched in 1971 by his Chicago LCN superiors to represent Chicago LCN in this area and to control and coordinate activities. Spilotro remains in his assigned capacity to this date." The date was October 15, 1978.

That got me thinking more and more about Spilotro. I was assigned to the New York godfather, kingpin Joe Bonanno, in Tucson, from where we believed he was running his long-held empire in Brooklyn by remote control. I was assigned to think more of the New York mob now than Chicago although, obviously, there were several Chicago hoods in the open territory of Arizona that I investigated also.

I recalled that a guy I will refer to as Nino was living and doing his thing in Tucson. I had known Nino in Chicago, but he had recently transplanted to Tucson, obviously with the approval of the Outfit. He was not the biggest mobster in Chicago but he was big time in Tucson. Obviously, I thought, he must be here with Spilotro's approval. He was close to Spilotro in Chicago, close to Mad Sam, very close to Philly Alderisio. He *must* be Tony's man in Tucson. Just as Chris Petti was in San Diego, Joey Hansen in Los Angeles and Paulie Schiro was in Phoenix. Everything west of Chicago *is* Chicago, the saying goes. Arizona was the one exception in 1978, the reason Joe Bananas could reside there and run Brooklyn.

I asked that Nino be assigned to me. We opened a 92 case on him. Soon after I interviewed Nino for the first time, in his lawyer's office at his demand, I decided to open another case on him. A 137. A PCI case to determine his potential to be an informant. We had developed a fairly cordial relationship during the meeting in his attorney's office. Now I invited him to lunch. We found common ground. We had a lot of mutual acquaintances in Chicago. I actually began to feel that Nino was lonely and that I served as a lifeline between him and his Chicago roots. Hard to fathom, but I came to believe it. I was an FBI agent and he was a hood, but we had a background in the same city. For the next two years, as long as I remained in the FBI in Tucson, we had lunch every couple of weeks. We got friendlier and friendlier.

Soon I was able to steer the conversation to Tony Spilotro. At first that was off limits, that was going too far. But then one day, Nino dropped something which interested me. Very much. Tony was coming to Tucson to "look something over."

Wow! Nino would tell me no more. I picked up the phone and called our Las Vegas office as soon as I got back to what is called the Tucson "resident agency." It is a downtown satellite office, reporting to its headquarters, Phoenix. I talked to the case agent on Spilotro. Did they know Spilotro would be coming to Tucson? It might not be big news for the Las Vegas Office, but it sure was for the Tucson resident agency.

A few days before Tony was to arrive in Tucson, I got another call from Nino. We sat down again.

"Look," I remember him saying, "if Tony spots you when he arrives, he'll know somebody tipped you off. That will put me in a bad spot. For my sake, wait until he is ready to leave before you do anything to alert him. Then, after he's been here awhile it could be anything or anybody who tipped you off. Listen, I'll tell you what he's up to. He's coming in to see Pete. You know the Detroit boys have the Aladdin. That's what he's coming in for. To see Pete about the Aladdin."

"What about the Aladdin?" I asked.

"That I don't know. But I'll find out, I think, after he goes. From him or from Pete. I'm gonna be with Tony for a while when he's here. I'll find out then."

Of course I agreed not to be waiting at Tucson International Airport when Tony arrived. I couldn't give Nino up.

As Nino would fill me in later, Tony came into Tucson that day in 1979 and was picked up at the airport by Pete Licavoli, a capo in the Detroit family of La Cosa Nostra who, like Bonanno, spent most of his time in Tucson although his interests were back east. They proceeded to the newly opened El Conquistador Resort on the north side of the Catalina Mountains and lunched. Then they drove to the Grace Ranch, Pete's home, on Wrightstown Road near the Rincon Mountains. There they conferred. The subject of Tony's visit was the

Aladdin, which was then in a state of decline. The Detroit mob
had skimmed the hell out of it. Now Joey Lombardo had instructed Tony to see if the Chicago Outfit could move in and
whether it would be worth the trouble. Tony had talked to the
Detroit people in Las Vegas but none there were as big as Pete
Licavoli. So he came to Tucson to confer with Pete.

I don't know what happened but the Chicago mob never
moved into the Aladdin. It went dark for a while, closed, and
then was sold to legitimate interests. Dennis Gomes, a highly
respected former top agent of GCB, got a multimillion dollar
contract to run it, but after a while he moved on. The Aladdin,
although in a nice spot about halfway between Bally's and the
great hotels on the southern end of the Strip like the MGM,
Excalibur, the Trop and the Luxor, all new or newly renovated,
plush hotel-casinos, continues its struggle today.

All this notwithstanding, I was not about to let Tony come
into what I now considered my town and get away without a
confrontation. I would be true to my promise to Nino not to
let anything splash on him, but I would not miss the opportu-
nity for what would turn out to be my last chance to have it
out with Tony Spilotro.

I had made contact with security at the airport and learned
that a Tony Brown had arrived on the flight I was interested
in and that he was scheduled to leave the next day at two to
fly back to Las Vegas. Brown was an alias both Tony and his
brother, John, used from time to time. So, at about one, I arrived at the airport to await Tony Brown.

Sure enough, here came Pete Licavoli, his driver and Tony.
The driver was carrying Tony's bag. I stood in their way. All
three recognized me at once. One of the first things I had done
after arriving in Tucson was to head out to the Grace Ranch
and confront Licavoli. I was always on the lookout for a PCI.

I saw Pete look at Tony. I got a flash that perhaps he was
worried that our surveillance of him had tipped us off to
Tony's presence.

"Having a good time in Tucson, Tony?" I asked. At that
point I did not exhibit a hostile attitude. I decided I would see
where the confrontation would take me.

But Tony was a volatile little pissant. "Roemer!" he exclaimed. "They told me you were out here. What's the matter, did we run you out of Chicago? Lost your steam? Getting old, aren't you? Out of the big time now. They put you out to pasture, I guess."

That got me. I had voluntarily transferred to Tucson to work on Bonanno, as big a man in the LCN as any in Chicago, a charter member of The Commission, the ruling body of La Cosa Nostra, from the time it was formed in 1931. There was plenty of good work in Tucson before we would convict Joe Bonanno. I sure didn't want anybody thinking I had left Chicago to get away from the heavy work, that I was winding down.

So I came right back at him. "Same little pissant, huh, Tony? Little body, little brain. Big mouth." I turned to Pete Licavoli. "Pete, how come you let the pissant into Tucson? I knew he was here when I noticed that old smell from Chicago!"

Now this riled Tony up. He had started off in command of the situation. Now I seemed to be gaining the upper hand.

"You know this guy, Pete?" he asked Licavoli.

"We've met," Pete replied. Licavoli had some sense. He had been through the wars with FBI agents like Bob Fitzpatrick in Detroit. He was swift enough not to court trouble with the FBI when he didn't have to. He more or less took a step back. If Spilotro was going to act tough with the FBI that was his business. He would make it clear he was not looking for such a fight. Smart!

Not Tony though. His nature was not to step back from any kind of fight, with a mobster or "the G." Of course, he usually approached from behind, with all the odds on his side. I'm sure he knew here, however, that it was not going to get physical, that I had no intention of physically abusing him. Really, I shouldn't have even been there. There was no official purpose. Nothing to be gained from the standpoint of standard investigation. Due to my intense dislike of the guy, however, I just wanted him to know I knew he was in my territory and that he couldn't just expect to walk in and walk out without being banged in some way by Roemer. Not too smart but that's why I was always just a street agent. But I suppose my purpose in confronting Spilotro that afternoon, at least unconsciously, was to recapture the old feeling.

So Tony had gotten under my skin—as usual.

I shot back at him. "Yeah, Pete knows me. But he's a gentleman. He's done more in his lifetime in his family than you'll ever achieve." Then it hit me. I threw another good shot. "This guy's a capo, Tony, not some soldier. I hope you kissed his ring when you came here!"

Of course, Tony didn't kiss anybody's ring! Maybe when he was with Mad Sam and Philly Alderisio. But now he was the king of Las Vegas. He kissed nobody's ring!

My last comment seemed to put Tony down for a moment. If I was still just a field agent, he was still just a soldier. He got beyond himself. Made a big mistake. He let his animosity toward me and what I was saying take over.

"*Some* soldier, huh!" he shot back. "Listen, Roemer, you come into Las Vegas, you'll see who runs that place. I don't sit in some shithole like this, waiting to see who might walk into this punk airport. In Las Vegas everybody kisses *my* ring! I'm the big man there. You'll never understand that, Roemer, you got no ambition. But I do. I left Chicago too, just like you, but my move was up, Roemer, not down. I'm the *man* in Vegas!"

Now this was very interesting. It was tantamount to an "admission against interest" in the law. Now I could do a report. I could include what, in effect, was Tony's admission. My mission, which started out to be just harassment, all of a sudden had an official purpose.

I goaded him with it. "Big man in Vegas, huh!" I hissed at him. "From what I hear you're nothing but a thief and a loan shark there. You're not the boss of anything but a pack of petty thieves and burglars! The big stuff, the skim, you aren't even a part of. Your people sent you out there to be a no-good cat burglar. We got twenty of them better than you right here in Tucson!"

"Oh, how that shot struck home!

"Nothing but a burglar, huh, Roemer," he spat back. "That shows just how far out of it you are! If you only knew what I do in Vegas, what I really do!"

"Tell me, Pissant, what do you 'really do' in Vegas?"

But Tony was not that upset, not that dumb. He turned to Licavoli and snatched his bag from Pete's driver. They had called his flight. Without a word to Pete or to me, he was gone.

It was to be my last sighting of Tony. I admit that I would miss the encounters with him and the direct investigation of him.

Nino would keep me advised of what he was up to. Nino would visit Tony in Las Vegas and report back. I would send 209s, my reports on his information, to Vegas. I would also develop another informant in Tucson who furnished information about Tony and his underlings, but that was scattershot, hit and miss. That guy, unlike Nino, was not working for Tony. He was a California mobster assigned to their interests in Arizona. Since California was part of Tony's territory, my other source picked up information from time to time on Tony, but not constantly. That would pretty much be the extent from then on of any personal investigation on my part of Tony and his activities. As my attention focused on Bonanno, Tony began to slip more and more from the front of my brain. Bonanno became my prime interest.

Tony Spilotro might have slipped in my priorities, but certainly not in the priorities of the rest of the FBI, the agents assigned to Las Vegas and Chicago. The full-court press continued.

23 Trouble in Paradise

There was a bump in the road for the Bureau agents assigned to Las Vegas.

Mike Simon was the Chicago C-1 agent who had been transferred to the field office in Las Vegas, primarily to attend to the investigation of the interests of the Chicago mob there. He was a sharp agent who had demonstrated to us on C-1 that he could do the job. During his time in Chicago he was a very popular agent. He worked closely with the others on C-1 and he and his wife, Dee, partied with us after working hours. I sometimes tarried for a drink with my colleagues on the way to my train home, but didn't do so regularly. But many of the other agents did. Especially my two partners, Marshall Rutland and Ralph Hill, and Johnny Bassett, who would soon become my partner before he, like Rutland and Hill, would go on to Washington, to FBIHQ. Those guys, with a handful of others, were the guts of C-1. They were the most productive agents although, of course, there were many others of the seventy agents then assigned to C-1 who carried their share of the load. Guys like John Roberts, Denny Shanahan Christy Malone, Gus Kempff, Elliot Anderson, Joe Shea, Merle Hamre, Max Fritschel, George Benigni, Bill Meincke, Hal Johnson, Lenny Wolf, and later younger guys like Bill Dougherty, Bert Jensen, Sonny Martin, Adrian Mohr, Mike Bryne, Ray Shryock and Curt Fitzgerald. All top agents with whom I was proud to be associated. And all close pals of Mike Simon before he transferred to Vegas to be what amounted to an extension of C-1 in the desert.

Now Mike had been in Vegas, doing a superb job on the organized crime squad there, for a decade or more. He and the "sound men," the technicians, had placed Title IIIs in two mobbed-up hotels, the Dunes and the Aladdin. Mike was the case agent in charge of monitoring the bugs, analyzing the results and reporting on a daily basis to FBIHQ. His supervisor, the supervisor of the organized crime squad, was Tommy Parker.

However, just a few days after the bugs were planted in the Dunes and the Aladdin, they went dry. Whereas the people overheard talked very freely for the first few days, all of a sudden they engaged only in desultory conversation. The purpose in planting the bugs, which took a great deal of work on Mike's part, work that he had learned with us back on C-1, was to discover just how the mob was skimming the Dunes and the Aladdin and how they were getting the skim to the mobs who had the points in those hotels, St. Louis and Kansas City for the Dunes and Detroit for the Aladdin.

Mike got very suspicious. He felt that somebody must have tipped off the people at the Dunes and Aladdin. He even suspected his boss, Parker.

Jack Keith was then the SAC, the Special Agent in Charge, of the Las Vegas FBI office. Parker was a supervisor, one of maybe four working under Keith, but he was in charge of the organized crime investigations, the most important in Las Vegas.

Simon took his suspicions to Keith. I don't think Jack felt they could be true, but Simon impressed upon him that Parker and some other older agents who had been assigned to Vegas for decades were accepting comps from the very people who were fronting for the various mobs that had hidden points in the dozen or so hotels then mobbed-up in Vegas. This practice was unacceptable to Mike Simon. Nothing like that had ever happened on C-1.

Keith's hands were tied. Mike had come to him officially with his complaint. Even if he didn't believe it, he had to pass it on. Besides, Mike was taking his concerns outside the FBI, to the U.S. Attorney's Office—and not just the one in Vegas but also the one in Los Angeles! Jack, a fine SAC and a hands-on one to boot, couldn't just sit on Mike's accusations. He reported them to FBIHQ.

Immediately, a team of inspectors was sent off to Las Vegas. Every field office of the FBI is inspected by such a team annually. Las Vegas had had their inspection just months before. But this was an emergency. If Mike Simon's suspicions were accurate, if veteran Las Vegas agents were accepting free meals, drinks and rooms at the very hotels they were investigating, then this was one hell of a mess!

The inspectors honed in on about a dozen agents, some of the very best ones, at least by reputation, in Vegas. Some of those who had been working the organized crime beat for many, many years.

The inspectors' report was never made public, never made known even to the agents in Las Vegas or to agents in other offices. Jack Keith got his orders, however. Within a couple of months there was a series of disciplinary transfers of old-time organized crime agents from Vegas to offices which certainly were not their offices of preference. There were also some early retirements. And a dozen or so letters of censure. Tommy Parker himself went, shortly thereafter. I will take his word for it that he retired due to the low morale of his squad. However, he took a position immediately upon retirement with the Valley National Bank, headed by a man who was perceived by agents on Parker's squad to be closely connected to people like Moe Dalitz and Lefty Rosenthal, a bank which more than any other loaned money to the mobbed-up casinos.

I remember going into Vegas at about that time. I met Tommy for a drink at the MGM, now Bally's. We intended to have dinner at Barrymore's, one of the restaurants there, but when I mentioned that I had also invited Mike Simon to join us, he abruptly got up and left. He made no bones about it. He was not about to have dinner with Mike Simon.

Years later, Mike retired. He applied for admission to the Society of Former Agents of the FBI, a group almost all former agents belong to and enjoy. He was blackballed by the Las Vegas chapter. Several of the agents who had been affected by his complaint objected to Mike becoming a member.

Mike called me and Ralph Hill, then retired in San Jose, California. We were happy to sponsor his request for reconsideration. It didn't matter. The ex-agents in Vegas were successful in keeping Mike out.

Mike was a fine agent. He worked hard and did the job. He was then and is now my friend. I have nothing but respect for him. I was not assigned to Las Vegas, then or at any other time, so I have no real way to assess the accuracy of Mike's complaint. As far as I know, the organized crime agents in Vegas were good, honest agents. There may have been some indiscretions on their part. I don't know. But it is extremely difficult for me to believe any of them would intentionally violate their duty to the FBI. It is hard for me to believe they would deliberately inform the mobsters of any of our activities—to compromise what the fine FBI agents like Mike Simon were doing. But Mike was there.

24 Las Vegas vs Atlantic City

Then came a major development. The voters in New Jersey approved a referendum legalizing gambling casinos in Atlantic City. This event would seem to have little effect on Tony Spilotro in Las Vegas. At the time.

Shortly thereafter, however, "The Commission" held a meeting in Fort Lee, New Jersey, just over the Hudson River, across the George Washington Bridge, from New York City.

Joe Aiuppa, the guy they call O'Brien in Chicago, was representing the Chicago family of La Cosa Nostra at this meeting of the ruling body of the LCN. All members of The Commission were present. Represented were the five bosses of the New York families: the Columbos, the Gambinos, the

Lucheses, the Genoveses and the Bonannos. The New Jersey mob was represented. The Patriarca family in New England was there. Philadelphia was represented by Angelo Bruno, shortly before he would be gunned down by his own—Nicky Scarfo. Pittsburgh was represented. Cleveland. Buffalo. Detroit.

Aiuppa made a proposal. That the Chicago mob be granted exclusive rights to Las Vegas. They would "grandfather" in the rights to the hotels already established, such as the Detroit family at the Aladdin and the New York mob at the Tropicana. But from there on out Chicago would have Las Vegas as its alone. In return, Aiuppa proposed that Chicago would relinquish the right to establish anything for itself in Atlantic City.

The proposed trade was cause for great concern. Las Vegas was a going business. New York had really got it going when they sent Bugsy to build the Flamingo. They had been first in such places as the Desert Inn and the Riviera, as well as the Tropicana. Those four places were among the very best hotel-casinos in the late Seventies. Of course, by that time Chicago had horned in on the Desert Inn, the Riviera and the Tropicana.

As a result, the eastern mobs, and that included just about all that were represented on The Commission, now had little left in Nevada.

Finally, they arrived at a consensus. It was a good deal for all.

From then on, the Chicago LCN would be the dominant, nay, the sole, mob in Las Vegas except for the few points the eastern mobs had grandfathered in.

We did not have a CTE on The Commission. We got some guys very high up but never one who sat on The Commission. But I did have a CTE in Chicago who had to be advised of such an action because it had a direct effect on him. I can't tell you, of course, who he was and what he did for the mob, but I can tell you that it wasn't too long before I got the word. I was still in Chicago, on my last legs there, and, of course, it was a most interesting piece of information.

It would increase the workload of Tony. But, first, let's ex-

THE ENFORCER
SPILOTRO–THE CHICAGO MOB'S MAN OVER LAS VEGAS

Tony Spilotro in the early 1960s.

The author, on right, winning his fourth Notre Dame boxing championship in 1949 in preparation for conflict with Spilotro and his pals.

Charles "Lucky" Luciano, top mobster in New York in the 1930s.

Sam Giancana, top boss of Chicago mob, 1957–1966.

Mug shot of Al Capone in his prime, 1929.

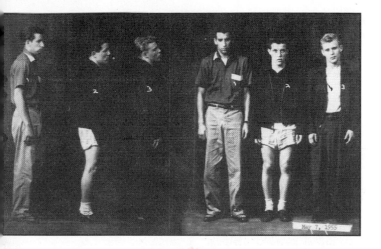

Tony arrested at age 17—in his undershorts yet! The guy at right is believed to be Joey Hansen, later his man in Los Angeles.

Tony Accardo, aka Joe Batters, in 1929 at the time of his participation as trigger-man in the St. Valentine's Day Massacre when he was a bodyguard of Al Capone.

Paul "The Waiter" Ricca (right), true name Paul DeLucia, when he was the Chicago mob's top boss in the early 1940s.

Tony Accardo (above), aka Joe Batters, "The Man" in the Chicago mob for parts of eight decades circa 1945.

Marshall Caifano, aka "John Marshall," the *representato* of the Chicago mob in the western United States and Las Vegas from 1958 to 1971.

"Mad Sam" DeStefano, the worst torture-murderer in history. Spilotro's first mentor.

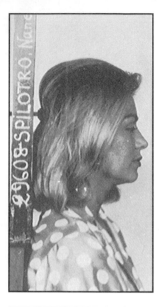

Nancy Spilotro, wife of Tony Spilotro, circa 1961.

William "Action" Jackson, victim of infamous Chicago torture-murder.

Police mug shot of Phil Alderisio.

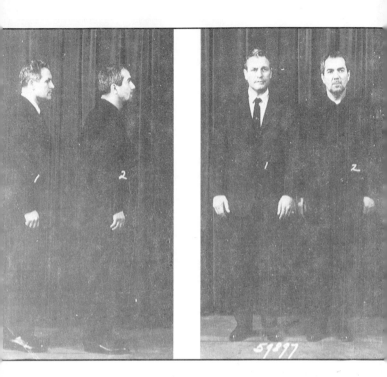

The Chicago "Hit Men." Chuckie Nicoletti on left, "Milwaukee Phil" Alderisio on right. Police photo taken after arrest while staking out a victim in 1965.

Philly Alderisio circa 1969.

FBI surveillance photo of Chuckie Nicoletti, mob "heavy," on left.

Chuckie English, top lieutenant of Sam Giancana when Giancana was Chicago mob boss. Both were murdered by their own people.

Sam Giancana, who, as boss of the Chicago mob, controlled their gambling interests in Havana, Cuba, in the 1950s.

Rap sheet of Tony Spilotro in Chicago PD up to 1969.

CITY OF CHICAGO / DEPARTMENT OF POLICE · 1121 South State Street · Chicago 5, Illinois · WAbash 2-4747
IDENTIFICATION SECTION

ARREST RECORD OF Anthony Spilotro M/W

DATE 12-14-62

DATE OF BIRTH 5-19-38

I.R.#13146

F.P.C. ○ U 00I 11
2 U 0IM

NAME & ADDRESS	C.R. NO.	DATE OF ARREST / ARRESTING OFFICER & DIST. / CHARGE	DISPOSITION
Pasquale Spilotro		Jan 11 55 River forest,Ill.Larc.	
	E12463	Apr 4 55 P.Larc.Judge Salter fine $10.Larc.	
		Offs.Poole & Biagi.Oak Pk. Ill.PD.	
		May 6 55 Inv.Off.Vojtech & Co. 16th Dist.	
		May 24 56 Evanston,Ill.#56273 G.P.	
Anthony		Jan 2 57 Inv.Off.Beilke & Co. 31st Dist.	
		Mar 9 57 Inv.Sgt.Lynch 31st Dist.	
		Feb 3 58 Inv.Off.Flynn & Co. 31st Dist.	
		Feb 28 58 Inv.Lt.Lynch & Co. DB.	
	E43080	Dec 9 58 Arr.Offs.Bennett & Tuszynski,Evanston,Ill.	
		Jan 14 59 Ind.Jan G.J. Poss.Burg. Tools.Jd.O'Connell.	
		June 2 59 Inv.Off.Dorband & Williamson Evanston,Ill.	
		Aug 12 59 Inv.Off.Hanhardt DB.	
		Aug 21 59 " " " " .	
		Oct 9 59 Inv.Off.Schofield & Co. DB.	
		Feb 29 60 App;.Cr Ct. Bondsman.	
		Mar 30 61 Inv.Off.Kanrand & Co. 35th Dist.	
	1173577	Dec 12 62 Off.Sgt.Hinchey DDA5.	
	1263369	7 May63 Parapinski DA#5 Inv Robb	7 May 63 Release
Anthony Spilotro	1355619	10 Sept 63 Lance DDA5 Inv Burglary Released	
2152 N Melvina		-17 May 64, Miami,Fla. SO, DC, Resist Arrest. $200 F	
		or 90 das in Co Jail on chg of DC, Resist Arrest...	
		released.	
" "	2342563	-8 Oct 67 Fusel & Co. IRS. Fed Wager laws Viol.	
		- 9 Oct 67, Fed. Watering Stamp- Delivered to U. S.	
		Marshal 9 Oct 67	
Anthony SPILOTRO	2844620	- 12 Sept 69 Kelly VCD-G(CD)Keeper of Bets	
1102 Maypole			
Oak Park,Ill			

ISSUED ON INQUIRY
BY NAME CHECK ONLY

Ben "Bugsy" Siegel, the New York mob's man in the west, who built the first luxury casino on "The Strip" in Las Vegas. Killed by his own people in 1947.

Benny "Bugsy" Siegel

"Milwaukee Phil" Alderisio under arrest, escorted to Chicago Police Department lockup by FBI agents John Bassett, Dennis Shanahan and the author.

Dick Cain, my double agent inside the mob, one heck of a courageous guy!

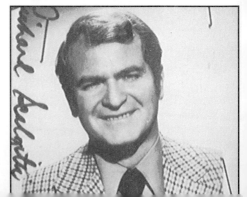

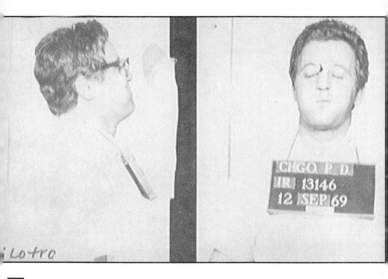

Tony Spilotro as he mugged for a mug shot following another arrest.

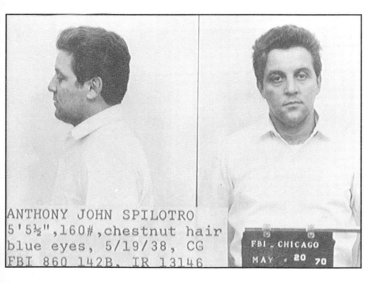

ANTHONY JOHN SPILOTRO
5'5½",160#,chestnut hair
blue eyes, 5/19/38, CG
FBI 860 142B, IR 13146

FBI - CHICAGO
MAY 20 70

Chicago PD mug shot of Tony Spilotro after his arrest for gambling in 1970.

Al Capone (above).

Meyer Lansky, the financial genius of the New York mob from the 1930s through the 1980s.

Frank Costello, top New York mobster 1930s to 1960s, who, with Meyer Lansky, sent Bugsy Siegel to Las Vegas.

Moe Dalitz (left), the "god-father of Las Vegas," being honored in 1976 in Las Vegas as the "Humanitarian of the Year."

Marshall Caifano, Spilotro's immediate predecessor as Chicago's "Mr. Outside" in Las Vegas. Replaced by Spilotro in 1971.

Jackie Cerone, Chicago mob boss, as he appeared in public, suave and well groomed.

FBI surveillance photo of Murray "The Camel" Humphreys (left) on his way to Washington to visit congressmen "on his pad."

Tony Accardo (right) as he appeared at the top of his game in 1954 when he was top boss of the Chicago mob.

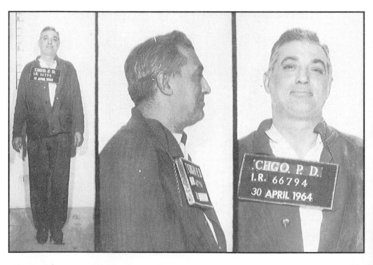

Mario DeStefano, killer.

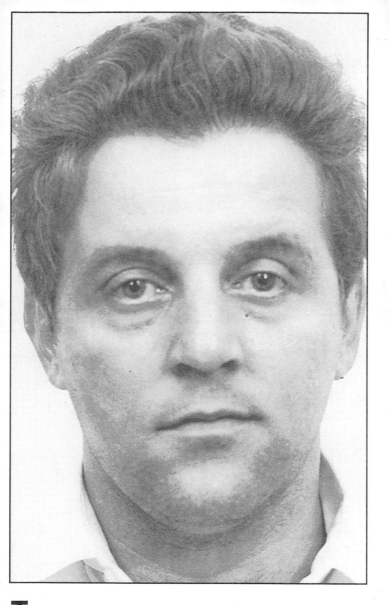

Tony Spilotro as he appeared about the time he was sent to represent the interests of the Chicago mob in Las Vegas and the rest of the west in 1971.

"**F**at Herbie" Blitzstein, top lieutenant of Spilotro in Las Vegas.

Pat Marcy, "made" member of the Chicago mob who, as a functionary in the Regular Democratic Organization of Chicago's First Ward, was the conduit of orders from the mob to corrupt public officials.

Joey Hansen, top lieutenant of Spilotro in Los Angeles.

Joe Lombardo, capo in charge of Spilotro's activities. Now released from prison on parole. Some feel he will soon be top boss of the Chicago mob.

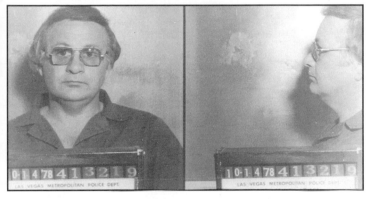

Frank Cullotta (above), boyhood chum of Tony Spilotro who joined him in crime as a teenager and was his top lieutenant in Las Vegas for many years. Cullotta was Tony's top man in the Hole in the Wall Gang, and became one of the country's most infamous burglars.

Irv Weiner, Tony's co-defendant in the New Mexico case—friend of many mobsters.

Frank "Lefty" Rosenthal, "Mr. Inside" in the casinos in Las Vegas to Tony Spilotro's "Mr. Outside."

Jimmy "Turk" Torello, former capo of the Chicago mob who was thought to be a challenger with Spilotro to take over as Chicago boss.

Murray "The Camel" Humphreys, "Public Enemy Number 1," in 1931 following the conviction of Al Capone.

Tony Accardo, the *consiglieri* of the Chicago mob from 1957 to 1992 when he died of natural causes after never having spent a night in prison.

Joe Yablonsky. The most vigorous FBI chief ever in Las Vegas.

Gus Alex, top Chicago mobster in charge of Loop and "connection guys," in Switzerland on his honeymoon.

Lenny Patrick, Chicago mobster, circa 1955. Patrick became a government witness in 1992 and testified against top associates in the mob, including Gus Alex.

Michael Spilotro, kid brother of Tony, in 1979 as he began to become more and more involved in Tony's criminal activities.

FBI - CHICAGO
MAY 17 1979

FBI - CHICAGO
MAY 17 1979

Joey Aiuppa (right).

FBI surveillance photo taken September 16, 1974, of Joey Aiuppa, top boss of the Chicago mob, on left, and Jimmy "Turk" Torello, mob capo, when Aiuppa was boss of the Chicago mob.

Rocky Infelice, top boss of the Chicago mob before he went to prison for the rest of his life in 1992.

Joe Bonanno, the boss of the "Bonanno Family" of La Cosa Nostra which has controlled a section of Brooklyn, New York, since 1931. Bonanno is currently a neighbor of the author in Tucson, Arizona.

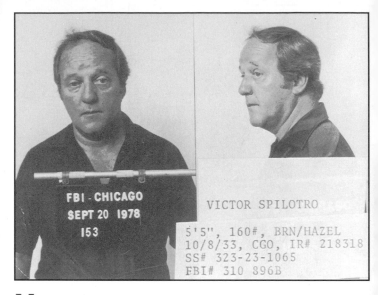

Victor Spilotro, Tony's brother, after his arrest by FBI in Chicago.

FBI mug shot of Joey Lombardo, Tony Spilotro's "capo," after his arrest in the Strawman case.

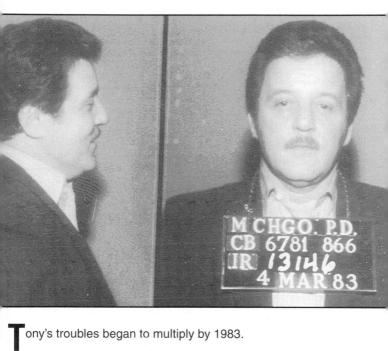

Tony's troubles began to multiply by 1983.

FBI surveillance photo of Frank Balistrieri (left), boss of the Milwaukee mob.

Jackie Cerone (right) as he appeared in a mug shot after his arrest by FBI in the Strawman II case in the early 1980s.

FBI surveillance photo of Tony Accardo on left and his protégé, Jackie Cerone, on right.

Angelo "The Hook" La Pietra, Chicago mob "capo."

Sam "Wings" Carlisi, Chicago mob boss 1992–93, as he appeared at a mob "sit-down" in 1986.

Ken Eto, Chicago mob gambling boss who turned to the FBI after the mob shot him three times in his head. Witness in the Strawman case in Kansas City.

Goodbye and good riddance: photo of top leadership of Chicago mob in the mid-1970s. Obtained during a search of the residence of Caesar DiVarco.

Tony Spilotro near his end.

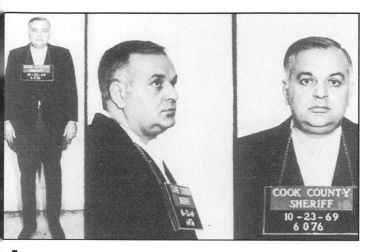

J oe Ferriola.

MICHAEL PETER SPILOTRO
5'6",170#,brn hair
9/12/44,CG
SSAN 340-34-1925
lka   1102 S. Maple,
      Oak Park, Ill.

M ug shot of Michael Spilotro as he appeared on the fatal day in 1986.

Johnny Bassett, the author's partner in the FBI for
fifteen years, as he appears in the 1990s.

amine what happened thereafter in Atlantic City. The eastern mobs, especially the five New York families, the Philadelphia family and the New Jersey family, but also Boston, tried their best to do in Atlantic City what had been done in Las Vegas. But the New Jersey legislature did something the Nevada lawmakers had not done until very late in the game. New Jersey established the Casino Control Commission. As I have mentioned before, Nevada did not authorize the GCB until after the hoods were well hunkered down in Nevada, almost twenty-five years after casino gambling had been legalized in 1931.

I saw the figures in the mid-Eighties. For every casino in Nevada there were 1.1 GCB employees. For every casino in Atlantic City there were 92.3 CCC employees. The state of New Jersey spent $3.4 million per year per casino. The state of Nevada spent $32,000 per casino. I'm sure had the eastern families of the LCN realized this was what was about to transpire they would have had no hesitancy in turning Aiuppa's proposal down. Flat. Chicago had hoodwinked them. They knew what they had in Nevada and they smelled it out that it would not be so easy in Atlantic City. They were right.

Nevada had had a grandfather clause of its own. When state officials finally came to the realization, in 1955, that they needed to regulate the gaming industry and that it was a necessity to license gaming executives, they passed the law that anyone already in place in the casinos would not be subject to the licensing requirements. They were grandfathered in. Well, of course, this was one hell of a loophole. By the mid-Fifties the mobs were well entrenched.

None of the governors in Nevada seemed to want to recognize there was a problem with organized crime. Certainly not Paul Laxalt, Mike O'Callaghan or Robert List. I remember Governor List telling the National Conference on Public Gaming that "the men," meaning organized crime figures, "have been cleaned out of the gaming industry." Wow. That was in the mid-Seventies when Tony, Lefty, Glick and so many others were sending millions of dollars a year in skim back to the Outfit in Chicago.

The difference between the efficiency of the Casino Control Commission of New Jersey and the Gaming Control Board of Nevada, both set up to combat the same thing, can easily be evaluated by looking at the case of Sidney R. Korshak. Hilton Hotels was easily granted the license to own and operate the Las Vegas Hilton and the Hilton Flamingo (Bugsy's old hotel) in Las Vegas. But when they applied for a license to operate in New Jersey they were turned down. Why? Because Sid Korshak was on their payroll. He was the attorney who has represented so many Chicago mob interests since the days of Frank "The Enforcer" Nitti, especially in Las Vegas. But hardly any in Atlantic City, where he was persona non grata. I remember very well how the Chicago mobsters, Murray Humphreys and Gussie Alex in particular, would contact "Mr. Lincoln" to do their bidding. I remember Hump telling Gus in front of Little Al how he had reamed Sid out. He was their guy. That made little difference to the GCB but it sure as hell did to the CCC.

The same thing happened with the Perlmen brothers, Clifford and Stuart. Nevada found them suitable in 1983 when they bought the Dunes from Morris Shenker for $164 million. But when Caesars World tried to obtain a license in Atlantic City, the CCC ordered them to get rid of the Perlmen duo if they wanted a license. The Perlmen brothers associated with Al Melnick, who in turn associated with Meyer Lansky. Caesars World obeyed. That association was enough for New Jersey but it didn't faze Nevada.

I admit the atmosphere in Nevada changed for the better when Richard Bryan became governor. The former Nevada Supreme Court Justice and current U.S. Senator from Nevada made it much tougher with his better appointments to the GCB. I had a long chat with then Justice Bryan in Carson City, and he impressed me with his capability and sincerity. Senator Bryan is very good for the honest, hard-working citizens of Nevada.

Of course, another fine thing for the good citizens of Nevada took place in 1980 when Joe Yablonsky was sent by Judge Webster, then the director of the FBI, to be the SAC in charge of the Las Vegas field division. Joe was a unique character. Talk about hands-on SAC's. Joe wrote the book! He had been a protégé of Jack Danahy, the great organized crime squad supervisor in New York, where he worked with some outstanding agents like Warren Donovan, Jim Mansfield, Jimmy Mulroy, Tom Emery, Jimmy Flynn, Frank Garritty, Billy Kane and Guy Berado. Then he transferred to Miami where he worked on the organized crime squad headed by Ralph Hill, my old partner. Eventually he became the ASAC in Boston and the SAC in Cincinnati. At the end of the Seventies, Webster sent him to Las Vegas to head up that office and handle its problems.

Joe did a fine job for the three years he was there. He became quite controversial to say the least. The good Senator Laxalt even made an appointment with Judge Webster and complained that under Joe, "law enforcement is too aggressive" in Las Vegas.

Joe had his problems. He and State Attorney General Brian McKay didn't take kindly to each other. In fact, Joe lent his support to McKay's opponent during the election for AG and McKay never forgot it. I worked closely with Joe and we are close friends. I recall traveling with him one time after we retired and were working together defending a news organization against a libel suit. We were in Chicago and Joe got a call from his wife, Wilma. She relayed a message that Joe was to call an assistant of McKay in Carson City, the state capital. When he did he found that McKay was attempting to rescind Joe's private investigator's license. The establishment held Joe's aggressiveness against him even after he left the FBI.

25 Informants

By 1979 Tony ran into more trouble. He would be charged with the murder of Sherwin Lisner. Lisner, a mobster, became an informant for Metro, the police force in Las Vegas which had been formed by a combination of the LVPD and the Clark County Sheriff's Office. He also was an informant for the Drug Enforcement Agency, DEA, in Vegas. Lisner had done a lot of things in Las Vegas although, of course, he was not "made." But he knew a lot about what was going on in Vegas and who was involved.

Though Lisner was not actually murdered by Spilotro, Tony had ordered it. It had been committed by Tony's underling, Frank Cullotta, who had chased Lisner through Lisner's house until he cornered him in a bedroom and plugged him full of holes. Tony had ordered the killing when he learned that Lisner had become an informant. That was *always* a *sure-fire* way to get killed.

The newspapers would refer to Lisner as a snitch. I hate it when they say that. Fink, Snitch, Rat and Stool Pigeon are the terminology of the underworld. They are derogatory terms. Informants and Sources are what we call them. PCIs, CIs and CTEs. Complimentary words.

In front of me as I write I have the editorial of the *Las Vegas Sun*, one of the city's two dailies, from the Sunday, September 12, 1993 edition discussing Geraldo Denono, my informant. The Denono case, according to the *Sun*, "provides a chilling example of self-seeking federal irresponsibility." It goes on. "Tell us your story, federal officials essentially say to sleazes like Denono. If we like what you say, we will protect, house, feed and clothe you in style. And we'll give you money. All you have to do is go where we ask and tell your story when we request it." It gets worse. "According to one expert, during the twenty-odd years Denono has avoided Nevada's prison, he has likely been supported under an assumed name, in a house or condo better than many Americans can afford." Then: "About a month ago, his federal sidekicks brought Denono to Nevada to plead for clemency before the Nevada Board of Pardons. Enthusiastically, they urged the board to allow Denono, who has never served a single day in prison, eligibility to apply for an immediate parole. . . . We regret to say our Board of Pardons got duped.

"The entire sordid practice of purchasing testimony from creeps like Denono needs to be examined and curtailed. Sadly, the witness protection program obviously has become an expensive and dangerous toy, which some misguided characters in federal law enforcement cannot be trusted to use in a restrained and reasonable manner."

First of all, Denono was never in the witness protection program run by the U.S. Marshall's Service. Gerry was in the witness program of the Bureau of Prisons. Still is. In other words he is imprisoned, has been for almost twenty years. He's gotten no pass at all. He's never been housed "better than many Americans can afford." Nobody has ever "protected, housed, fed and clothed" Denono—except the guards. I know. I've visited him there. As Sandy Smith, my old friend on the *Chicago Tribune*, *Sun-Times*, *Life* and *Time*, used to say, "Some reporters never let the facts interfere with a good story."

I'm sure you remember my reference to Denono when I wrote about the Denono Diary, the skim ledger of the Vegas casinos. I'm not about to say that his cooperation matched that of many of my CTEs. But he was very helpful. Not so much for me but for several other federal and state law enforcement people. The state of Arizona went to bat for him just as I did at his hearing before the Nevada Board of Paroles. They did so since he helped by giving testimony regarding the murder of Don Bolles, the reporter for the *Arizona Republic*. He got up in court and testified about one of the murderers of this crusading reporter.

The point I'm trying to make here is that informants are crucial to law enforcement. We can't get along without them. Up until 1985 we were only able to turn two of the made mobsters of organized crime families into witnesses in court against their fellow mobsters. Joe Valachi and Jimmy Fratianno. Since 1985 there have been more than a dozen. It is not a coincidence that during this same period we have had many more convictions of the upper echelon of organized crime than ever in our history. I'm not saying it's *all* due to such witnesses. But it's part of the one-two punch with Title III, the hidden mikes in mob meeting places. In the Nineties we've had several prosecutions of top bosses predicated on the one-two punch, including those of John Gotti in New York, where the FBI penetrated Gotti's headquarters, the Ravenite Social Club on Mulberry Street in Little Italy, lower Manhattan. This evidence, combined with the crucial testimony of Gotti's underboss, Sammy "The Bull" Gravano, got us a conviction. Another example is the recent case in Chicago where B. J. Yahoda, a former top lieutenant of Rocky Infelice, the Outfit boss, carried a wire and recorded his conversations with Infelice and his lieutenants—and then completed the one-two punch by testifying in court against them. Or the recent case in San Diego where "No Nose" DiFronzo and Donald Angelini were convicted on the basis of Title IIIs from a roving wiretap and by testimony by such men as Lenny Patrick, the former Chicago gambling boss.

I have developed dozens of informants. Some have been CTEs who have met with the worst killers in our history and then come to me and told me about it. Some have gotten up and testified in open court, eyeball to eyeball with the mobster-defendants, telling the story of corruption, murder and mayhem. Don't you think that takes courage? Balls? Guts? Would you call that guy a rat or snitch? I sure don't.

What I call the action of those kind of people is bravery. Courage. Sure, up to that point in their lives they were bad guys. Scum, as I call them, and slime. And there is an element of self-preservation, self-interest in what they do. Some do it for money. More do it for leniency, sometimes even immunity. But when it is done for leniency, it is always because we are getting the bigger law violator in exchange for their testimony. We're using the minnow to get the shark. As bait.

Let's assume that Denono came over to our side from their side because he had a self-interest. I say forget his motive. He saw the light. He's now on our side! For whatever reason, he's now doing the right thing. The effect is to put some very bad people, very guilty people, in prison. Look not at the motive but at the result. In his case he hasn't gotten much out of it. Maybe the guards treat him a little better than they do John Gotti or "No Nose," but if so, let's be happy they do. It's a small concession. And I'm not even sure they do.

Or take the case of Jimmy "The Weasel" Fratianno, who entered the U.S. Marshall's witness protection program. He lived in a nice house during and after he brought down many mob bosses. I know he did since I met with him in a western city in the mid-Eighties. Don't you think he deserves that? If the mob had ever found him—he died of natural causes in the summer of 1993—don't you think they might have put his head in a vise, squeezed his eyes out, and so on. Jimmy even got what he considered was a bum deal. He wrote a best-selling book with Ovid Demaris, *The Last Mafioso*. As best-selling authors sometimes make a great deal of money, the U.S. Marshall's Office felt he had enough to support himself in security. They put him out of the program. For his last several years he had to fend for himself, watching over his shoulder every moment, hoping not to see someone like Tony Spilotro coming after him, a real fear because he was living in the area covered by Chicago, the family Jimmy was made in. Jimmy used to call me with his bitter complaints. There was nothing I could do but commiserate with him. He died a broken man. He felt he had been deserted by the people he had joined. I could understand his situation. He had enough money to be comfortable, thanks to his book, but not enough to wrap himself in complete security.

The point I'm trying to make is that when a guy like Tony

Spilotro orders the killing of a guy like Sherwin Lisner, then the whole law enforcement community gets involved. Lisner was an informant for Metro and for the DEA. Rather than wonder why the security surrounding him, or which *should* have surrounded him, was penetrated, all of law enforcement, federal and state, would now band together in cooperation to develop the evidence necessary to bring Tony to justice for the murder.

One of the real problems in Las Vegas at that time was the fear of the FBI that there might be another Blasko or Leone inside Metro. We had already been burned when Blasko had turned our reports over to Spilotro. How far could we go in cooperating with Metro in the Lisner investigation? This was not a problem with the DEA. I was the official liaison with the DEA in Chicago for the Bureau shortly after it was formed in the mid-Seventies and I got to know those guys well. They are a talented, hard-working bunch of agents. Just as the Alcohol, Tobacco and Firearms agents are. And also the IRS, especially the Intelligence Unit of IRS. And, maybe most of all, the Secret Service. I never had a bad experience in sharing information with any agent of any other federal law enforcement agency.

Sad to say, Tony would never be prosecuted for the Lisner killing.

26 Tony and His Bosses

In 1979 there was a big move. Allen Glick was forced out of the Stardust, Chicago's main casino. The old reliable.

As we would find out later, when the Kansas City, Milwaukee and Chicago mob chiefs went on trial in Kansas City, the mob tired of Glick, who had lost his gaming license. And Lefty had become too high profile, with his TV talk show from the Stardust, featuring interviews with the stars appearing there, like Don Rickles or Shecky Greene, or others like Sinatra, who were prodded by the Outfit to appear.

In December 1978, GCB refused once more to reinstate Lefty's gaming license—after heated hearings at which Lefty hurled charges of corruption at some of the GCB commissioners including Ed Reid, now a U.S. Senator from Nevada. The hearings were televised and the citizens of Las Vegas got a full dose of just how their regulators conducted their business—which wasn't good for Lefty or for the GCB. Following the denial of his license, Lefty took the GCB to court and won. Then lost on appeal in the Nevada Supreme Court.

He was less and less of a value to the Outfit. Both Glick and Rosenthal, code-named respectively, "Genius" and "Potzo" by the mob—Potzo being Sicilian for crazy, demented—were marked for killing. In fact, Carl DeLuna, a top leader of the Kansas City family of the LCN, would be overheard at that time on a Title III in Kansas City saying Lefty's chances were "finito," Sicilian for finished.

Now the Chicago Outfit had to find a new licensee, a new front who could obtain approval from the GCB even though he would be working for Chicago, making sure nothing impeded the flow of skim to the Windy City. This hunt did not involve Tony. It was outside the realm of his responsibility. He was Mr. Outside; the people who worked inside were his to discipline but not to appoint, although he sometimes overstepped his bounds. When it came to finding top executives to operate the casino, Tony was not consulted.

The mob finally came up with two guys, Al Sachs and Herb Tobman. A GCB agent was assigned to get the rundown on those two prior to the hearings that would determine whether they could be licensed. If GCB turned them down, they couldn't participate in the operation of the Stardust. Jimmy "The Weasel" Fratianno was asked to testify. He testified that Sachs was a front for Chicago. The report of the GCB agent who had investigated Sachs, Dick Law, reflected that Sachs had been employed at the Jockey Club, a Chicago gambling joint run by the Chicago mob. At that time, one of my CTEs in Chicago, who I still maintained contact with although I was now in Tucson, told me that whenever he wanted somebody comped in Vegas he called Sachs. He told me that Sachs had previously worked for Les Kruse and Rocco Fischetti, major Chicago gambling bosses.

At the time Richard Bunker was a member of the Gaming Control Board. The FBI, which had my information and considerably more, however, did not trust Bunker. They declined the request of GCB for information in FBI files. The Chairman of GCB at the time, Roger Trounday, advised later that he was pressured by Governor List to speed up the licensing although both List and Bunker deny they were applying any pressure on behalf of Sachs and Tobman. Trounday would soon thereafter quit the GCB, partly because of the pressure he received. GCB agent Law's report recommended that Sachs "should not be the individual who should inherit Glick's gaming properties." It was ignored and Law was soon thereafter fired, for what he considered to be a trumped-up charge. He sued for reinstatement, charging his refusal to write a favorable report on Sachs was the real reason for his discharge. He won a partial victory.

When the dust settled Sachs and Tobman were licensed and the Outfit had their fronts. But it would turn out to be a rocky road.

It was about this time that Ivan Harris, a member of the organized crime squad of the Chicago FBI office, developed a new informant who was a well-placed Chicago mobster. The hood advised that he had been in recent contact with Tony and that Tony had informed him that when he moved his headquarters from the gift shop at Circus-Circus to the Dunes he had desired to take legal action against GCB, which was putting pressure on Al Sarno to force Tony out. However, Joey Aiuppa ordered him not to do so due to the publicity it would cause, the attention it would focus on him.

The same informant advised that the Chicago Outfit was

concerned that Tony was not "keeping his head down" and was drawing attention to himself as their rep in Las Vegas. On his next trip to Chicago, Tony was cautioned by his superiors.

The informant also related to Harris that Spilotro told him that the Chicago bosses "constantly use me for murder contracts."

It was at about the same time that another fine OC agent in Chicago, Pete Wacks, was developing Alva Johnson Rodgers as an informant. Pete had come onto C-1 in 1970 or so and had quickly developed into one of our very best. Rodgers was a close associate of Marshall Caifano and to a lesser extent of Joey Lombardo, Tony's capo. One of the first things Rodgers told Pete Wacks was that Lombardo was the guy who killed my pal Dick Cain in Rose's Sandwich Shop. He had done so, Rodgers said, after Cain had been set up by Caifano. The most interesting thing to me, however, was Rodger's information indicating that neither he, Caifano nor Lombardo was aware that Cain was a double agent inside the mob and that this, therefore, was not the reason for his murder.

Rodgers also told Pete Wacks around this time that he met with Lombardo and Caifano at a driving range on River Road in Chicago the day after Danny Seifert had been killed. Seifert, of course, was the prospective witness against Lombardo and Spilotro on the Deming, New Mexico case. Lombardo and Caifano did not admit that they had been involved in the slaying but were very gleeful about it. Lombardo told Rodgers, "He won't be able to testify now," and then laughed.

Incidentally, Rodgers is also the informant who advised Wacks that Caifano had told him that he, Caifano, had requested permission from Lombardo, who was his capo as well, to kill Ray Ryan, the Indiana oilman who Caifano extorted. At first Lombardo refused, but subsequently Ryan was blown up in southern Indiana, where he lived. Caifano made mention to Rodgers shortly after the murder that Ryan had been hard to follow because he had no set pattern of movement.

It was also about this time that Charley Parsons, one of the top agents assigned to the organized crime squad in Las Vegas, developed a top informant. This guy was very close to Spilotro

in Las Vegas. He would later testify that he worked directly
for Spilotro, both in Chicago and Las Vegas. He advised that
Spilotro on numerous occasions told him that his capo was
Joey Lombardo and that any significant criminal activity he
engaged in had to be approved by Lombardo. This information
was very significant because it indicated that Tony was operating in Las Vegas in some respects "out of control." For instance, his involvement as the boss of the Hole-in-the-Wall
Gang was not known to Lombardo or to any of the other top
bosses in Chicago.

This informant then advised Parsons of something very interesting to me. He told Parsons that he had been instructed
that when he was in Chicago, anything he did, inasmuch as he
was "with Tony," had to be cleared by Lombardo and that
when there he should reach out for Michael Spilotro, Tony's
kid brother, to get to Lombardo. This was the first indication
to me that Michael was involved to any extent in the affairs of
Tony and the Outfit. I knew that Michael was the owner and
manager of Hoagie's, a well-known bar and restaurant that
was the hangout for a number of mid-level Chicago made
guys, but I had not received any indication that Michael was
involved in Tony's affairs or that he was in touch with Tony's
boss, Lombardo. Not only could Michael put the informant in
touch with Lombardo, but Michael could discuss the informant's business with Lombardo and bring back to the informant
Lombardo's decision as to whether he could proceed.

This same informant advised that on one occasion he had
wanted to murder a man in Chicago. He was put directly in
touch with Lombardo, who instructed him that he should just
break the individual's arms, legs and head. However, if the
problem occurred again, then he could kill him. On that occasion, the informant said, he was told by Spilotro that any hit
he, Tony, wanted to perform had to be approved by his capo,
Lombardo.

This is the same informant who advised that on one occasion he had been disciplined by Lombardo when the son of
Louis Eboli, a member of Lombardo's street crew in Chicago,
had been beaten in a bar owned by the informant. Lombardo

ordered the informant to submit to a similar beating by Eboli. He did as he was told and permitted Eboli to beat him with a brick. The informant said that he readily submitted to such discipline because if he refused, the matter would be taken all the way up to Joey Aiuppa, the mob boss, and his decision might have been to kill the informant.

It was also in 1979 that still another informant advised that Lombardo's function in the Chicago family of the LCN included supervision of the activities of Allen Dorfman, then the administrator of the Central States Pension Fund. Dorfman, according to this informant, acted as a clearinghouse and conduit for all loans to organized crime entities. In this regard, the informant advised that not only was Dorfman close to Lombardo, his supervisor, but to Nick Civella, then the boss of the Kansas City family of the LCN. Dorfman got his payoff for the high risk loans he was making from the fund by having the loan insured through Amalgamated, the insurance company he owned in Chicago at The International Towers at 8550 Bryn Mawr Avenue. The informant pointed out several Las Vegas casinos that had taken out insurance with Dorfman's company. In this manner Dorfman was able to receive what amounted to a kickback for arranging and approving the loans from the pension fund of the Teamsters.

Another informant told the FBI that Dorfman inflated the insurance premiums he charged Las Vegas hotel-casinos when he issued insurance policies on the loans the Teamsters made to them. He then split these inflated premiums with the organized crime figure who was involved.

This informant also advised that Lombardo frequently consulted Dorfman on matters of financial interest to organized crime entities. Dorfman also maintained an active role in establishing and managing numerous business investments on behalf of his associates in the mobs, not only the Chicago mob but others.

A different source advised that he was present in Dorfman's offices in the International Towers when Tony Spilotro and Joey Lombardo arrived to meet with Dorfman. During the meeting they discussed a number of illegal activities. It was apparent to this informant that Lombardo exerted a great deal of control over Dorfman and, therefore, the Teamsters pension fund. This informant advised that at the time Joey Aiuppa was the Chicago LCN boss, Jackie Cerone and Joey Lombardo were capos answerable to Aiuppa and that Cerone was the underboss who took command when Aiuppa was not available. The informant pointed Lombardo out as a "killer."

This is the informant who then provided specific information about the killing of Danny Seifert. He informed us that Tony Spilotro gave him a vivid description of how he and his Chicago LCN companions killed Seifert in front of Seifert's wife and child. Spilotro told him in no uncertain terms that the killing was done to insure that Seifert did not testify against him and his co-defendants, including Lombardo and Dorfman. The Chicago mob could not afford to lose these guys. Spilotro told the informant that he had been criticized by his Chicago bosses because they considered the murder to have been badly handled in that it was done in front of Seifert's family, a fact that caused the killing to get widespread attention in the media. On that occasion, Spilotro indicated to the informant that he not only killed Seifert, but pistol-whipped him first.

It was also at about this time that the Kansas City office of the FBI conducted a review of their file on Joey Aiuppa. A great deal of information on various elements of mob activity was discovered. For example, it was found that Aiuppa, as boss of the Chicago Outfit, had approved all gangland slayings involving Chicago mobsters. These included eight individuals who the Chicago mobs suspected were involved in the burglary of Tony Accardo's home in January 1978. The burglars had ripped off a jewelry store on the north side of Chicago just prior to the Christmas rush. The owner just happened to be a friend of Tony Accardo. He went to Accardo and requested that the jewelry be returned because otherwise his Christmas season, the time when he did most of his yearly business, would be ruined. Now, as I have mentioned, burglary is not something the Outfit involves itself in. But Willie "Potatoes" Daddano had the responsibility for insuring that the mob got a street tax from every Chicago burglar. Therefore, Daddano had the Outfit responsibility of knowing who every Chicago burglar and thief was and what they were doing. Accardo contacted him, and the burglars involved in the robbery of Accardo's friend were quickly identified. They were firmly instructed to return the jewelry. They did. But then they had a change of heart. Tony Accardo and his wife, Clarise, had now departed from their River Forest home to spend Christmas at their condo in Palm Springs. The burglars, feeling they had no reason to return the jewelry and that they were entitled to their score, invaded the now-empty Accardo residence in the belief that the cache would be located there. They didn't find it because it had already been returned. The next day, Marie, one of the daughters of the Accardos, checked the house. She found it ransacked. She told her father in Palm Springs. He ordered that the police be notified. He also ordered something else. Soon thereafter, every one of the burglars was found. All dead. All with their throats slashed. One, an Italian who should have known better, was castrated and had his face burned off with a blowtorch! That would teach them. And anybody else who might decide to fuck with the Outfit!

The review of the Kansas City FBI files also found that information had been received showing Aiuppa had approved the murder of Marty Buccieri. Buccieri had been employed at various mob casinos in northern Kentucky and then had been sent out to Las Vegas. Spilotro had been the prime suspect in that mid-Seventies killing. The files indicated that the murder had been requested by Frank Balistrieri, the Milwaukee LCN boss who reports to Chicago. I remember Mike Simon, the Las Vegas agent, telling me about the Buccieri murder, which he had investigated. Marty Buccieri was a made member of the Chicago mob. He was pretty well placed in Vegas. When the Stardust was sold by Glick, Marty felt he was owed a finder's fee. He confronted Glick in the rear of the Hacienda. Lefty Rosenthal was also present at that confrontation between Buccieri and Glick. It got quite nasty. Shortly thereafter Buccieri was murdered.

The files also contained information that Aiuppa had sanctioned the murder of Chuckie Nicoletti. Surprisingly, the motive for the killing was that Aiuppa had been led to believe that Nicoletti was an informant. To my knowledge, this was not true. I had met with him but he never turned.

Aiuppa had also authorized the killing of George Vandermark. Vandermark had been employed by the Stardust to supervise their slot action. He had a background of being the expert on how to skim slots. He did so for the Chicago mob. But then he was suspected of going a little too far—of helping himself to some of the skim. He fled when he realized he was under suspicion. Shortly thereafter, not being able to find George, the mob murdered his son. Vandermark himself has never been found. It is believed that he fled to South America and that the mob located him there and took care of him.

Aiuppa also had authorized the murder of Sam Giancana in 1975. This, of course, had to be true. Giancana could not have been killed if the then-current bosses of the Outfit had not approved. Aiuppa, himself, was not involved in the actual murder, any more than he was in any of the others. He just gave the nod.

It was disclosed that the best information at this time was that although the Chicago mob was not involved directly in prostitution or narcotics, they exacted a street tax from pimps and pushers, forcing them to pay a tariff in order to operate in Chicago. This did not surprise me.

There were also further indications in the files that the Chicago family of La Cosa Nostra "has control of all LCN activities west of the Mississippi River," and that "the final decision when conflicts arise between organized crime families within that territory is always made by the Chicago LCN boss, Joseph Aiuppa."

And it seemed that the Civella family, the Kansas City family of the LCN, had a *representato* in Las Vegas just as the Chicago family had theirs. The rep for KC was Joseph Vincent Agosto, who handled their affairs in Vegas from 1975 until 1979.

Finally, the files indicated that a dispute took place between the Civella family of Kansas City and the DeCalvacante LCN family of New Jersey over money owed by the Civellas to the DeCalvacantes. This dispute was resolved through the efforts of the Chicago family acting as the arbitrator between the other two La Cosa Nostra families.

27 Tony's Books Are Closed

In May 1979, another arrest warrant was issued for Tony, relating to a large sports betting and juice empire in Las Vegas. He had set up illegal betting establishments throughout southern Nevada.

You might wonder how illegal betting could be profitable in Las Vegas, when there are scores of casinos with sports and race books and scores of other free-standing betting parlors. Why go to an illegal bookie when there are a hundred or more legal ones, all licensed by the GCB, which vouches for their honesty?

There is a big reason. To gamble in the legal places like the casinos you need cash or a good credit standing. You can go to the casino cage, give cash or establish credit and get chips. But you need good credit. If you don't have it, or if you lose it by being "grinded" down at the slots or tables, then you can't gamble there.

But you can gamble at an illegal sports book, in Vegas, Chicago or wherever. Because they have an edge. They have the hammer. You fail to pony up with the mob and they send you to their juice guy, their loan shark. You then hand over to the bookie what you got from the loan shark. You fail to pay your six-for-five every week to the juice guy and then you put your life into his hands. Watch out for your kneecaps! The first week. Got a pretty wife? *She* better watch out the second week. Soon you're gone. Knowing how it works, any bettor at an illegal joint does whatever it takes to pay his shylock off. Many times that involves criminal activity.

This is what I feel right now, in the mid-Nineties, is so frightful about legalizing gambling on Indian reservations, on riverboats, in casinos in cities such as Deadwood City, New Orleans, Foxwoods in Connecticut, perhaps Chicago as I write this, and so many other places. I was contacted some time ago by the Chicago Better Government Association, a civic organization. Terry Brunner, the Executive Director, told me that they were part of the Chicago Ethics Coalition, a group of organizations and churches in opposition to Mayor Richard M. Daley's proposal that casinos be built near McCormick Place on the near south side. Brunner asked if I had any thoughts on the proposal. After we discussed it he asked me to go to Las Vegas to be filmed there making my objections to legalized casino gambling in Chicago. I was videotaped outside the Excalibur—not that that hotel has ever been mobbed-up— where I gave a forty-five-minute dissertation that was played at a hearing in Chicago on the casino situation.

I didn't address the moral problems with gambling. I left that to the churches in the coalition. My problem with legalized gaming is that a person goes into the nearby, convenient casino after seeing all the enticing advertisements in the newspaper or on television. He is conditioned to understand that some people get very lucky in a casino. Win hundreds of thousands. He is not conditioned to understand that the odds are fixed so that they eventually grind you down. You can win today. Maybe tomorrow. But the longer you play the less chance you have to win. Casinos are not in business to lose money. The odds are set so that they can't. Over time they have to win. Maybe this person wins for a while. He enjoys the excitement. He enjoys the high he gets when he pulls the lever on the slot machine or makes his point at the crap table. He comes back tomorrow, and tomorrow, and tomorrow. Soon he finds he's losing. At first it's just discretionary income. But pretty soon he's losing money that should have gone for groceries, to pay the light bill, maybe eventually the mortgage.

Now he has no more cash. He goes to the cage and arranges for credit. He wins today. His habit is fortified. But eventually, of course, he's bound to lose. Now what does he do? He's addicted. He can't give it up, but he can't gamble any longer in the legal casinos. No cash, no credit.

So his recourse is to go to the mob-controlled bookie. Every book is mob controlled. The bookie may be like Hal Smith in Chicago, who was not connected. But if such a bookie doesn't go 50-50 with the Outfit he winds up just like Hal Smith did. Dead. That's what Rocky Infelice and Lou Marino were convicted of in 1993 and sentenced to prison for the rest of their lives. Among other things, the killing of Hal Smith was because he wouldn't go 50-50 with Infelice's street crew. Very few bookmakers have the guts of Hal Smith. They either work directly for a guy like Infelice or go 50-50 with him. And if they're caught holding out they wind up like Smith. Trunk music.

So our guy goes to the bookmaker. He has no recourse if he cannot break the addiction which the legal casino caused. Had there never been a legal casino he never would have become addicted. But now he has to have the high which went with a bet on a horse, or more likely a football, basketball or baseball game. He gets bored if he doesn't have some action when he's watching sports. He's got to "get down" on games he wants to watch. So he goes to the bookmaker. He wins some and he loses some. Eventually, because of the odds, he loses more than he wins. Now he must go to the juice guy if he wants to continue. Soon he has to pay. He can't. But to try, he becomes a criminal.

It's a steady progression. That's the essence of my problem with legalizing gambling. Along with problems concerning the infiltration of the mob. We couldn't keep the mob out of Las Vegas thousands of miles from Chicago. Now they're talking about putting casinos in Chicago?

For these reasons, Tony built an illegal sports betting and loan-sharking empire in Las Vegas, among all the legal casinos. He found hundreds of players who spurned the casinos and placed their action with Tony's bookmakers.

However, the walls began to crumble on June 19, 1978. On that date FBI agents in Chicago and in Las Vegas conducted sweeping searches. We've already seen some of the effects of that operation, but the agents were also looking for records pertaining to the Spilotro sports betting and loan-sharking operation. They announced that the operation grossed $1 million a month. Scores of FBI agents participated in the searches with search warrants for fifty locations and/or persons. Three of the searches were in Chicago and the rest in Las Vegas.

The agents were seeking information concerning violations of statutes dealing with Interstate Transportation in Aid of Racketeering, Interstate Transportation of Wagering Paraphernalia, Interstate Transportation of Wagering Information and Interstate Transportation of Stolen Property, as well as evidence of organized crime activity and loan-sharking.

It was determined that Tony relied on three guys to oversee his books, Fat Herbie Blitzstein, Frank Cullotta and Sal Romano. Cullotta and Romano were also important figures in the Hole-in-the-Wall Gang. Especially Cullotta, a most accomplished burglar. He was Tony's right hand in the betting ring and in the Gang. He was accomplished in both areas and was very close to Tony, very much trusted.

Based on the evidence uncovered in the searches, arrest warrants were issued for Tony, Cullotta and Blitzstein ten months later, on May 16, 1979. The press headlined the arrests in Chicago and in Las Vegas. They heralded the ring as "the multimillion dollar illegal sports betting and loan shark operation." The affidavit supporting the arrest warrants also disclosed that the FBI had developed information that "the Chicago mob had hidden interests in the Argent Corporation and that money was diverted from the casino of the Stardust and sent to Joseph P. Balistrieri, whose father, Frank, is described by the FBI as the 'organized crime chieftain in Milwaukee and answerable to the Chicago organized crime family.' "

The affidavits also reflected that the probable cause had been built during a six-month investigation by the FBI in Las Vegas in 1978. It indicated that the information was developed primarily by the use of Title IIIs at Gold Rush, Ltd. where "calls were made to and from the store dealing with a loan-sharking operation, with associates of Spilotro apparently traveling to other states to collect debts."

The FBI had also learned that Tony had meddled in the affairs of the Fremont and the Stardust by calling executives there and ordering them to place people on the payroll who were wanted there by Tony. He even ordered that the Stardust fire one girl and hire another "he would send them." This was seemingly in contradiction to Tony's role as Mr. Outside. But, as we were learning, Tony had a big ego. He did not want to be confined.

28 Cops

Tony went nuts! "How the fuck did this happen?" he reportedly shouted. "How did we ever let that guy in? We should have our fuckin' heads examined!"

The affidavit for the raid had disclosed that an undercover FBI agent, Rick Baken, had infiltrated Tony's operation at Gold Rush Ltd. Posing as a jewel thief known as Rick Calise, Agent Baken had wormed his way into Tony's confidence and that of John, his brother. He had actually obtained stolen jewels from Gold Rush for resale on commission. This was all part of the probable cause for the arrests. In fact, just to make things legal, Oscar Goodman, Tony's Las Vegas attorney, and Tony were summoned to Strike Force Attorney Geoffrey Anderson's office where Anderson and Jim Powers, then the SAC of the Las Vegas FBI office, officially notified Goodman and Tony of the true identity of Rick Calise. Jim Powers had been the ASAC of the Chicago Office while I was there and is now the security director of The Mirage Corporation, which owns three of the best hotels in Vegas—the Mirage, Treasure Island and the Golden Nugget. All controlled by Steven Wynn, who has had his problems but has never been mobbed-up.

Now the attorneys for Argent and for Tony—Frank Rothman and Oscar Goodman—went to work attacking the warrants. They're both sharp guys who know their business and will go to any lengths—any lengths—to win. Remember also that they were operating in Las Vegas, the seat of judges like Harry Claiborne, the first sitting federal judge ever to go to federal prison.

U.S. District Court Judge Roger Foley took a good hard look at the situation. Finally, on November 9, he ruled that the FBI searches at the Stardust lacked probable cause and ordered the FBI to return the voluminous documents it had seized.

Then Tony was involved in an incident in Atlantic City. Remember Gene Clark? He was the police captain, the former deputy police chief in Las Vegas, who borrowed some money from Allen Glick. When the search warrants were executed at the Stardust, documents were found there by the Bureau indicating that Chief Clark had accepted $181,000 from Allen Glick, the front for the Chicago Outfit at the Stardust.

Clark had retired from the Las Vegas PD after twenty-eight years on the job. He had taken a job as director of security for Penthouse International, Inc., which not only published the magazine but owned a hotel in Atlantic City. He had then applied for a gaming license in Atlantic City and put down a nice chunk of money as an investment in a casino there. Was it some of the $181,000 Glick had advanced him? Who knows. But he was doing pretty well for a former cop. When that became public, Clark was discharged from his position with Penthouse. And any dreams he might have had of becoming a licensee in strict Atlantic City went down the tubes.

The situation was a real shame. Clark had been a cop for twenty-eight years. He faced temptations there that can only be imagined. Nick Civella said, at about that time, on a Title III in Kansas City when he was the boss of the KC mob, "In time, everyone out there, the fishes out there, gets corrupted. They can't help it. You know, they live right in the midst of it."

It was true. Las Vegas was a tough place for any law enforcement officer. We have seen the allegations of Mike Simon, substantiated or not, in the most incorruptible law enforcement agency of all time, in any country: the FBI. I have talked to many former FBI officials in Las Vegas like Joe Yablonsky, Jim Powers, Dean Elson, Charley Parsons, John Shreiber, Herb Hawkins and Red Campbell. Many of them feel that no FBI agent should be assigned to Las Vegas for more than several years. That's a tough call. The longer an agent stays in a town the better he gets to know his way around it. The more informants he develops—and many times turning an informant turns on a substantial rapport, a friendship and trust built up over many years. I was in Chicago twenty-four years and most of the CTEs I developed were the culmination of a long period of preparation. I never succumbed to any temptation—and there were some—but, on the other hand, I never worked exclusively in Las Vegas.

Clark, of course, maintained his innocence. It was hard to feel for the man when it was clear he had gotten, by loan or gift, the amount of money he did from Glick. And, as Deputy Chief of Police, he must have known who Glick was. And who he represented. Clark referred to the fact that the only dealing he ever had with Spilotro was when he arrested "and harassed" him. He pointed out that he had been an honest cop for twenty-eight years and that the loan came following his retirement from the force. He claimed that there was nothing in the files of the Intelligence Unit of the LVPD to indicate that Glick was anything but honest. Now, of course, that, if true, was a real indictment of the Intelligence Unit of the LVPD! On the other hand, as I have previously pointed out, the FBI had developed a mistrust of the LVPD, and may not have felt that it should be trusted with factual information that might tend to compromise the source of that information. And, of course, the FBI was perhaps the only agency with the ability to ferret out the information that Glick was the front for the

Chicago mob in Argent. So perhaps Clark was not evading the truth when he made that statement.

I have great sympathy for local policemen. They have a tough job. I give them all the credit in the world. And I am among the last to come to the conclusion that a cop is dirty. It is easy to paint a black picture with a broad brush. We hear about dirty cops in Chicago, New York, Las Vegas, Philadelphia, Miami, Los Angeles and most of the big cities. But 99 percent of police officers do their job well and honestly. Local cops work a lot in the muck, unlike FBI agents who very seldom have to work a night shift in the worst neighborhoods.

If in fact Clark did not know that Glick was the front for the Chicago LCN, then he might not be guilty. If he had taken the money as a loan from what he felt was a legitimate hotel owner and had every intention of paying it back—as might just have been the case—then how was that different from the case of so many law enforcement people retiring or resigning to take a high position in the gaming establishment? I gave him the benefit of the doubt. I might not furnish Clark with the identity of an informant, but I wouldn't arrest him either.

Such was the environment that Tony wallowed in. Las Vegas, especially at this time, was a tough town. Even for cops.

29 Joe Bonanno Attempts to Take California

Shortly after I transferred to Tucson it became obvious to those of us investigating Joe Bonanno that he was in conflict with the Chicago mob for California.

Bonanno had been one of the most powerful mob bosses in the country for decades. When La Cosa Nostra was instituted in New York in 1931 and territories were parceled out, he was given Brooklyn and named the boss of his own family, one of the five LCN families in New York. With the exception of Lucky Luciano, perhaps Bonanno was as influential in the affairs of La Cosa Nostra as any other mob boss. He was a charter member of The Commission, the name they had given to the ruling body of organized crime. And his chief rival for influence on The Commission, Luciano, was convicted in the mid-Thirties and would thereafter wield little influence, being deported from the country in the mid-Forties. In LCN history, mob figures like Frank Costello, Meyer Lansky, Albert Anastasia, Tony Accardo, Sam Giancana, Angelo Bruno, Vito Genovese, Frank Nitti, Raymond Patriarca and one or two others might command as much respect as Bonanno, and even that is doubtful, but none commanded more.

However, Joe got into some trouble in 1964 when he was perceived by his fellow bosses in The Commission to have plotted the murder of two of them. He was summoned by the bosses to appear at a hearing. At the same time, he had been subpoenaed to appear before a federal grand jury in New York. I had served that subpoena on him, my first of several meetings with him. What Bonanno did then is history. He alleged that the LCN boss in Buffalo, his cousin, Stephano Maggadino, had him kidnapped during some gunfire on Park Avenue, and then for the next eighteen months held him captive in various places in the west. None of this story, in my opinion, is true. I believe that Joe faked the kidnapping in order to avoid having to appear before the grand jury and at the hearing called by his fellow Commissioners.

These strange doings were followed by the "Bananas War," when Joe tried to elevate one of his capos to be acting boss of his LCN family. It so happened that the capo was his son, Salvatore, ordinarily called Bill, whose seniority was much less than some other capos, who were considered more capable and certainly had more experience. But Joe, still in hiding, kept out of it.

Finally, Joe suddenly appeared in the federal courthouse at Foley Square in New York and gave himself up to federal authorities. He claimed he should not be held in contempt of the grand jury. By then, however, the government had apparently lost interest in the case.

We never knew for sure, but The Commission also seemed to abandon its inquiry. Joe had achieved his purpose. However, there may have been some sanction imposed on him at the time. He may have lost some of his territory. We had no device, no informant, who could tell us for sure. In any event, Bonanno returned to his home on Elm Street in Tucson and, as far as we could tell, resumed control of his section of Brooklyn from Tucson.

When I arrived, four of us were assigned to organized crime investigation. The other three agents were very well qualified and great guys to work with. Bill Christiansen had been the case agent on Bonanno for years. Although the OC supervisor in Phoenix, the headquarters city which Tucson reported to, asked me to take over the case, I graciously declined. As far as I could see, Bill was doing a fine job. I sure didn't want to cause any friction there. Donn Stickles had been a supervisor at FBIHQ and was as good an agent as I ever knew in the Bureau. Louis "Skip" George, a younger agent, had all the potential of being just as good and proved it as the years went by. He had Pete Licavoli assigned to him. As I write this Skip is now the OC supervisor in Oakland.

Soon after I arrived in Tucson we put a full-court press on Bonanno. We picked through his garbage since we found that he wrote notes to himself outlining his daily agenda and then tore them up into four pieces and threw them into his garbage at the end of his day. We found indications that he was in close touch with Brooklyn and that he may even have had a hand in the sanction of the killing of Frank Bompensiero, our informant in San Diego. We also surveilled him constantly, by car, foot and airplane. We had found that he never used his home phone. He was driven by one of his underlings to pay phones all over Tucson. We got court orders under Title III to tap those phones as he used them. We listened to those conversations for months. Then we raided his home. He kept a "buco," a safe, in the cement floor of his bedroom closet. We penetrated it. We found some more evidence. Soon we had enough to indict him and then convict him. We sent him away for the first felony conviction of his life, his first federal prison time.

That, in a nutshell, was Joe Bonanno. But I'm a little ahead of my story and why it is pertinent here. One of the things we also found was that Joe Bonanno was in conflict with Tony Spilotro!

The Chicago family of La Cosa Nostra historically has had the right to everything west of Chicago except for the open territories. Now, however, Bonanno wanted California!

That, of course, brought him into conflict with Chicago. And with Tony, since Tony was responsible for all the west.

We estimated at the time that the operations in California were worth up to $10 billion a year. Quite a prize!

Already there was an LCN family in Los Angeles and another in San Jose. They were vulnerable for a couple of reasons. Three of the top guys in California had recently died, including Frank DeSimone, the boss, one of the attendees at Apalachin. Joe Cerrito had been the boss of the San Jose family for nineteen years until his death in 1978. And we know what happened to Bomp, the Los Angeles capo who was their boss in San Diego. Nick Licata, who had succeeded DeSimone in Los Angeles, had also recently died.

We believed that the notes found in Bonanno's garbage implicated him in the killing of Bomp and that Bomp's murder was part of his attempt to gain control of California for his family. We also believed that Joe didn't want it so much for himself but for his two sons, his capo, Bill, and his other son, Joe, Jr. They had been sent to San Jose and were operating there. In fact, that is where they would be convicted in the near future.

Never has there been a strong crime family in California. Not in Los Angeles, not in San Diego, not in Fresno, not in San Jose, not in San Francisco.

The Los Angeles family has always been laughingly referred to as The Micky Mouse Mafia. They tried, but they never really succeeded in building a strong empire in the City of Angeles. The FBI there, ramrodded by their fine supervisor, Jack Barron, and the LAPD, really a fine department in spite of recent troubles, and one noted in those days for its tough Intelligence Unit, kept a tight lid on LA.

The San Diego mob was really a part of the LA mob, hence the presence there of Bomp, a capo out of LA.

The San Jose family had tight control of that area. For years Cerrito held control over a nice money-making operation. But it was small, peanuts, compared to such cities as Chicago, New York, Philadelphia, Detroit, Kansas City, Cleveland, Boston and even Pittsburgh and Buffalo. It didn't even have a spot on The Commission, just as no city west of the Mississippi did—they were all represented by Chicago.

San Francisco has never really had an LCN family. Jimmy "The Weasel" Fratianno operated out of the Bay Area for several years but he was more active in Los Angeles, where at one time he had been acting boss. He was a made soldier of the Chicago mob, never even a capo.

Fresno had some organized crime. Joe Sica ran the San Joaquin Valley from his ranch in the San Fernando Valley, further south. I visited him there on one occasion. He was not very hospitable.

No other area of California had any vestige of real organized crime.

Fragmented as it was, Joe Bonanno must have felt that it was ripe for the picking. That's why he sent his sons there and why, although they lived in San Jose up north, they also spent considerable time in Los Angeles, especially Bill, the capo.

There was another long-time Mafioso in California. James Lanza had spent most of his life in San Francisco without much success, and now he was ailing at the age of seventy-seven. So Bonanno didn't worry much about him.

In 1976 the California Department of Justice had delivered a report to the California Legislature outlining the power struggle which had begun for control of California's organized crime. The report stated that the power struggle was between New York and Chicago. The two factions were headed by two of my targets in 1978. Joe Bonanno and Tony Spilotro.

At the outset of our inquiry, I recalled a conversation that Little Al had given us. The mike had picked up a conversation between Tony Accardo and Sam Giancana in September 1959. Accardo for years had been the Chicago member of The Commission. Now he had been succeeded as boss of the Chicago LCN and, therefore, as a member of The Commission by Giancana, who had just returned from his first Commission meeting. He informed Accardo that Joe Bonanno had "planted a flag" in Arizona and was claiming it as his own. Accardo was furious!

"Arizona has always been an open territory. Anybody can go there. He has no right. He's just trying to open up something for his sons. We've got to nip that in the bud. The next thing you know he'll move on California out there. That's probably just what he wants, California. Move to Tucson, close by, and get set up to move on California. We got to watch that prick, Sam. You keep your eyes on that bastard. He's no fucking good! You watch him. He can't have Arizona. And he sure as hell can't have California!"

Now, twenty years later, it was déjà vu all over again. Bonanno still had his eyes on California. Giancana had been killed in 1975, but Accardo, the tough old Joe Batters, was still around. In fact he had a second home in Palm Springs, California.

Accardo called Tony Spilotro to Palm Springs in 1978. As we learned from an informant who had driven Tony from Las Vegas to Tucson to Palm Springs and back, Joe Batters had some advice for Spilotro. He gave pretty much the same instructions that he had given to Giancana in 1959.

"Watch that fucking Bonanno. He's a no good bastard. He wants what's ours. What's always been ours. California. Now we put you out here, Spilotro, to watch these things for us. You watch that Bonanno!

"Listen, kid, I get some disturbing stories about you. That you're not tending to our business in Vegas. That you've got something going on the side which is personal for you. Not for us. Now listen, Spilotro, we didn't fucking send you out here to do things for yourself. We sent you here to watch the store for us. We got another guy here now, Korshak, who sometimes forgets who he works for, who brought him up. And we've had guys out here before you, in your spot, who sometimes had to be brought up short. One was Roselli. He wound up in a fucking drum at the bottom of the fucking ocean in Florida. You know that. And the other guy before you, Caifano. He went to the joint and when he came out we gave him nothin'! He's in Chicago now, in my old neighborhood, getting any garbage thing he can find. We give him nothing. He's made but he might just as well not be. We tell Lombardo to keep an eye on him, don't let him go broke but don't give him anything much, nothing somebody else could get. You want to be like them guys, Roselli and Caifano? The guys we sent out here before you? If you do, just keep it up. You'll find out."

It was good advice. An excellent indication of the thin ice Tony was treading on.

Serendipitously, we did more to thwart the ambitions of Joe Bonanno than Tony did. We did all but lock-step Joe in Tucson. I was in charge of the on-the-street surveillance. We code-named him The Lone Ranger and we were like his Tonto. Just as close. But he didn't know it until it was too late. Then we pounced.

We found on our wiretaps that he had been coaching witnesses scheduled to testify before a federal grand jury in San Jose against his sons in their attempts to get things going in California. We convicted him of obstruction of justice, and soon Joe was on his way to federal prison in Springfield, Missouri. His ambitions in California were over. Tony Spilotro had us to thank. He stayed out of trouble from Tony Accardo on that occasion, no credit to him.

I don't think Bonanno had much of a chance to take over California. He might have made some inroads, especially in the San Jose area, but not in Los Angeles, San Diego, Fresno or San Francisco. San Jose is a much bigger city than most people are aware, one of the largest in the country really. Bonanno's effort to take over organized crime there would have been worthwhile if successful. But it wasn't. Thanks to our efforts against him. Tony wound up the beneficiary of our success. Not that I relished that.

Today, as I write this, Joe is my neighbor in Tucson. We have even exchanged autographed books. His, entitled *A Man of Honor*, says nothing about his efforts to infiltrate California. In fact it says nothing about his failures. Just his successes in his "tradition," La Cosa Nostra. Joe is almost ninety now but he's still up and about. But not in California.

30 Tony Gets Listed

A funny thing happened to Tony one day while he was on his way up the Strip to the Stardust. He was driving his Chevrolet Monte Carlo, the latest model of course. He got too carried away with his passenger, maybe a little starstruck. He banged into a tour bus full of senior citizens enjoying the sights of Las Vegas, at that moment watching the fountains of Caesars Palace. They all piled out of the bus.

Then Tony's passenger jumped out of Tony's car to look over the damage. He was immediately recognized by just about every citizen on the bus. But when he saw he was recognized, he jumped into Tony's Monte Carlo and they sped away. Moments later, Tony returned—alone.

Now a traffic cop had arrived. He was told that Tony had not been alone when the accident occurred. The cop asked Tony who his passenger had been. He replied that it had been his kid brother, Michael.

The passengers let out a yell. They knew it had not been Michael. They quickly told the cop it had been Robert Conrad, the movie and TV star.

Robert readily admitted it when reached by the press. He

made no bones—then and now—that he was a pal of Tony. "I wasn't aware of Tony's reputation when I first met him," he said. "I met Tony through his brother Michael. I consider Michael one of my dearest friends. I don't shy away from friends. I've read that Tony is allegedly tied to the Stardust Hotel. I don't know what Tony did before I met him. But he's treated me right. I don't know anything kinky about him." Conrad said further that he met Tony "years ago" as a result of his friendship with Michael, who at the time was the manager of Hoagie's Pub on the far west side of Chicago.

Conrad said he originally met Michael through Larry Manetti, his co-star on the TV series "The Duke" and "Baa Baa Black Sheep." Conrad saw to it that Michael got a cameo role in "The Duke," appearing as a stick-up man, appropriately enough.

At the time, we had little investigative interest in Michael—he never seemed to be called Mike by anybody. I knew him to be Tony's youngest brother and that he managed Hoagie's. But none of the top guys in the Outfit hung out there, none of the capos. I knew that Michael had been arrested once for aggravated assault with the brother of Joey Lombardo, Rocco, and with a former Notre Dame football player who knocked around a little, Pete Schivarelli. However, I also knew that the trio had been acquitted. They had pleaded that the guy endangered them and that they had acted in self-defense. Judge Louis Wexler had found them not guilty after a bench trial. Of course, there were the usual suspicions about the wonderful Chicago judges, so many of whom have been convicted of corruption in recent years, but I had no reason to believe that Judge Wexler had improperly used his judicial discretion. After all, it is possible that one guy could attack three guys, one a former ND football player, and put them in fear of their lives.

Sometimes I think we are too hard on people whom we judge and find guilty by association. There is no suspicion whatsoever that Conrad and Manetti have ever been involved in any illegal activity, with or without the Spilotro brothers.

Conrad had the guts to attend funerals in Tony's family—and made no effort to hide his appearances there.

I *do* have problems with attempts made by celebrities to sway public opinion in favor of a racketeer. Witness obvious appearances of such stars as Mickey Rourke and Anthony Quinn at the trial of John Gotti in New York, where they submitted to interviews outside the courtroom alluding to their admiration for Gotti, the most publicized mob boss in New York in years.

There was no such attempt on the part of either Conrad or Manetti for Spilotro. Manetti had the sense to stay out of the public spotlight. He didn't appear publicly with either brother. Conrad attempted to keep the association sub rosa also. And when he was jackpotted in Las Vegas in Tony's Monte Carlo he had the good sense to quickly lam.

Tony got some more notoriety in December 1979 when his name and photo were added to the Black Book, the listing of names of those whose presence in a Nevada casino or hotel may cause that establishment to lose its license. At the time Tony was added there were just nine people listed. Only nine "undesirables" in the whole world.

The "Black book" really is black. It is a loose-leaf folder bound with a black cover and it is disseminated to every hotel-casino in Nevada. It was initiated on June 13, 1960. Alas, by that time there were dozens of mobsters in Nevada. But from that time on any listee found in a casino caused the owners great woe. Witness Frank Sinatra when he allowed Sam Giancana to frequent the Cal-Neva at Lake Tahoe. Even though the GCB was unaware that Giancana was a hidden owner of the Cal-Neva, Sinatra lost his license in Nevada. It wasn't until later, at Caesars Palace, when his buddy, Ronald Reagan, went to bat for him that Sinatra was able to regain his gaming license. Witness Marshall Caifano, Tony's predecessor, who lost a lawsuit over his inclusion in the Black Book.

Tony was incensed about his inclusion in the book. It curtailed, at least to some extent, his activity. He did not work inside a casino but his function included some observance of what his minions were doing inside the casinos the Outfit was skimming. His attorney, the ubiquitous Oscar Goodman, called the Black Book "Un-American." It is unconstitutional, he claimed. He filed suit in the Clark County Court to declare it such and to have Tony's name removed from it. He lost.

Ironically, Tony was listed on the last page of the book. Who do you think was on page one? Caifano. Caifano was then sixty-six, had just spent ten years in federal prison and was living in Wood Dale, a western suburb of Chicago. He hadn't been known to be in Las Vegas since he went to prison. Certainly not since Tony replaced him. Yet, there he was on the first page.

Actually, the book was pretty tame. The only other mobsters in it in 1979 were Nick and Carl Civella, the two bosses of the Kansas City mob (and Nick was in prison in 1979!); Louis Tom Dragna, a small-time Los Angeles LCN member (notorious mainly because his uncle, Jack Dragna, had been the boss in LA years before), who was about to go to prison for his involvement in the murder of Bomp; and Joe Sica, the mobster from the San Fernando Valley. None of the top LCN leaders from around the country were included. No Accardo, Aiuppa, Bruno, Patriarca, Corrallo, Salerno, Castellano or any of the other prime guys. The Black Book was a fine idea, no doubt about it. As far as it went.

It was about the least of Tony's problems. Other more serious ones were about to cascade down on him in the next six years.

I retired from the FBI in February 1980 after almost thirty years in the Bureau. I would still involve myself in organized crime investigations as a Special Consultant on Organized Crime for the Chicago Crime Commission and later for the New Orleans Crime Commission. I would be retained as an investigative attorney for the defense team in some ten libel suits, all involving organized crime figures or associates, including some with Las Vegas involvement. That would bring me back to Las Vegas, Tahoe, Reno and Carson City on some twenty-five occasions. Some of these impacted upon guys like Moe Dalitz, Tony Accardo and Guy Alex. But not on Tony

Spilotro. From 1980, unfortunately, I had no official investigative interest in him. He was now on his own. At least from me.

31 Pendorf

In 1980, I heard about a sensational operation taking place in Chicago.

When I transferred to Tucson in May 1978, I believe I was the last of the original seventy agents from the Kennedy administration's Criminal Intelligence Program to leave. By then it had been renamed The Organized Crime Program and a new generation of fine C-1 agents was taking over its leadership.

Two men, in particular, were most capable of continuing the investigative activity of the scores of us who had preceded and, in a sense, trained them. Pete Wacks and Art Pfizenmayer had both come onto C-1 in about 1970 and had since worked closely with those of us involved in organized crime investigations. It was up to younger agents like them to carry on. And carry on they did. I'll say.

What they did was commence Operation Pendorf. Wacks was the case agent but Pfizenmayer would carry a big burden of the investigation also. Eventually some twenty or thirty other agents would be assigned to assist.

Operation Pendorf stood for "Penetration of Dorfman." We knew Allen Dorfman to be the mob's guy in the Central States Pension Fund of the Teamsters. We knew that his father, Paul "Red" Dorfman, had been the guy who brought Jimmy Hoffa to the attention of such mob figures as Murray "The Camel" Humphreys. Hump at the time was the mob's main guy in labor racketeering although Paul Glimco, the Teamsters' chief of the Taxicab Drivers Union, Local 777, in Chicago, functioned almost full-time in this capacity also. The Chicago mob, on the recommendation of Hump, then boosted the career of Hoffa all the way into the presidency of the union. As a payback, Hoffa gave the son of Paul Dorfman, Allen, the spot where he could influence loans to mob fronts.

The full name of the fund is the Central States, Southeast and Southwest Pension Fund. It was established in 1955 in order to provide the basis for the comfortable retirement of members of the Teamsters, mainly truck drivers, taxicab drivers and warehousemen. All members paid a percentage of their weekly paychecks to build the fund, counting on it for their days in retirement. Trustees, appointed by the president of the International Brotherhood of Teamsters, invested the money. The first loan made to Las Vegas interests was benign enough. It was made to Sunrise Hospital, built by Moe Dalitz. Then came a loan of $45 million to Rancho La Costa, the resort located thirty miles north of San Diego. It was owned by Moe Dalitz and three of his Las Vegas and Hollywood partners in Paradise Development. Then followed a torrent of loans to Nevada casinos, including $2 million to the Riverside in Reno; $30 million to Hyatt; $146 million to Allen Glick's Argent casinos (the Stardust, Hacienda, Fremont and Marina); $50 million committed to Morris Shenker of the Dunes; $26 million to Circus-Circus, Tony Spilotro's landing spot in Vegas; $21.9 million, initially, to the Aladdin, which eventually was the recipient of $34.2 million; and $15.1 million to Caesars.

The original intention of Wacks and Pfizenmayer was to uncover evidence of hidden ownership in the Vegas gaming establishments on the part of Allen Dorfman. They knew that Dorfman was a key figure in the relationship between the mob and the Teamsters pension fund. They had evidence showing that he was actually controlled by the Chicago family of La Cosa Nostra and that he had strong ties to other LCN families in Detroit, New York, New Jersey and especially to the Civella family, the LCN family in Kansas City.

In late 1978, Pete and Art prepared an affidavit showing probable cause for a Title III court-authorized microphone to be placed in Dorfman's office at Amalgamated Insurance. The U.S. District Court of Northern Illinois authorized the installation and, in January 1979, the hidden mikes were put in place by FBI sound men.

It wasn't long before Pete and Art, and the other agents working under them, got something they had not expected. An apparent bribery plot was being carried out. The scheme involved seven acres of land owned by the Teamsters Union near the Las Vegas Hilton Hotel and Casino. The Vegas Hilton, the scene of the infamous Navy Tailhook party years later, is one of the top hotels in Vegas. It is located a short distance from the Las Vegas Convention Center, almost a mile off the strip. Surrounding it are acres of undeveloped land.

A group of investors, including a U.S. Senator from Nevada, Howard Cannon, was trying to purchase this land. A son-in-law of Senator Cannon, Robert Bjornsen, was also involved and was overheard on the hidden mike discussing Dorfman's efforts to get a competing bid withdrawn, thereby allowing Senator Cannon's group to obtain the seven acres of prime land. One of the main reasons the Teamsters preferred to have Senator Cannon's group obtain the land was their interest in a bill then pending before the Senate involving deregulation of the trucking industry. Senator Cannon would have a key vote in the committee reporting the bill to the full Senate. (I should say at the outset that Senator Cannon was never indicted in this scheme and would testify for the government in the ensuing trial.)

For more than two years the Chicago agents monitored the mikes and followed the leads. Pete Wacks was responsible for coordinating the overall investigation, and he reported on its progress to higher-ups in the Bureau and to the Justice Department Strike Force, which would be responsible for prosecuting the case. Art was in charge of the physical monitoring. He rented a location near Dorfman's office and supervised the crew of agents who listened to the conversations, the transcripts of which were given to Wacks.

In May 1981, a federal grand jury in Chicago returned an eleven-count indictment charging five defendants with conspir-

acy to bribe Senator Cannon and to defraud the Central States
Pension Fund of the Teamsters. The defendants were Dorfman;
Joey Lombardo, the mob capo in charge of overseeing Tony
Spilotro and also the pension fund; Roy L. Williams, then the
president of the International Brotherhood of Teamsters; a Chicago trucking company executive who was a trustee of the
pension fund; and a Chicago businessman who was director of
labor relations for the fund.

The charges involved an attempt by the defendants to have
Senator Cannon arrange for his Commerce Committee to handle trucking deregulation legislation. The Teamsters had a
strong desire not to have this legislation passed. Senator Cannon had waged a successful jurisdictional fight against Senator
Ted Kennedy of the Senate Judiciary Committee over which
committee would hear the proponents and opponents of the
bill and, hence, control the legislation. The scheme was that in
return for Cannon's opposition to the bill, including shelving it
in committee, the Teamsters would insure that his group would
get the property near the Hilton in Vegas. The indictment
charged that Williams and his co-defendants attempted to influence the other bidders on the land purchase to withdraw
their bids so that Cannon and his group would have an exclusive to purchase it at a nice price.

Before the trial began I became very interested in just how
the agents in Chicago had been able to penetrate Dorfman,
how they had been successful in putting the bug in his office.
I had been involved for years in installing electronic microphones, and I wanted to be kept up to speed in the event we
needed one in Tucson on Bonanno. What I found out was that
the Special Operations Squad, a squad of FBI sound men, exercised their expertise anywhere in the country where court-
authorized installations were needed. The squad's leading
member in 1980 was Special Agent H. Edward Tickel. He was
building an enormous reputation at that time in the Bureau.

I found out that what Ed Tickel had done was to enter the
building housing Dorfman's Amalgamated Insurance Company
through the building's underground parking garage. Knowing
that the building was well guarded by private security guards,

he could not take the elevator up to the second floor. Instead he walked up a back stairwell. There, on the second floor, Tickel dismantled and then decoded a lock on another office in an effort to evaluate the master key system for the entire building. As a result, Tickel was able to make a master key. He tried it on several floors of the building and found that he could now use the key to get into the second floor stairwell door and into the outer offices of Amalgamated. But now he needed another key to get into Dorfman's private office, always locked during nonworking hours.

I could relate to all of this. It was similar to what I had done at 620 North Michigan on the Magnificent Mile when we penetrated the general headquarters of the Chicago mob in 1959. I had obtained a key to the outside door of the building, now called the Briskin Building, but could not obtain a key to the tailor shop itself, the location on the second floor that housed the private office of the mob. We would have to pick that.

This is just what Tickel did, though he did even more. He hid in the general offices after he had made the key, and then, while cleaning women opened the door to Dorfman's private office, he snuck inside in order to inspect the elaborate and sophisticated alarm system Dorfman had installed according to Joey Lombardo's orders. Tickel made a note of the serial numbers and the model numbers of the alarm system and made an inspection of the "shunt" locks to the security camera and the phone room.

With the master key he had made, Tickel opened the door of the phone room, which was essential to the operation. In order to bring the wires from the hidden mike which he would plant inside Dorfman's private office, he had to get into the mainframe room to make connections with spare pairs in existing telephone cables. He gave all this information to another member of the Special Operations Squad who was more knowledgeable about alarms and they were able to "defeat" Amalgamated's very expensive and very efficient alarm system. After that it was relatively simple for the rest of the squad to make the actual installation.

I knew Tickel to be just the man for this work. He was our

best. He also did the work necessary for Operation BRILAB, the sting operation in New Orleans that netted the boss of the New Orleans mob, Carlos Marcello. He had handled some two hundred other such operations, all in preparation for Pendorf.

Unfortunately, Ed Tickel later ran afoul of Bureau regulations—and even the law. He was fired from the Bureau in 1982 after the first of two indictments. He was acquitted of an attempted larceny charge but convicted of possession of stolen jewelry. It was a real disaster. When doing his job, Ed was the very best in his field. Ethically, legally, under court order. Perhaps it was the strain and the stress. Probably was.

At about the same time Ed Tickel was leaving the Bureau in disgrace after having done such unprecedented good work for his country, a jury trial commenced in Chicago in which much of the evidence was developed from his work. All the defendants were convicted and received long prison terms. Lombardo got fifteen years. He would be paroled in 1992. Roy Williams agreed to step down as Teamster president in order to stay out of jail pending his appeal. When it was denied he went to prison but later redeemed himself by appearing as a government witness in more than one case involving the mobsters who controlled the Teamsters during the years Jimmy Hoffa, Frank Fitzsimmons and he had ruled the union. He would later die of natural causes.

Dorfman would not have it so good.

I had one of my most embarrassing moments in 1980 and it involved Dorfman. After I retired I worked for nine years as an attorney representing news organizations who were being sued for libel for reporting about different organized crime associates. One of the ten I represented in this manner was *Penthouse* magazine which had carried a story by respected journalists Lowell Bergman (now a producer for "60 Minutes") and Jeff Gerth (then and now with the *New York Times*) that La Costa, the resort just north of San Diego, which had been financed by the Central States Pension Fund of the Teamsters Union, was used by mobsters when they wanted to get away from the heat in their cities. La Costa was then owned by Dalitz and his partners in Paradise Development

Company—Allard Roen, Merv Adelson and Irv Molasky. Adelson was later married to Barbara Walters and he and Molasky were the top principals in Lorimar Productions, located on the MGM-United Artists lot in Culver City, California. They produced such hits in those days as "Dallas," "Knots Landing," "The Waltons" and "Falcon Crest," and such movies as *An Officer and A Gentleman*.

Penthouse was sued for $522 million, then the largest libel suit in legal history, by Moe Dalitz and his partners. We were engaged to prove that what the magazine had reported was factual, truth being a perfect defense in any libel action. The case did go to trial, but eventually was settled to the satisfaction of everybody concerned, including Bob Guccioni, *Penthouse*'s publisher.

We decided to subpoena Allen Dorfman, I was to serve the subpoena on Dorfman in his offices at Amalgamated Insurance. Ralph Hill, my former partner on C-1, was working with me. We waited for Dorfman in the underground parking garage. When we observed him arriving, we quickly jumped out of our car, slammed the doors shut (an old Bureau habit) and intercepted him to serve the papers. However, we had locked ourselves out of the rental car. What did we do? We swallowed our pride and went up to Dorfman's offices, then being bugged. We told Dorfman of our problem. He graciously, under the circumstances, ordered his chauffeur to drive us to the rental agency where we obtained extra keys. Wacks and Pfizenmayer got a huge kick out of that! Listening on their bug, they found it very amusing to pick up our conversation.

As I said, Dorfman wouldn't have it so good. The mob no longer trusted him. He was considered soft although he had completed one prison term in New York for fraud just a couple of years before his latest conviction. But he was soon once more under indictment in San Francisco for extortion charges involving a kickback to a Skokie, Illinois property developer. Coupled with his long sentence in the Pendorf case, the mob considered him a likely target of the FBI as an informant.

All signs pointed to Tony Spilotro. Dorfman and his pal, Irwin Weiner, once a co-defendant with Tony in the Deming,

New Mexico case, were walking to lunch in Lincolnwood, a northwestern Chicago suburb. It was January 1983, just weeks after the Pendorf sentences had come down. Weiner probably set him up. Probably for Tony and one other. Once again, the job was accomplished with a .22. The mob would worry no more about Allen Dorfman. Just another day in the life of Tony Spilotro. One more job well handled for the Outfit.

32 Tony is Harassed

Tony's troubles back in Las Vegas would escalate as the Eighties dawned. He didn't have me to be concerned about, but I'm sure he didn't worry about that. I was a thorn in his side in many ways through the years but it had always been somewhat at a distance. Duncan Everette and Mike Simon had "the ticket," the assignment card, on the substantive investigation, and while I had many functions which impacted on him, I never was charged with the direct task of putting him in prison. Now Dunc had been embarrassed and Mike had had his problems in Vegas. New agents in Chicago and Las Vegas, like Charley Parsons and Joe Yablonsky, were assigned to put the cuffs on Tony.

In March 1979, Tony had filed a lawsuit in the U.S. District Court in Las Vegas to enjoin the multitudes of ongoing investigations of him. The last straw for Tony had come when the IRS placed a large lien against his house on Balfour in Las Vegas for evasion of wagering taxes in connection with the arrests made of Tony and his pals in the betting ring. In 1980 the suit was dismissed.

In 1980 the Hole-in-the-Wall Gang was still in full bloom. Tony's pals then were Frank Cullotta, Sal Romano, Joe

Blasko, Thomas Amato, Robert Doldot, Ernie Davino, Leo Guardino and Larry Neumann. Neumann and Cullotta, in particular, were tough guys. They did the "heavy" work for Tony just as he had in his younger days for Philly Alderisio—not that Tony wasn't still quick with the gun in the Eighties himself. The Hole-in-the-Wall Gang continued their jewel, fur and all kinds of home and store burglaries, but Frank Cullotta spent a great deal of his time robbing drug dealers in Las Vegas—and then selling the dope to addicts all over Vegas.

Another associate was Eugene Cimorelli, who had ties to the Kansas City mob and had been a key employee under Allen Glick at Argent when the mob was skimming the slots and tables. Then he was observed playing golf with none less than Tony Accardo in Palm Springs. No punk played golf with the great Joe Batters! His front was the Fred Astaire Dance Studio in Vegas. Later, Frank Sinatra would get some heat when he arranged for a job for Cimorelli at Caesars Palace after Ole Blue Eyes had gotten his license back.

Other pals of Tony's in Vegas in the Eighties included Jaspar Speciale, the leading loan shark in Vegas until Tony arrived, Frank Masterana and Gus Gallo. All would be convicted of various crimes during the Eighties. Another pal was Fred "Sarge" Ferris, another guy with dubious ties. Most of them were associated with the New York, not Chicago, organized crime families.

It was also in 1980 that a meeting of the top leaders of La Cosa Nostra took place in Philadelphia solidifying the Commission pact deeding Las Vegas to Chicago. Two insiders later tipped off the FBI about the meeting and it was the focal point of a conference of FBI agents in Los Angeles where Charley Parsons gave a presentation featuring Tony. The conference in LA was attended by representatives of a dozen or so field offices in the western part of the country and by two of the top agents in the Chicago office, Ray Shryock and Jim York. Ray was one of my closest friends and York took my place as the coordinator of TECIP, the Top Echelon Criminal Informant Program, when I transferred to Tucson. Shryock, Wacks and Pfizenmayer were considered the top agents in Chicago.

The mobsters were informed in Philadelphia that anyone "working" in Nevada would be required to report to Tony Spilotro and that, since he was in charge of Chicago's interests in Nevada, any work out there must be cleared with him.

Information was disseminated by the FBI to the IRS concerning the Philadelphia "sit-down." IRS then included it in the affidavit filed in U.S. District Court in Nevada pertaining to the lien on Tony's house. The affidavit stated, in part: "Spilotro extorts a percentage from profits derived from all major illegal bookmakers and from other organized illegal activity in Las Vegas."

At about the same time, Metro noted that during the past twelve months there had been what they considered to be an influx of Chicago hoods, apparently arriving in Vegas to beef up Spilotro's operation and its increased role in organized crime activities. Metro reported that there were thirty former Chicagoans, answerable to Spilotro, who were living in Las Vegas and involved, either then or in the recent past, with loan-sharking, extortion, illegal bookmaking, labor racketeering, jewel thefts and burglaries. All thirty were seen meeting in recent months with either Spilotro or his top people like Cullotta. Licensing records also indicated that Tony financed the $45,000 purchase of a popular supper club just outside Las Vegas city limits for a former cook at the club. The supper club and its grounds were appraised at $350,000. A nice deal.

Tony wasn't satisfied with his operation in 1980, however. Now he dodged a subpoena calling for his testimony in Santa Fe, New Mexico. It seems that Tony and Jimmy "The Weasel" Fratianno, with others, had hidden interests in the Alfa Chemical Corporation, a New Mexico firm that manufactured detergents and other cleaning products. The firm had supplied its products to Las Vegas casinos, where a word from Tony was all that was needed, as well as to the state government of New Mexico. The grand jury in Santa Fe was attempting to verify allegations that New Mexico officials were involved in offers of bribery to purchase Alfa Chemical products to clean state offices. I got involved in the case when I represented the *Albuquerque Journal* after it was sued for libel by an

Albuquerque attorney who allegedly was a pal of some dubious characters, including Fat Tony Salerno, a New York mobster. Tony Spilotro was involved in that libel case since Alfa Chemicals became a point of contention.

Then came the Frankie Blue incident. One day in 1980 officers assigned to Metro were shadowing Tony. They found him conferring in a Vegas restaurant with a man unknown to them. So when the meeting concluded, a detail of Metro was assigned to tail the man. He entered Sunrise Estates, a high-security private community where he lived. The police busted through the gate and challenged the man. He pulled a .22 and aimed it at them. They shot him dead! It turned out he was Frank Bluestein, an old pal of Tony's from Chicago whom he had placed as the maitre d' at a restaurant in the Hacienda Hotel, one of the Argent hotels.

Frankie Blue was the son of Steve Bluestein, an organizer for the Culinary Workers Union, Local 226, in Las Vegas, a local of the Hotel and Restaurant Employees International Union. I testified before the U.S. Senate Permanent Subcommittee on Investigations in 1983 that Ed Hanley, the president of that union, was first brought into the union by Joey Aiuppa, later the boss of the Chicago mob. The father of Ed Hanley, known as "Stick" Hanley, had come to the attention of Aiuppa when he dealt cards in illegal card games at gambling joints controlled by such Chicago mobsters as Rocco Fischetti, Les Kruse and Ralph Pierce. The younger Hanley had been elevated to the presidency of the union after having started with Local 450 in Cicero, a local which had been chartered by Aiuppa in 1957.

Again, Tony filed a lawsuit through his attorney, Oscar Goodman. He complained he was again being harassed by Metro. He was joined in this suit by Steve Bluestein, Fat Herbie Blitzstein and Art Nasser. The first two were understandable, they were close pals of Tony, and Bluestein was the father of the victim, Frankie Blue. But Nasser was a Chicago lawyer, the former IRS appeals attorney whom I had previously warned about associating with dubious people.

It was about this time I attempted to serve a subpoena on

Tony. Again I was representing a news organization being sued for libel.

On October 27, 1980, I went to Tony's home at 4675 Balfour in Las Vegas with Mike Simon, now also retired. We surveilled the residence most of the morning and afternoon, trying to spot Tony. When we finally gave up, we went to his door. Nancy, Tony's wife, refused to open the door to us but we conversed through it. Nancy advised that she was sick but eventually she agreed to allow her niece to come to another door and accept my card, on which I asked Tony to call me at Caesars Palace, where I was staying. Nancy promised to give Tony my card. Mike also placed his home phone number on the card.

We then proceeded to the Stardust Hotel where we contacted Yale Cohen, a "Mr. Inside," who answered to Tony. We hoped to put some pressure on Tony by letting him know we would meddle in his business in Las Vegas until he accepted our subpoena. On the same theory we then went over to the Riviera where another "Mr. Inside," Charley "Babe" Baron, was the official host. Charley was some piece of work. I would serve a subpoena on him years later in another case when he was lunching with Moe Dalitz at the Las Vegas Country Club. But on this occasion, it was our job just to harass him a little, let him know we'd be around doing such things until Tony took our service, knowing full well that each "Mr. Inside" would get the message to him posthaste.

Baron, who had just been elevated to the position of general in the Illinois National Guard, was a proud guy. He really did consider himself a general—which I guess he was, to some extent. I started talking to him about how ironic it was that he was now at the Riviera. He had been a bookmaker in Chicago's Loop when he shot a competitor there. Then, when Sam Giancana was the Outfit boss, he was sent to the Riviera—in Havana, Cuba. Now he was once again at a Riviera. The proud Baron didn't like to be reminded of the old days. Then I mentioned to him that we had never talked but that I had heard his voice several times before, when he came to mob headquarters in Chicago and Little Al reported how he was there to "rat on Johnny Roselli." Oh my, now he didn't like me at all! He got right up and walked out of his office, saying "This conversation is over!"

Then we went to the residence of another "Mr. Inside," Fred Pandolfo. Freddy was then a shift manager at the Stardust, in on the skimming. We couldn't find him so we went back to the Stardust, where Mike and I made contact with the secretaries of Al Sachs and Herb Tobman, the two "owners" of the Stardust, who fronted directly for the Chicago mob. Now we were right at the top of the pyramid of Mr. Insides. We were informed that Tobman was at the Sundance, downtown, which we found was probably a subterfuge because when we got there we were told that Sachs and Tobman were back at the Stardust. Nonetheless, we were accomplishing our purpose, stirring things up in Las Vegas.

The next day we repeated the process. First at Tony's house on Balfour, then back to Sachs, Tobman, Cohen and Pandolfo. With the same results. So then we decided to bust in at Gold Rush, Ltd. At about five that afternoon we pushed in and found John Spilotro, who ran the jewelry portion of the operation. We informed him of our purpose but, of course, he reported that Tony was not there. Since John seemed fairly cordial I asked him a question.

"John, when I worked for the FBI in Chicago we always called you guys Spil-ott-tro. But then I transferred out to Tucson and found that everybody here pronounces your name Spil-oh-tro. I'm confused. Which is it?"

"Any fucking way you want it. Just call us for dinner." It was an old joke.

"How did Patsy pronounce it?" I asked.

"Patsy? Patsy who?"

"Your father."

"How do you know so much about us?" John asked.

"I spent more than twenty years investigating your brother, John. He knows that. That's why he will know Mike and I aren't about to give up before we put this subpoena on him."

"OK, I get the message," John said.

"Well, John, do all of us—him, you and us—a favor. Let

him know it's Mike and me looking for him. He already knows that but make it clear we're here for the duration. Now how *did* your dad pronounce his name?"

"Spil-oh-tro. But most people say Spil-ott-tro."

"OK, John, thanks," I said. "Now don't forget my message to your brother."

At about eight, I rejoined Mike at the Outfit's flagship casino, the Stardust, to start a round of evening harassment there. He had news. Just before he left he had received a phone call. I was to call my casual friend Art Nasser, in Chicago.

When I called Nasser, he told me to go the next morning to the office of Oscar Goodman, who would have Tony there to accept our subpoena. Then Art said, "For Christ sake, Bill, why stir up all this shit in Las Vegas! Why didn't you come to Oscar or me first off. We would have saved you all that trouble."

"Yeah," I replied, "and miss out on all this fun?"

The next day we accomplished our purpose.

Later, we got wind that Yale Cohen had been particularly upset with our visit to him. When we contacted him at the Stardust we had asked him about his knowledge of what Mike referred to as the "Roselli incident." What it concerned was a dispute between Moe Dalitz and Johnny Roselli over the sale of the Desert Inn to Howard Hughes's Summa Corporation. It seems that Johnny Roselli, the erstwhile Chicago *representato* in Vegas preceding Tony Spilotro, had gotten a $400,000 finder's fee from Dalitz when the sale was completed. Peanuts when you consider the millions of dollars involved. So Roselli thought he had been cheated. He complained to Bomp, their man (and our man) in San Diego, a capo of the Los Angeles "Mickey Mouse Mafia." He asked Bompensiero to accompany him and Yale Cohen when he had it out with Dalitz. At the meeting Dalitz flared up. "Let's all get in my private plane and fly down to Miami and we'll settle this in front of Meyer Lansky!" he shouted. Lanksy, of course was the New York mob boss who had initiated the building of the Desert Inn and who had brought Dalitz from Cleveland to Las Vegas to operate it. Lansky was nobody to screw around with. That threat ended it. Roselli, nobody's fool, acquiesced. He suddenly decided $400,000 was enough. Later he and Bomp would be severely criticized by Tony Accardo for attempting to squeeze Dalitz.

It became a story nobody wanted told. And up to this point it had not surfaced. But now Mike brought it up with Cohen, one of the participants, letting him know we knew a lot of things about matters the mob wanted to keep sub rosa. Shortly before, the dismembered body of Johnny Roselli had been found floating in a drum in Key Biscayne, not far from Meyer Lansky's condo on Collins Avenue in Miami Beach. It had been weighted down but came to the top anyway and was discovered by a curious boater who notified the police. Yale Cohen did not want to be found in Lake Mead!

That same month, October 1980, Tony had some more trouble. He had stopped in the casino at Sam's Town Hotel, one of my favorites, located a long way from the Strip off Boulder Highway on the way to Nellis Air Force Base. It doesn't cater to high-brows, and features local country musicians. As I have reported, Tony is in the Black Book. If he were caught, all kinds of trouble for Tony and for the Boyd family, the owners of Sam's Town, could ensue. Years later the Boyd family would buy the Stardust. I put no sinister connotation on that. They seem to be honest and respectable. In fact, after they operated the Stardust for a few months they were amazed at what a good deal it was. Their gross was far above what it had ever been before. I wasn't surprised. Now it wasn't being skimmed!

Tony almost got out of the Sam's Town jam. When he was spotted by a member of the Intelligence Unit of Metro, the officer radioed for backup. As usual, the call on the police radio was picked up at Gold Rush. Tony was paged at Sam's Town and told to get the hell out of there right away. He did. But Metro filed an affidavit with Clark County Justice of the Peace Joseph Bonaventure and secured a warrant for Tony's arrest. He surrendered on the Monday following the Friday he had been at Sam's Town. Nancy had been with him. She was used to lamming when Tony was rousted. Shades of Monaco! The

Black Book violation by Nevada statute is a "gross misdemeanor" that carries a maximum penalty of a year in jail and a $1,000 fine. However, Tony would never serve the time.

33 Lefty, Geri and Tony

Tony Spilotro and Lefty Rosenthal grew up on the west side of Chicago and had known each other there even though Lefty was ten years Tony's senior. Lefty was already working for Donald "The Wizard of Odds" Angelini's handicapping-bookmaking emporium on Clark Street just north of the old Sherman Hotel—now the site of the State of Illinois Building—when Tony went to work for Mad Sam DeStefano. They had worked together in Miami, and then the Outfit sent them both to Las Vegas, Lefty in 1968 and Tony in 1971. They had to work closely together if they were to produce the skim and make sure it was huge. And to get it back to Chicago.

When Tony was arrested on the Chicago murder warrant on September 1, 1972 and needed a character reference to reduce his bail, it was natural he called on the one guy he knew best then, Lefty. As a result of Lefty's influence in Vegas, the bail was reduced to $10,000, a paltry sum when you consider a bondsman will put it up—just 10% is needed with any kind of collateral. In fact, that favor for Tony was used as evidence four years later at Lefty's license hearing. His obvious relationship with Tony cost him the chance to be licensed.

As soon as Tony arrived in Vegas, it was Lefty and his wife, Geraldine, better known as Geri, who acted as Tony and Nancy's big brother and sister and assisted them in their move—in so many ways.

Geri grew up in the San Fernando Valley, graduated from Van Nuys High School, had a bad love affair and took off for Las Vegas. She became a cocktail waitress and then a show-girl. She met Lefty soon after they both arrived there. Lefty had just been divorced. He sent her a two-carat, heart-shaped diamond ring after their first date. They were married within a year.

As would be expected, the Rosenthals and the Spilotros be-came the best of friends. Nancy and Geri shared all their con-fidences. Geri introduced Nancy to her hairdresser and manicurist. They spent most of their time together while their husbands tended to their nefarious business. In 1974, Nancy was arrested for DUI. It was Geri who came to the police sta-tion to get her and who was listed as the person to be con-tacted, not Tony. When the Spilotros applied for membership in the Las Vegas Country Club it was the Rosenthals who sponsored them. Lefty and Geri lived in a million-dollar house on the fourteenth hole of the exclusive enclave of the Country Club. Lefty drove a yellow Cadillac Eldorado. Geri had a Mercedes. Lefty flew in a tailor from Beverly Hills to fit him for ten to twelve suits at a time. Geri did him one better. She flew off to Rodeo Drive in Beverly Hills and bought her clothes from Giorgio. You can't get out of there—I'm told—for under a couple of thousand a dress.

Tony and Nancy, however, kept their heads down as Tony Accardo had commanded. They bought their clothes off the rack, drove Monte Carlos, joined the PTA, and sent their son Vincent to Bishop Gorman Catholic High School where the rest of the middle-class Catholics sent their kids. When I saw the home of the Spilotros on Balfour I was surprised at how middle class it was. Mine was almost as nice.

Lefty and Geri had two kids, both of whom have grown up to be Olympic-class swimmers. They trained in the Olympic-size swimming pool at the Country Club where they had the best swimming instructors. Lefty devoted a great deal of time to the kids, whom he loves. Still does. First in Vegas, then in Orange County, California, and now in Florida. He even be-came the swimming tournament announcer and timer.

But trouble loomed. Geri got a drinking habit. While Lefty trained the kids in the pool water Geri trained at the posh watering holes. Lefty would turn off the pool lights at ten and put the kids to bed. Geri wouldn't have gotten home by ten—sometimes not until ten in the morning. Now all of a sudden she started wearing new furs, not her old ones.

Now she came up with a "sponsor." In Las Vegas parlance that meant a protector, somebody who would share her goodies and take good care of her. The fact that she had Lefty, in a great position to take care of her, seemed to matter little.

She made no bones about it. Her sponsor was Tony!

Wow! When Mike Simon heard that he thought about what Ralph Hill had done years before, in 1958, when Sam Giancana had sponsored Marshall Caifano's wife, Darlene. Only we didn't call it that in Chicago. Not in my circles.

Now Geri was just one of Tony's playthings. Power is the ultimate aphrodisiac. He could command the favors of many a showgirl in Vegas—some much prettier and sexier than Geri. But now he had a chance to screw his pal!

Not only did Tony take Geri, he flaunted it. He made no pretence of it. Mike Simon offered to show Lefty pictures of his wife with Tony at the local nightspots. Not at the casinos, Tony couldn't be seen there, but in places like Alpine Valley Inn or the Golden Steer, the fine free-standing Las Vegas restaurants.

It had to happen. It did. On the morning of September 8, 1980, the neighbors were aroused when yells and shouts engulfed the neighborhood at the Las Vegas Country Club. It was one of the nights Geri hadn't come home and now the sun had been up for hours. Lefty had finally had enough. He had locked Geri out! She went nuts! Rosenthal would later charge that she was high on drugs and alcohol. A security guard at the Country Club, hearing the ruckus, called the police. Just as they arrived, so did Nancy Spilotro. Geri was ramming Lefty's Caddy with her Mercedes! Lefty charged from the house, enraged at the damage to his beautiful car. Geri pulled a gun! A snub-nosed, silver, pearl-handled .38—engraved with her name on the handle. A gift from Tony.

Geri shouted obscenities at Lefty. "I'm going to the FBI. I'm going to tell everything," she screamed.

Lefty shouted right back. "Go right ahead, you fink!"

When the Metro police arrived, the first thing they saw was the gun. And an out-of-control woman brandishing it like it was a water pistol. They jumped out of their cars and took cover behind them. According to the police report, it was two-bit-sized Nancy, five inches shorter even than The Ant, still dressed in her pajamas, who made the collar. She jumped on Geri and, according to the police report, "grabbed her around the arms, wrestling her to the ground at which time [the officers] closed in and assisted Nancy Spilotro in taking the weapon from Mrs. Frank Rosenthal."

The day had just started, however. Now Geri did the unthinkable! She announced that she needed police protection. She was going to the bank. Metro escorted her—with three squad cars of police yet—to the Valley National Bank where Lefty kept his safety-deposit boxes. In Geri's name! Lefty brought up the rear in his banged-up Cadillac.

He protested. Like hell he protested! But the police hemmed him in, kept him from interfering with Geri's mission. They watched, as did the enraged Rosenthal, as she quickly scooped up $200,000 in cash and an estimated $1 million in rubies, sapphires and diamonds. Oh, did Lefty scream and holler. What a show! The bank employees and customers watched in awe!

Then, while Metro kept Lefty back, Geri charged off, got into her Mercedes and left. Leaving Lefty in a fit of rage!

Geri hightailed it to Van Nuys. Almost before she arrived her father, almost eighty, got a phone call. Not from Lefty. From Tony. The words were not those of endearment. Tony's words made a deep impression. "She don't know nothin', you understand! You know what I mean!" Geri's father got the idea. So did Geri.

Mike knew a good PCI when he heard of one. He had the Los Angeles office hurry out to the San Fernando Valley, to Van Nuys. But Tony had gotten the word there first. Geri was scared. Now that she had come down off her high she realized what she had done. Mike Simon never knew how or when, but Lefty got the cash and jewels back.

Now Lefty, still enraged, flew back to his roots. Chicago. He had made an appointment with Joey Aiuppa and Jackie Cerone, the mob bosses there. He put the problem in their hands. Calmly and without rage. Tony had violated the oath of *omerta*. Joey and Jackie had to make a hell of a decision. In 1980 Tony was doing his job. Things weren't going too badly. The skim was getting back to Chicago in heavy quantity. Could they afford to jeopardize that over some pussy-whipped rep they had out there? When the guy who was cuckolded was not made, was a Jew. As another Jew, Joe Yablonsky, would say about the matter: "When push comes to shove, if it's an Italian against a Jew in the LCN, you know who's going to win *that* battle."

Lefty would soon thereafter file for divorce. He also filed a million-dollar lawsuit against Metro, which he blamed for his loss at the Valley National Bank. That suit never got anywhere. In January 1981 he reached a settlement with Geri. Lefty got what he really wanted—the kids. He agreed to give Geri $5,000 a month alimony.

For the next two years, Geri frequented the Sunset Strip night spots. At first she frequented the nice spots. Then some of the more seedy ones. Finally, on November 6, 1982 she fell onto the floor of a rundown motel. She was taken by ambulance to Cedars-Sinai Medical Center, one of the country's best. They could do nothing for her.

She had bruises all over from being beaten by a no-class boyfriend. The Los Angeles County Coroner found that death was accidental. There were large traces of cocaine, Valium and tranquilizers in her system. She was forty-six. Lefty and the two kids were notable by their absence at the funeral and the burial at Mount Sinai Memorial Park.

Lefty remained in Las Vegas. He and Tony were under the gun to work in close harmony for the interests of their bosses in Chicago. The mob had decreed that a little thing like this would not spoil the close working relationship of their two top guys in Vegas.

34 Tony's Pal Comes Over

As 1980 turned into 1981, Tony's problems continued to pile up. However, it wasn't until the Fourth of July that they hit the fan. The FBI under Joe Yablonsky in Vegas, and Metro under Commander Kent Clifford, put a surveillance on six of Tony's stalwarts in the Hole-in-the-Wall Gang. They tailed them, in four cars, to a well-known home furnishings and antique dealer. The cops waited until the six were well into the process of cutting through the vault. Then they pounced.

Frank Cullotta, Tony's boyhood chum who had been with him from his youth in Chicago, was one of those arrested, as were Wayne Matecki, a well-known Chicago burglar who Tony had brought to Vegas; the volatile Larry Neumann, yet another former Chicagoan; Leo Gardeno and Ernest Devino, veteran Hole-in-the-Wall Gang members; and Joe Blasko, the former Metro detective. What a shame!

Blasko hadn't actually been in the store. He was outside, listening to police radio broadcasts, keeping his pals inside alert by walkie-talkie. However, the FBI agents and Metro officers were alert for this ploy and made no broadcasts that would alert Blasko.

The vault was found to contain about $1 million in jewelry, antiques and cash. It would have been one hell of an Independence Day celebration for the gang! One of their biggest heists yet.

Cullotta was getting a lot of publicity now. His mug shot was featured in the Las Vegas and Chicago papers, since anything that happened to Spilotro and his crew was big news in

Chicago. For instance, Ron Kozial, the *Chicago Tribune*'s reporter in their west coast bureau, spent many days in Las Vegas tracking Spilotro, Rosenthal, Cullotta, Sachs, Bluestein and Blitzstein.

Neumann was a late arrival in Las Vegas. He had been convicted of murdering three people in a Chicago tavern and had been sentenced at age twenty-nine to three concurrent terms of 125 years each after he pleaded guilty. He went to the Illinois State Penitentiary in Joliet, but he was out in twelve years! Justice! Now he was back to his old tricks.

Then, two weeks later, worse news for Tony. Once again he was indicted and arrested. He was charged with racketeering, conspiracy to deal in stolen property and possession and concealment of stolen property. Also arrested with him were Blasko, now retired from Metro; Blitzstein; and brother John. U.S. District Court Judge Harry Claiborne, who would later be convicted himself, appointed two appraisers who were to accompany FBI agents to make a detailed inventory of all items at Gold Rush Ltd., including the jewelry, most of it stolen from all over the country. Included in the indictment was the charge that the four men conducted an illegal bookmaking establishment out of the store. This raid was in coordination with the FBI's Gold Rush raid made three years earlier. Maybe now they might put it out of business.

Part of the evidence was garnered by the undercover role of FBI agent Rick Baken. Much of the $100,000 worth of jewelry given to him by Tony Spilotro to sell on commission had been traced to jewel thefts in the Chicago and Kansas City areas. That jewelry was part of the evidence against Tony as were the reams of tapes from the bug the FBI had placed inside Gold Rush.

Back home in Chicago, the press likened Joe Blasko to Dick Cain. Both had been cops in high places who, the press believed, had sold out to the mob. I cringed when I read those stories. Cain had been a made guy who had infiltrated the Chicago Police Office and then the Cook County Sheriff's Department where he became Chief Investigator. However, Cain had redeemed himself, unknown to any but a few of us in the FBI.

He had become a double agent for me inside the mob after he had been convicted and fired by the sheriff. He had then become the closest confidant and aide to Sam Giancana, as well as a top gambling operator. So in 1981, when I read the many comparisons of Cain to Blasko, I was saddened.

Actually, lack of oversight by his Chicago bosses was one of the reasons Tony was able to get away with the crimes he was now committing in Las Vegas. Joey Lombardo was now in prison following his conviction in the Pendorf case. No one else in Chicago seemed to have the background to comprehend what Tony was now doing in Las Vegas. This void left Tony free to go his own way out in Vegas.

As long as Tony Accardo was alive no Chicago mobster was allowed to deal in dope. One did. Chris Cardi. The mob found out when he was arrested. They let him go to prison and serve out his full sentence. Three weeks after he was released they killed him. Slashed his throat. Trunk music. Now, however, the FBI began to get rumblings that Tony was selling narcotics also. What wouldn't this guy do?

Then, in May 1982, came the bombshell. Frank Cullotta had been indicted in the antique and jewelry store robbery. He had a similar conviction in Chicago years before Tony had brought him to Vegas. Cullotta had been held in the Clark County Jail since his Vegas arrest. The first indication came when his attorney, John Momot, withdrew from the case saying that there had been a breach of trust and confidence in his client. This is normal. Criminal attorneys, "members of the defense bar" as they term themselves, do not allow themselves to represent mobsters who are about to flip, go over to our side and become government witnesses. If they do, they will not get many more clients who are mobsters—the Outfit will not let them. They become renegades to the defense bar if they allow their clients to turn.

I'm dealing with such a case as I write this. A mobster has contacted me to take him to the FBI in Chicago to cooperate with them. I've had two other such cases in the past. Mobsters from my days in Chicago or those who have read my books feel I am a stand-up guy who can be trusted to take them to the FBI in Chicago where they can discuss cooperation. I always tell them they don't need me to do that, but in some cases they are willing to pay my fee and expenses to get the deal accomplished. In the current case, the mobster wants to make sure his attorney does not know. He does not trust him. He feels that the mob would immediately be alerted if his attorney should suspect his intentions—in order that the attorney can "keep himself clean" with the mob and thereby expect additional mob clients in the future.

The next indication came when Elaine and Frank Cullotta's young son was taken from their home in protective custody. When Tony found out about that the same night, the lights were burning in Tony's house on Balfour long into the night.

Then Joe Yablonsky made the announcement. "Frank Cullotta has been undergoing debriefing by agents of our office of the FBI and by Las Vegas police for the last two weeks." Wow! It was true. Frank Cullotta, who knew more about Tony Spilotro than anyone else in the world, was being debriefed (one of my favorite words, FBI jargon for vetting everything an informant knows). Oh, how I always loved to debrief! Now, I wished I could have been in on it. There was nobody I'd rather debrief. Frank Cullotta could be a gold mine about the Gold Rush Ltd. and everything else Tony Spilotro had done since he reached puberty! If he could be influenced to tell it all. That was still unclear. Like almost any prospective informant, Cullotta would want to be very clear about just what was in it for him. That's just natural. He would want leniency or even immunity, and life in the witness protection program for his wife, child and himself. Can you blame him? Without guys like him, law enforcement would lose many of the cases against the worst offenders.

Then, in 1982, came something which had become close to my heart. At the time I was working on the *Penthouse* magazine libel case, and Jack Barron, the former supervisor of the OC squad in Los Angeles, and Ralph Hill, my old partner on the C-1 squad in Chicago, were working for *Penthouse* as well. The Los Angeles FBI office had developed an informant,

Gene Conrad, who was very close to California mob figures, such as they were. He testified in the trial in Compton, California, that in the early Seventies he observed Tony Spilotro conferring at La Costa with Marshall Caifano and Lou Rosanova.

Marshall, as we know, was Tony's immediate predecessor in the west. Lou Rosanova was a unique character. I had interviewed him once in Chicago when his brother, a Notre Dame graduate and a friend of mine, asked me to "sit down" with Lou and persuade him to "straighten himself out." We had a pleasant conversation, but I don't know that he straightened himself out. Lou was very close to many Chicago mobsters—especially Jackie Cerone, who was to boss the Chicago mob on two separate occasions—but also to a whole bunch of others. Lou was a scratch golfer and owned a country club down south, in Savannah as I recall, where Cerone, also a fine golfer, traveled regularly.

Conrad also testified that he saw Moe Dalitz conferring with Rosanova and Caifano at La Costa in 1973. He described Dalitz as "a senior mentor among the criminal aristocracy." That's one way to put it.

Then it was learned that the Chicago Outfit, at the urging of Tony, had set aside $200,000 to locate and kill Cullotta. I felt a bit slighted at this piece of news. In the Sixties, Sam Giancana had set aside just $100,000 to set me up for a hit. I felt better when I decided that inflation would have escalated the fund in twenty years.

One of the big items on Cullotta's plate was the old M & M Murders, the murders of McCarthy and Miraglia some twenty years before. You'll recall that Tony had tortured one of them by putting his head in a vise and popping his eye out to force him to give up the whereabouts of his partner. Cullotta had the details of that hit.

Cullotta also talked at length about the killings of the burglars who invaded the home of Tony Accardo in 1978 and who were all later found as trunk music with their throats slashed from ear to ear. Cullotta told the FBI that that is when he decided to take Tony up on his long-standing offer to come to Las Vegas and work there for him. He felt things had gotten too dangerous for burglars in Chicago at the time. Not because of law enforcement so much but because of the mob.

Joe Yablonsky was quoted in the papers as saying that "Cullotta is even better and has more information than we first believed."

Cullotta then furnished information about the gangland hit of four businessmen in Park Ridge, at one time the biggest hit since the St. Valentine's Day Massacre.

Cullotta would later say that he decided to turn on Spilotro and the mob when he was turned down for membership in the Outfit. He decided when he was not made that he was in danger and then decided to flip. He had come to Chicago to meet with Jackie Cerone, a meeting he set up through Dominic "Large" Cortina. Cortina was one of those convicted by the testimony of Lou Bombacino. One day, Cullotta said, he was at a mob gathering when he approached Spilotro. Tony yelled at him "Get away from me." It was then he decided things had gotten too much out of hand and that his salvation would be with the FBI and Metro. First, however, he asked Tony to post the $30,000 bond he needed on the Gold Rush case. Tony refused. Cullotta spent five months in jail awaiting trial and during that time the mob never helped him or his family. Had he been made they would have been obligated to do so under the rules of La Cosa Nostra.

Shortly after Cullotta turned he was debriefed by Ray Shryock, a former C-1 squad member and later my supervisor for a short time. He had become the head of the OC squad of the Cook County State's Attorney's Office, Richard M. Daley being the State's Attorney at the time. Ray was dispatched to Las Vegas to learn all he could about the involvement of Tony in the M & M Murders. He got an earful. He would later return to Vegas to bring Tony back to Chicago in handcuffs.

35 Brothers

Before Tony would get into more troubles, Pat would. Pasquale, the older brother of Tony, had been a respected oral surgeon and dentist in Des Plaines, a northwestern suburb of Chicago, for some years. Then he had applied to the Chicago Mercantile Exchange for a seat. His application was denied.

In March 1982, Pat sued the Exchange. He claimed that he was unjustly denied a seat solely because of the notoriety of his brother, Tony. Pat claimed that he was allowed to purchase a seat on the International Monetary Market division of the Exchange in the summer of 1981 for $165,000. However, in the fall of 1981 the Board of Governors of the Exchange reexamined the situation and rejected Pat.

Pat did one thing right. He hired a fine, very respected attorney, Tony Valukas. Tony had been an Assistant U.S. Attorney, where he had served with considerable distinction during my days in Chicago, and he would return in years to come to be *the* U.S. Attorney.

Actually, the reasons for the rejection of Pat's application not only included his brother's notorious reputation "as the head of the Chicago crime syndicate's alleged activities in Las Vegas," as the rejection letter read, but because "Dr. Spilotro is a close associate of other individuals who allegedly have been the subject of grand jury investigations." Valukas pointed out that Pat's son, Mark, had been a well-regarded runner at the Exchange who was now pursuing a business major in college. Pat would eventually succeed in gaining his seat at the "Merc."

Apparently following Pat's example, his brother John became involved in what looked to be a legitimate business. He opened the Food Factory, a hot dog, hamburger and taco dining room located a block off the Strip. John's wife, Arlene, and Tony's wife, Nancy, were listed on the incorporation papers as vice president and secretary-treasurer, respectively. They were never seen in the place flipping hamburgers, however. The speculation was that John wanted to set something up for his family's future in case he went away. None of us could argue with that.

In July 1982, Frank Cullotta was sentenced in the Clark County District Court of Las Vegas to eight years in prison. However, under the terms of his plea bargain, Judge Paul Goldman suspended eighteen months of the sentence. He would be eligible for parole in twenty-six months.

At the sentencing Cullotta was guarded by thirty Metro detectives and federal marshalls. At the time he was granted immunity for any other crimes he may have committed in Nevada in return for his continued complete cooperation with local and federal authorities and his truthful testimony in trials of his former confederates.

One of the matters Cullotta was being debriefed on in 1982 was his band of hotel room burglars. He advised that he and his pals looked for patrons of the casinos who flashed big bills and women wearing expensive jewelry. They would put those people under surveillance and follow them to their rooms in the hotels. Then when they were again spotted in the casino the burglars would pick the locks of their hotel rooms and make off with whatever they could find.

This modus operandi reminded me of the scheme Gerry Denono tipped me off to when I conducted my investigation of the theft at the luxury resort, the Camelback Inn in Scottsdale. Gerry pointed out that the Camelback has balconies which can easily be seen from the parking lot. Gerry and his crew would register and then make a duplicate of the key to their room. They would then come back the next evening and observe the room they had rented from inside their car in the parking lot. When the guests departed for dinner or dancing they would enter the room to burglarize it. Then they would take the jewels and furs they had stolen to the Gold Rush Ltd. and fence them. That was all well and good in the Sixties and Seventies. Now, however, the Camelback Inn, like most good hotels, uses digital key-cards which they discard and change for the next guest. This was done as soon as I informed my client, Fireman's Fund Insurance, of the method of operation of the thieves.

Another item Cullotta was dropping on his debriefers was that Tony was allowing his crew to deal dope. As I have mentioned before, that was in direct contradiction to the policy of the Chicago Outfit under Tony Accardo. Cullotta confirmed that. He advised that Tony's action was carried on without the knowledge or approval of Joey Lombardo or any other of the top people in Chicago. Out of sight, out of mind. None of the big people in Chicago suspected Tony of doing this because it was unthinkable. You could get killed for that, as Chris Cardi did.

Cullotta also advised that as soon as Tony brought him to Las Vegas he was put in charge of the Hole-in-the-Wall Gang, always subject to the orders of Tony. Cullotta had knowledge of 150 burglaries, robberies and jewel heists and provided indirect information on about 300 more. He estimated that burglaries and robberies in Las Vegas in just three previous years netted over $4 million in cash and valuables.

Cullotta advised that his crew had also preyed on casino dealers and stickmen as well as cocktail waitresses in the casinos. They were likely victims because when they left work they were carrying hundreds of dollars in cash from the generous tips they received from the players.

When Ray Shryock of the Cook County State's Attorney's Office arrived in Vegas he brought with him a list of 128 gangland-style murders in Chicago—all unsolved and all believed to be a result of Outfit action. Ray would tell me that although I had developed better informants with information about the Chicago mob itself, "this guy knows more about the kind of stuff Tony Spilotro and his crew are involved in than any informant we could ever dream of in our wildest fantasies." Ray also told me that during his debriefing of Cullotta he obtained "good information on eighteen of the murders in Chicago. And he's given the Las Vegas people solid information on a dozen or so more out there."

Perhaps one of Frank Cullotta's most interesting stories, according to Ray, was of how he and other members of the Pancsko gang held up a Brink's truck for more than $200,000 in 1964. What was interesting to me was the identity of his fellow burglars. Here is what they did, a classic example of just what made these guys tick. First, they forced their way, wearing ski masks, into the rectory of Divine Savior Catholic Church in Norridge, a northwest suburb of Chicago. Almost every one of the robbers had been raised in the Roman Catholic religion. God save them! They tied up the two parish priests they found in the rectory and then sat back to await the Brink's truck. But just for fun they discovered the church's Christmas collection, which was the reason the Brink's truck would be arriving, to take it safely to the bank. The bunch had determined that the church would be the forty-seventh and last stop on the truck's route that day.

When the truck arrived, it was evening, dark. The truck was manned by two men, a driver and the guard. The guard left the truck and entered the rectory. The driver stayed inside the locked truck, guarding the cache of money already collected.

Immediately upon stepping inside the rectory where he could not be seen by the driver, the guard was clubbed on the head. His uniform was stripped from him. One of the robbers quickly donned it. He then went outside, knocked on the truck door. The driver, not really alert after his tiring day, opened the door. He was immediately slugged and subdued.

The robbers, all six of them, then drove the truck into Westlawn Cemetery where they had stashed a "work car." They unloaded the money, taking only big bills, and sped away. The case would never be solved until Cullotta talked. By then the statute of limitations on robberies had long run out. The haul totaled $285,000. Cullotta would tell Ray that it took the bandits some eight to nine hours to count it.

Not all profit, however. Don't forget the street tax! The Outfit cut in for its percentage. They had nothing to do with the heist but they got a piece of the action. Nice work if you can get it! And the Outfit could.

As I say, when Ray told me of what Cullotta had informed him, I was especially interested in Cullotta's partners in crime. It was now almost twenty years later and I had a good handle on the career paths, so to speak, of the gang. Peanuts Pancsko was busted so many times, mostly with his brothers, Pops and Butch, that you can't count his arrests. They were all the subject of a great book by my friends John O'Brien and Ed Baumann in 1993, *The Polish Robbin' Hoods*.

Frank DeLegge was found as trunk music with his throat slashed in 1978 after he had attempted to retrieve his stolen loot from the home of Tony Accardo.

Mike LaJoy and Joe D'Argento both preceded Cullotta into the witness protection program, having provided considerable information to authorities.

Gerry Tomaszek was the remaining member of the gang. He went on to become one of the most prominent Top Jewel Thieves in Chicago, a special target of the FBI C-2 squad. I understand he is living quietly in Chicago today, too old for that kind of stuff now.

I often wonder whether any of the nominal Catholics ever reconciled with the Divine Savior.

I would also wonder whether Frank Cullotta would "stand up" as a witness against his old cronies or whether he would do a Harold Lurie and collapse, more or less, when he had to face the steely eyes of the defendants. As it would turn out, Cullotta would face Michael Spilotro, Tony's kid brother and now more and more his sidekick. Michael would be seen in attendance at just about every trial at which Cullotta would testify. Shades of *Godfather II* when the brother of a mob witness was brought from Italy to sit in the audience while his brother was scheduled to testify against his mob boss. It worked in the movies. Maybe Michael thought it would work in real life. After all, Cullotta had been just like a brother to Tony for all those years.

36 Moe Dalitz

I first met Moe Dalitz in 1982. No book on the mob in Las Vegas would be complete without a chapter discussing him.

Morris Barney Dalitz, who would become known as the "godfather of Las Vegas," got his start in Detroit during prohibition. There he was known as the "admiral" of "the Little Jewish Navy." This title referred to his role in rum-running, bringing booze from Canada across the Detroit River into the city. But those were the days of the Purple Gang in Detroit, and although popular fiction states that Dalitz was a member of the gang that ruled Detroit during prohibition, he was not.

Dalitz soon discovered that his bread was not buttered in Detroit but in another city, one on the other side of Lake Erie. He moved to Cleveland. There he established the Mayfield Road Gang, headquartering it in the Hollenden Hotel. He got involved in all forms of gambling and even expanded to northern Kentucky where he had the Beverly Hills Club and The Lookout House, two luxurious nightclubs with large casinos for illegal gambling. He catered primarily to the citizens of Cincinnati who poured over the Ohio River to try their luck. He also built a dog track in southern Ohio. Many were the public officials who were corrupted in Ohio and Kentucky by Dalitz and his Mayfield Road Gang.

During his days in Cleveland, Dalitz became very close to many of the mobsters around the country. These included Frank Costello, Longy Zwillman, Meyer Lansky, Bugsy Siegel, Lucky Luciano, Boo Hoff, Angelo Bruno, Joe Bonanno, Carlo Gambino, Albert Anastasia and many others from the east. He also got close to Frank Nitti, Jake Guzik, Murray Humphreys, Paul Ricca and Tony Accardo in Chicago. All recognized a keen intellect in Dalitz.

At some of the famous mob sit-downs prior to Apalachin, Dalitz was present with the top leaders of La Cosa Nostra from around the country. One he even set up in Cleveland.

Then Bugsy Siegel developed the Flamingo, the first plush casino on the Strip in 1946, but then got in trouble with his own people. The New York mob now needed somebody who was clean, one with a background without arrests, one who could be a good front. They thought of Moe Dalitz. They sent him out to Las Vegas to do a feasibility study—to "look the place over and see what you think," as they described it. Moe went out and came back. Great potential, he reported. Would he front for the New York mob? He would.

So it was that he built the Desert Inn, one of the nicest hotels then and still one of the nicest today.

Then the Chicago mob asked him to operate their place, the Stardust. It was a nice combination, the Stardust for the "low rollers," the Desert Inn for "high rollers."

Then, in January 1961, Little Al told us about complicated machinations involving Hump, Gussie Alex and Les Kruse of Chicago and Moe Dalitz and Morris Kleinman of Las Vegas. These machinations culminated in a meeting at a hotel in Chicago attended by Sam Giancana at which the Chicago Outfit gained additional leverage in Las Vegas. They would then have interests in the Stardust, the Hacienda, the Desert Inn, the Riviera and the Fremont and later the Tropicana. All very plush hotel-casinos.

Moe became a big man in Vegas. Not only inside the casinos but as a man-about-town. The former governor of Nevada and U.S. Senator, Paul Laxalt, would say of Dalitz: "My general opinion of him, as a citizen of Nevada, is favorable. He's been a good citizen." Of course, like so many other politicians in Nevada, Laxalt never had problems taking major contributions from "the godfather of Las Vegas." That does seem to tend to help mold opinion.

Soon Moe Dalitz and his associates would help build some

of the major developments in Vegas, the Sunrise Hospital, the Valley Bank Plaza, the Las Vegas Convention Center, the Las Vegas Country Club and several University of Nevada–Las Vegas buildings. It is not difficult, therefore, to understand why Dalitz was highly regarded in Las Vegas. He fronted for the mob but he helped build Las Vegas—and not just on the Strip. Not just with casinos, not only in the gaming industry.

In 1982 Dalitz would be listed by Forbes Magazine as one of the richest people in the United States. They estimated his worth at $110 million.

That was the year I first met Dalitz. At the time I was in the midst of investigating the *Penthouse* libel case. We were deposing all of La Costa's owners. I found Dalitz to be an engaging and personable guy. Just what I had been led to believe by Mike Simon and his cohorts in the Las Vegas FBI. Just what he had to be to front for the people he was representing—the New York and Chicago mobs.

I sat down with Dalitz again around 1986 when I was working on a different libel action. This time the target was the *Sacramento Bee*, which had disclosed that Paul Laxalt, after he left the governorship of Nevada and before he became a U.S. Senator, had run into financial problems while he owned the Ormsby House Hotel and Casino in Carson City. He had run out of collateral and now needed a new loan. He got it from Chicago's largest bank. All well and good, but it appeared that the Teamsters had put a corresponding deposit in the bank, thereby guaranteeing the loan to Laxalt, so to speak. In return, the *Bee* alleged, an executive of the Riviera in Las Vegas who was fronting for the Outfit, Bernie Nemerov, was transferred to the Ormsby House to oversee skim there which would be couriered to the Chicago mob. None of this was ever proved and the case was settled just days before it was to go to trial, to the satisfaction of both sides.

In any event, we also obtained a subpoena for Moe Dalitz to be deposed in that case. Leo Stevens, a former FBI agent, and I served it while Dalitz was lunching at the Las Vegas Country Club. We had a cordial talk. He told me then that he was dying from kidney failure and was on dialysis every other day. Shortly thereafter he died.

Some people say Moe Dalitz built Las Vegas. He certainly became one of the town's leading citizens. I can understand the reverence with which some there hold him. If you understand how he got there, why he got there, and who he represented when he got there you might put a different spin on the story.

37 Lucky Lefty!

Lefty Rosenthal's life was not exactly in a shambles, thanks to his deep devotion to his two children, but things had not gone well for him in the last year or so. He had now been banished as the boss of the Argent operation controlling the Stardust, Hacienda, Fremont and Marina hotels, and had lost his wife.

By that time, Lefty was getting careless. Every mobster—even every FBI agent—is taught to vary his habits. When leaving his house, for instance, he should not take the same route every day to his destination. But now Lefty was following the same routine every evening. He would leave his house after overseeing the swimming lessons of his kids, drive to Tony Roma's restaurant in Las Vegas, park his car in the same spot, dine at the same table with the same pals and almost like clockwork leave the restaurant at eight-thirty to drive the same route home to get his kids ready for bed.

It was now eight-thirty on the evening of October 4, 1982. Lefty left his pals at Tony Roma's, walked to the parking slot where he had left his 1981 yellow Cadillac a few hours before, slid behind the wheel and turned on the ignition, leaving the driver's side door open. That he had been trained to do in Chicago. It's a favorite precaution among Outfit members. It probably saved his life. That and the fact that Cadillacs have a steel floor plate under the front seat.

A charge of C-4 explosive had been fastened under the trunk, close to the gas tank. It was wired to the ignition and it detonated when Lefty turned the ignition key!

The roof was blasted sixty feet away. Lefty was still inside. The gas tank would explode within seconds!

Instinctively he jumped from the car. Two seconds later the gas tank exploded and the car went up in flames.

Lefty was severely wounded. Many ribs were broken. Metal car parts were embedded in his body. He collapsed, just feet from the fireball, badly burned. The ambulance arrived but it looked bad.

When he awoke in the hospital emergency room, he could see a circle of people peering down at him. One was Charley Parsons, the FBI agent who had replaced Mike Simon as the case agent on Tony and Lefty when Mike Simon retired. Charley, who at this writing is the SAC of the Los Angeles FBI office, wanted Lefty to know that if he wanted to talk—about anything—he was anxious to listen.

When Lefty was discharged and brought home, one of his first visitors was Commander Kent Clifford of Metro. Commander Clifford put it bluntly—very bluntly. "Lefty, you're a walking dead man. But we won't protect you unless you become an informant!" Wow, that was blunt! Sheriff John McCarthy, Commander Clifford's superior in Metro, had to apologize. "Of course we protect all citizens of Las Vegas, even those like Lefty Rosenthal."

Charley Parsons expressed the opinion, privately, that it had been Tony Spilotro's work. Tony had obviously gotten the sanction of the Outfit back in Chicago, through his capo, Joey Lombardo. He had failed by a hair. The fact that Spilotro and Rosenthal had gotten sidewise because of Tony's sponsorship of Geri probably added some fuel to the flame, but the prime reason was Chicago's paranoia. They are always on the lookout for one of their own who might become one of our own.

Loose cannons And if there was ever a loose cannon, it was Lefty. We have seen how the Outfit felt about Allen Dorfman. They would take him out in January, just a few months after Lefty's close call. Charley Parsons let Lefty know that he was in serious trouble. That was no news to anybody, certainly not Lefty. Charley made the offer we make to all people in Rosenthal's circumstances. "Come on over, join us, and we'll take good care of you—and your kids. The witness protection program might not be the greatest way to spend the rest of your life but take a hard look at the alternative. Look what a slim chance you have staying on the street. Come with us, we'll put our arms around you, put you in a faraway town, make sure you get what you need and that your kids are well taken care of. You'll be comfortable the rest of your life." Hundreds have taken the FBI up on this kind of offer: a life. Thanks to the fine U.S. Marshall's Service, like the FBI a part of the Justice Department. It's not luxurious but it is livable. And that's the idea.

Rosenthal made sure his people in Chicago knew his answer to Charley's offer. He announced it in his usual style. Lefty was back in form. He called a press conference, of all things. His message to the Outfit and to the world was simple. Thanks but no thanks. That wasn't his style.

Charley Parsons and another outstanding FBI agent, Al Zimmerman, continued to pressure Lefty to turn. He never did. He stayed in Las Vegas for a while, then moved near Anaheim in Orange County, California, and then moved back to the scene of his former escapades, Florida. Lefty never flipped, but I have always regarded his devotion to his grown kids with admiration. God bless him!

PART THREE

1983 to 1986
THE FALL

38 Tony's Tough 1983

In January 1983, Meyer Lansky died at the age of eighty. The old fox succumbed to cancer. At the funeral held in Beth Jacob Synagogue in Miami, he was praised as a devoted husband of Thelma (Teddy) and friend of Israel by Rabbi Shmaryajhu T. Swirsky. Lansky, the former Prime Minister of Organized Crime and member of Murder Incorporated, had left behind a deep legacy. Now the media speculated on his successor.

It was theorized that the Chicago mob would make deeper inroads into the open territory of Miami. First it was speculated that Joey Lombardo would be the man sent to Miami to ramrod the Outfit's ambitions there. Then it was realized that Lombardo was about to go away on the Pendorf conviction.

The next guy down the line was Tony Spilotro. The press recalled how he had worked in Miami with Lefty Rosenthal and was well-acquainted with the landscape down there. One article concluded that "Spilotro apparently favors the move" since he desired to avoid the continued spotlight of investigation in Las Vegas. "In Miami, he will use his organizational talents to gain control of the Miami operation with the help of some of his former close associates from Chicago."

I did not place any stock in these speculations. I knew that Tony was in deep trouble and that his stature in the Outfit was not such that he would now be considered for the invasion of Florida, should there be one, by Chicago.

Sure enough, the same month, the indictment came down. Tony was indicted in Chicago for the M & M Murders! Frank Cullotta had gone before the grand jury after his debriefing by

Ray Shryock and told the story of how Tony had bragged to him about killing McCarthy and Miraglia. The murders had established Tony's reputation in Chicago. How Tony had squeezed McCarthy's head in a vise until his eye popped out.

The statute of limitations runs out after several years on most crimes but never on murder. The torture-murders of McCarthy and Miraglia had happened almost twenty-one years before. Now finally they might be solved.

At the same time, documents filed in connection with Tony's arraignment in Las Vegas reflected that immediately upon the execution of Allen Dorfman in Chicago, just days earlier that month, Tony had been sought for questioning about it. They wanted to know if he was in Chicago, as they could not find him in Las Vegas. He continued to be a prime suspect in any heavy work of the Chicago Outfit. And the Dorfman killing was very heavy.

Ray Shryock then hustled out to Vegas once more. Not only had Tony been indicted for the murders by Cook County, in Chicago, but he had also been indicted by the federal government for unlawful flight to avoid prosecution. On January 27, 1983, U.S. Magistrate Phillip Pro, in Las Vegas, set bond for Tony at $2 million. Later, after the FBI took Tony into custody on the federal charge, it was dismissed and Tony was turned over to Shryock and his people to take back in handcuffs and leg irons to Chicago. Tony would not be exactly returning to his home town in style.

Tony would be the only defendant in the M & M Murders case. The other two participants, Milwaukee Phil Alderisio and Chuckie Nicoletti, had long gone on to be judged by a higher authority.

In September 1983, Tony was indicted once more! This time for involvement in the killing of Sherwin Lisner (the DEA and Metro informant who was murdered) and for Tony's command of the Hole-in-the-Wall Gang. The indictments were the result of the work of the FBI under Joe Yablonsky, the SAC in Las Vegas, and Cullotta was on our side now. He had taken the offer Lefty Rosenthal had turned down.

Of considerable interest to me at the time was the identity

of one of the defendants in the Hole-in-the-Wall Gang indictment. He was Michael, Tony's kid brother. During my days in the FBI looking at Tony, I had not found Michael to be involved in his brother's activities. I had considered Michael to be under the influence of Pat. I knew John and Victor, other brothers, were with Tony. And I knew Michael had been arrested for beating a man in a barroom fight, but that had not involved organized crime. In 1983, the agents assigned to Tony had reason to believe, to know, that Michael was deeply involved in his brother's work.

Also indicted in the second part of the indictment were Fat Herbie Blitzstein, Peter Basile of Wilmette, Carl Urbanotti of Chicago, Ernest Lehnigg of Addison, Illinois, and Wayne Matecki, a former Top Jewel Thief in Chicago who had been brought out to Vegas by Tony to take a major part in the gang.

These were hot times in Chicago. Ken Eto, a mob gambling boss, was shot three times in the head from the back seat of the car he was driving. He would survive to later testify about the Outfit. And 1983 was the year that Allen Dorfman was killed. It was also the year that Gerald Shallow, the former partner of my pal Dick Cain in the Chicago Police Department, filed a $250,000 lawsuit for back pay as a detective even though he was now confined in federal prison for Interstate Transportation of Stolen Motor Vehicles! These were curious times in Chicago.

I remember that year well. I was retained to come back to Chicago in January, just after Dorfman was hit and just before the Eto shooting, to represent the Chicago Crime Commission in hearings scheduled for March by the U.S. Senate Permanent Subcommittee on Investigations. The CCC is the fine private organization, funded by charitable donations from concerned private citizens in Chicago, that looks into corruption, organized crime and the efficiency of the courts in Chicago. It has been in existence since 1919 and has been headed by such legendary crime fighters as Virgil Peterson, Pat Healy, John Jemilo and now by Bob Fuesel, Jerry Gladden and Jeannette Callaway. I was retained then, and still am, as a Special Consultant on Organized Crime. My function in 1983 was to prepare and present to the U.S. Senate a complete picture of the history of organized crime in Chicago, going back even before Al Capone to the present, to tell the story of the structure of the Outfit and to let the public know of the history of public corruption on the part of politicians, cops, judges and labor leaders up to the then-current reign of Mayor Jane Byrne. I garnished my testimony with the story of how the Outfit, through the efforts of their man in the First Ward, John D'Arco, had influenced Jane Byrne to "dump Duffy," demote the foremost expert on organized crime in the Chicago Police Department, Deputy Superintendent William J. Duffy, as the mob desired.

And now the Chicago press speculated not so much on whether Tony Spilotro would succeed Meyer Lansky in Florida but on who would succeed him in Las Vegas. They hit on Joey Cusamano after conferring with Commander Preston Hubbs of Metro. Hubbs reported that Cusamano, who was spending much of his time at the Sahara where Paul Lowden was, and still is, the owner, had recently become a close associate of Spilotro. With all of Spilotro's other close associates being indicted with him, Cusamano was the logical choice. Cusamano had been noticed with Tony when Frankie Blue had been rushed to the hospital after being shot by Metro officers. Cusamano, Tony and Fat Herbie Blitzstein had come together to check the situation at the hospital. This speculation was not well-founded. Although Cusamano remains a figure of some stature in Las Vegas today, it would not be him who succeeded Tony as Chicago's man in Las Vegas.

Tony was not the only person in Las Vegas with problems that year. Even my pal Joe Yablonsky had some trouble. As I mentioned, Joe and Nevada Attorney General Brian McKay were not exactly compatible. In fact, when McKay ran for re-election in 1983, Joe is alleged to have provided some information, not altogether complimentary, from the Air Force personnel files of McKay, a former Air Force officer. When McKay publicly complained, Joe denied he had done this. But the Air Force made public some information indicating Joe might have used his FBI office to dig up information that was not part of any official FBI investigation. As a result, the wonderful Las Vegas *Sun* put a lot of pressure on William Webster, the FBI director, to replace Joe. However, Webster recognized that Joe was the right man for the job, so he kept Joe in place until he reached the mandatory retirement age of 55.

Joe's departure from his position as boss of the FBI in Las Vegas enabled Tony Spilotro to have a little breathing room. Not that Joe's successor let up on organized crime investigations and not that there weren't many capable and dedicated agents working in the Las Vegas field division. But Joe was sui generis, one of a kind. He made no attempt while in Vegas to pacify the gaming establishment. He knew that many of the casino people had been fronts for the mob and he saw no reason not to let the public know how he felt—at all times. That loud voice of a strong man continually stirring up the pot would be missed. As a result, some of the pressure on Tony Spilotro would be eased.

Then in September 1983, the U.S. Senate Subcommittee on Investigations, headed by Senator William Roth of Delaware with Cass Weiland as the general counsel, took up hearings concerning the Hotel and Restaurant Employees Union. Weiland had questioned me before the Subcommittee about the union and I found him to be a most capable guy. Not only that, he could beat me in one-on-one basketball. He is now practicing law in Texas and we joined briefly in 1993 when G. Robert Blakey, the Notre Dame Law School professor, filed a RICO suit against the union in Las Vegas and retained us to serve as co-counsel. Blakey is the former Justice Department attorney who drafted the RICO Act.

An investigator for the Subcommittee, Barbara Cart, testified in Washington that Tony Spilotro "established virtual control of Local 226," the Vegas branch of the union and the largest of its locals, with 26,000 members, most of them employees in the hotels and casinos. Testimony was taken that mobsters had gained control of the administration of dental plans, which are contracted out, and then charged the union trust fund for administration services that were either not provided or greatly exaggerated in cost.

At the same hearing, Senator Roth announced that the panel was continuing its investigation of organized crime in Chicago and that a subpoena for Tony Accardo had been issued. At the hearing I not only stressed the role of Tony Spilotro in Las Vegas but the lengthy role of Accardo from his days as the bodyguard to his position as *consiglieri*. The Subcommittee thereafter hauled Accardo before it in Washington and questioned him about my allegations against him. It made good copy but not much else. On the other hand, I am all for such hearings. It puts the kleig lights on organized crime. They operate best sub rosa. When the public becomes aware of their notorious activities it arouses public officials to do something about them.

As 1983 went on, Tony spent most of it in the Cook County Jail. He won a court order allowing him to confer with one of his underlings, Larry Neumann, whom Frank Cullotta would testify against in a murder trial stemming from the 1979 killing of another Chicago Top Jewel Thief, Robert Brown. Eventually a jury would vote unanimously to convict Neumann on Cullotta's testimony, but the very next day one juror would recant his vote and throw the case into a deadlock, causing a mistrial.

As Spilotro's trial in the M & M Murders case neared, he hired two attorneys. One was old reliable Oscar Goodman from Las Vegas and the other was the only attorney in the law firm of Bieber and Brodkin whom I respected, Herb Barsy. George Bieber and Mike Brodkin were the mob's mouthpieces in Chicago. George was close to most of the burglars and thieves although his office was a regular meeting place for Philly Alderisio. Brodkin, the other of the B and B boys, was close to most of the upper echelon of the Outfit. He was a frequent visitor to Little Al, the mike in the mob's headquarters on the Magnificent Mile, one of just two or three non-made guys who knew the location of the headquarters and its importance. Both Bieber and Brodkin had a large handle on the corruption of judges which the "connection guys" accomplished and were, in my estimation, nothing but extensions of the

Outfit—more important in the affairs of organized crime in Chicago than probably 250 of the 300 made guys.

We learned from Little Al that Bieber and Brodkin were not at all well versed in the law. In fact, Murray Humphreys would often tell them to "run this by Barsy" or "check this out with Barsy." We all knew that Herb was the brain of the B and B Boys. Now Tony reached out for him. I could understand why. I never made an informant out of Barsy, but I could talk to him. More importantly, he talked to me—not in ways to compromise his clients, but let's just say I was never thrown out of his office. There are good defense attorneys in Chicago like Pat Tuite and then there are sleazy ones. Barsy was with Bieber and Brodkin but he was a huge cut above them in character.

In September 1983, as I have previously stated, Tony was indicted in Las Vegas on the Sherwin Lisner murder and, with seventeen others, on the Hole-in-the-Wall Gang racketeering charge. He pleaded not guilty on October 3.

In late October he went on trial in Chicago on the M & M Murders case.

It was a weak case in that it was based on a twenty-one-year-old murder. The only evidence of any substance was the testimony of Frank Cullotta. I was given to understand that many of the top prosecutors in the State's Attorney's Office of Richard M. Daley, including Daley himself, did not want to handle the trial work. It all hinged on Cullotta. On direct examination, Cullotta detailed his almost lifelong association with Tony. He testified that "Tony was telling me he was present" when McCarthy's head was put in the vise. He further testified that Spilotro told him he took Billy to the murder site, grabbed him by the neck, pulled him into a car and took McCarthy's gun while at least one other man beat McCarthy. He then told the jury that before Miraglia was strangled he told Spilotro, Alderisio and Nicoletti, "I know you guys are gonna kill me so do it. Then my wife can collect the insurance. Strangle me because she can't collect any other way." Cullotta testified that "they strangled him and dumped him in the same car as McCarthy." Cullotta charged that Vincent "The Saint" Inserro was among the killers. Vince Inserro is not to be confused with

Vince Inser*r*a, the former supervisor of the C-1 squad. Inser*r*o, a made guy, was very bad, a real killer.

The case was heard as a bench trial before Judge Thomas J. Maloney. I'll not say more about Judge Maloney except to note that he was convicted in 1993 of accepting bribes to acquit defendants in his court. The decision in the M & M Murders case would be all his. No jury.

The next day Cullotta would return to the stand to continue his testimony about the killings. It was then he testified that McCarthy's head was "put in a vise. His eye was popped out of his head." He testified that he himself had been involved in the murder when he made a telephone call "to set up" his friend, McCarthy, for the meeting with Spilotro in Melrose Park, a close-in western suburb. He told how James Miraglia had been lured to a tavern and locked in the liquor room where he "got himself drunk out of his mind with the liquor." Then Spilotro and Inserro took Miraglia out and threw him into a car. "He was screaming. He was punched in the throat and started gurgling. He couldn't talk. They threw him in the trunk of one of the work cars." Cullotta had earlier explained that a "work car" was a car not easily traced and which was used for "work," for committing crimes.

Cullotta also testified that the reason he had become a government witness was that the FBI in Las Vegas told him a very believable story which he put credence in. That Spilotro had put out a contract on him—he was to be killed. After palling around with Spilotro since the age of thirteen he took the FBI's information seriously. And put himself in their hands. He agreed to testify truthfully against Tony and others of his pals in return for protection in the witness protection program.

Again, kid brother Michael, although he himself was now under indictment in another case, attended every day of the trial, sitting in the second row, keeping his eyes on Cullotta. It was obvious that Cullotta was keenly aware of his presence, of the fact that Michael, a member of the Spilotro "family" in more ways than one, was free to come and go. The attempt at intimidation wasn't even subtle.

Then Judge Tom Maloney took the case under advisement.

I guess if we had the benefit of knowing what charges would be provided against the integrity of Judge Maloney some ten years later—when he had become one of the top judges in Chicago—we wouldn't have been surprised.

Maloney acquitted Tony Spilotro of all charges. He decided that he could not "accept as proof beyond a reasonable doubt" the testimony of Frank Cullotta.

Barsy and Goodman were ecstatic. Tony was stoic. He may have known all along that Judge Maloney was not going to convict him. I don't know. Maybe Judge Maloney was honest in this case though not in others. Maybe.

Barsy waxed eloquent. Talking about Frank Cullotta, he said: "That man admitted to almost every conceivable crime a person could commit. Jesse James, John Dillinger are the worst criminals in history. But there has never been a person who admitted to almost every crime in the criminal code like he did. And seemed to be so proud of them."

Metro was still looking into the bombing of Lefty Rosenthal's car. They discovered that one guy who had the expertise to do it had been in Las Vegas at the time And that guy had already been indicted with Tony Spilotro in another matter. He was Ron DeAngelis, the electronics expert of the Outfit, the guy who had been indicted with Tony in the Deming, New Mexico scam on the Teamsters pension fund. Who, with Tony and Dorfman and Irv Weiner, had skated after the prime witness against them, Danny Seifert, had been murdered. DeAngelis was now living in Houston and his presence in Vegas at the time of the bombing cast a long shadow of suspicion on him—and on his boss, Tony Spilotro.

1983 was also a bad year for yet another Spilotro brother. Victor was convicted in Chicago of gambling and tax fraud charges in connection with a messenger-betting operation. Off-track messenger betting was a big thing in Chicago for several years in the late Seventies and early Eighties. In those years, a bettor could go to an off-track betting shop and place a bet on a horse race at any of the Chicago tracks. A messenger would then take the bet to the track where the bet would be placed legally. The only problem with this was that the off-track betting parlors were either operated by fronts for mob bosses like Joe Ferriola, then rising to become the top boss in Chicago, or were "50-50," subject to the street tax. Unlike Tony, Victor went to prison.

Now the "good" brother would come under scrutiny. The IRS opened an investigation of Pat. Documents filed in the U.S. District Court of Northern Illinois disclosed that Dr. Spilotro was under investigation by both the criminal and civil divisions of the IRS, although the inquiry was specifically aimed at determining whether Pat had "violated any of the criminal provisions of the Internal Revenue Code." One of the finest IRS agents of all time, Roy Suzuki, was deeply involved in almost every IRS investigation of any substance at this time. Along with Bob Fuesel of the Intelligence Unit of IRS, I'm sure they had a huge hand in any investigation of a Spilotro. At this time the Chicago Mercantile Exchange reconsidered their previous decision not to allow Pat a seat on the Merc. He was now allowed to join.

I never learned whether Pat was indicted. As far as I know, Dr. Pat remains the good Spilotro, sui generis, one of a kind. It would appear that the only smear to splash off on him and stick was the fact that he was his brother's kin.

In December 1983, just to complete an awful year for Tony, another blow came. On December 5, the Nevada Gaming Control Board, working with undercover FBI agents, seized control of the casino at the Stardust. The Stardust yet! The source of the largest amount of skim being siphoned off and moved to the Chicago mob! GCB charged that the skim had amounted to $1.5 million in 1982. That's just what could be shown. I believe that was just a portion of the skim in 1982, the height of the Chicago mob's operation there. Strict GCB control of the casino at the Stardust would obviously put a tremendous crimp in the income flowing from Las Vegas to Chicago's mobsters. They did control other major casinos at the time like the Fremont, a big moneymaker for them, a well-kept secret in Las Vegas since it is located on Fremont Street downtown, not on the Strip where most of the tourists go. Chicago also had control of the Sundance at the time, another large casino downtown, built on land owned by Moe Dalitz. Dalitz had applied for a license to operate the Sundance but by the early Eighties his organized crime connections were well known in Las Vegas and he withdrew his application before it could be acted upon when he felt he had no chance to be approved. The Outfit also controlled the Hacienda, another moneymaker, and the Marina, not much then although it had a nice location on the Strip, between the Aladdin and the Tropicana. It has since been torn down to make way for the MGM Grand, the magnificent hotel-casino-entertainment entity which opened in December 1993.

I guess 1983 was something like 1957 in the annals of law enforcement, or at least I think Tony Spilotro would agree. It was in 1957 that J. Edgar Hoover finally brought the FBI into the fight against organized crime, after which nothing would ever be the same for the crime syndicates. Looking back, 1983 seemed to be the year when the guns aimed at Tony Spilotro finally hit their target. Not all, but some did. And the biggest gun had fired in October.

39 Strawman

Unknown to Tony, what would become his biggest problem yet got started in May 1978.

Two of the finest FBI agents ever, Bill Ouseley and Lee Flosi, happened to be assigned to the Kansas City field office of the Bureau. I was aware of the good work they were doing in KC but at the time had not met them. Now they are good friends.

Bill's father and mother met in Italy and married there. She is Italian and Bill learned the Italian language from her. That

ability, and his heritage, would stand him in good stead when
he reached out to those mobsters in KC who had the potential
to become his sources and informants. Bill is now the security
representative of the National Football League in KC and lec-
tures all over the country. Lee grew up on the west side of
Chicago, just like Tony Spilotro, and went to law school with
Jackie Cerone, Jr., the son of Jackie Cerone, the two-time boss
of the Chicago mob. Jackie Sr., like Donald Angelini and John
Spilotro, was responsible enough to keep his son out of the
"family business" and guide him into the right side of the law.
Lee is now supervisor of the organized crime squad in
Chicago—the old C-1 squad, although that is not what it is
called today—battling the mob in his old neighborhoods.

In May 1978, the same month that I was transferring from
Chicago, Ouseley and Flosi began an investigation in Kansas
City that would rank right up there as perhaps the biggest case
against the mob any time, any place, though it was not begun
with any grandiose objective. It started out as an average case.

Actually, there came to be two cases and they acquired the
code-names Strawman I and Strawman II.

I have discussed the Strawman cases in great detail with
both Ouseley and Flosi. Bill Ouseley was retained by me in a
major libel suit after we both retired and we spent a great deal
of time working together in Los Angeles and Kansas City. Lee
Flosi is a frequent conferee since I am a consultant for the
Chicago Crime Commission these days.

By 1978 Ouseley was a senior member of the Kansas City
FBI organized crime squad and considered an expert in the
field, having been assigned to organized crime work in Kansas
City since 1964. Gary W. Hart was supervising the organized
crime squad in Kansas City then. He had come to KC the year
before from his position as a supervisor at FBIHQ in Washington. In Hart's mind, there was nothing the FBI could not
accomplish and the word "impossible" was not in his vocab-
ulary. We were also blessed with an extremely competent and
aggressive Justice Department Strike Force attorney in Kansas
City, David B.B. Helfrey.

In April 1978, Ouseley and Flosi received information that

the "family" had marked someone for murder and was actively stalking their prey. Unfortunately, their source did not identify the intended victim. A decision was made by Hart and his agents to prepare an affidavit to support an application for a Title III, a court-authorized electronic surveillance. With information the agents had already developed about prior slayings, they strongly felt there was probable cause to support the installation of bugs in certain cars being used by different LCN members in Kansas City known to be capable of murder.

In May 1978, the U.S. District Court in Kansas City authorized such electronic surveillance. However, due to technical difficulties there was a delay at that time in getting the plan operational. The delay was literally fatal. In mid-May, three or four mob hit men entered a local tavern and killed one and wounded two of the intended victim's brothers, leaving one paralyzed.

Having information that more killings were in the works, Ouseley and Flosi continued their investigation and developed enough information to support another request for a Title III. This time they were successful in planting a microphone in a local restaurant where key mob figures were known to hang out and talk "shop."

They hit pay dirt. But not about the murders being investigated. Rather, they intercepted a conversation between the acting LCN boss of Kansas City, Carl "Cork" Civella, and the underboss of the mob in KC, Carl "Tuffy" DeLuna. At this time, Carl Civella's brother, Nick, was the boss of the KC LCN but he was in federal prison and Cork was acting in his place. The conversation between Cork Civella and Tuffy DeLuna concerned the Kansas City mob's interests in Las Vegas!

Fortunately, the agents' expertise, not only about the affairs of the mob in Kansas City but of OC activity in other cities, such as Las Vegas, allowed them to grasp the full implication of the conversation.

Since the conversation had occurred during a phone call placed from the outside by DeLuna to Corky Civella at the restaurant, the problem now was to locate the phones used by DeLuna so that the Bureau could initiate a Title III on them as well. Continuous surveillance was set up on DeLuna. It paid off. He was discovered using pay telephones at a hotel located in the eastern industrial section of the city to receive incoming calls from a *representato* of the Kansas City family of La Cosa Nostra in Las Vegas. Their man in Las Vegas was Joseph Vincent Agosto. Joe Agosto had the official title of Entertainment Director of the Tropicana Hotel, but in fact he was calling the shots at the Trop, taking his directions from DeLuna!

The results of the Title III on the pay phones utilized by DeLuna were extraordinary! Agosto provided a blow-by-blow account of moves being made by other mobs that were attempting to buy controlling interests in the Argent Corporation. These calls also revealed the influence of the Kansas City family of the LCN in the Tropicana, including skimming of gambling proceeds from the casino.

As the investigation expanded, authority to electronically surveil other locations was obtained from the court. Telephone taps were placed on DeLuna's home phone and a law firm Nick Civella was using (he had by then been paroled due to poor health). The agents tapped the telephones of LCN member Pete Tamburello, Nick Civella's driver, and of LCN member Charles Moretina, a known enforcer and middleman in the receipt of the skim coming in from the Tropicana.

By November 1978, the Bureau had coverage of a six-hour meeting held in the residence of a Civella relative. The meeting was attended by Nick Civella, Carl DeLuna and, from Las Vegas, Joe Agosto and Carl Thomas. The main topic of discussion was the methods being used by Agosto and Carl Thomas to skim the Tropicana casino. However, Carl Civella arrived before discussion of the main topic got under way—he did not stay for the main meeting—to talk with Nick, his brother, about the need to murder a mob rival who was causing problems. They also discussed the methods they would use to kill this rival.

The first phase of the Bureau's investigation culminated on St. Valentine's Day in 1979. On that day, selected because intercepts indicated that $80,000 in skim from the Tropicana was being delivered to Kansas City by a mob courier, numerous search warrants were executed in Kansas City and Las Vegas. Ouseley chose to execute the warrant for the skim and, along with several other FBI agents and Kansas City Police Department officers, dashed to the airport to meet the plane. It almost didn't happen. Weather conditions were so bad that for a while it appeared that the flight from Las Vegas would be diverted to another city. There were tense moments but all ended well. The agents were there in time to execute the warrants and relieve the courier of the $80,000 in skim. It was the first such seizure, although skimming had been going on forever.

The other highlight of the day was the search of Carl DeLuna's home. As it turned out, he kept a meticulous record of everything he did! These notes were the best example yet of what might be called the "books" of a mob operation. They turned out to be devastating evidence, implicating mobsters in several cities, connecting them to the skim. Their seizure played a key role in the two major trials that would result from this investigation.

The next major step was to utilize the wealth of information that had been developed to seek revocation of Nick Civella's parole. Eventually, the agents were successful in this endeavor. As the investigation continued, evidence was developed that Civella, once he was reincarcerated, continued to call the shots for the KC LCN from Leavenworth Penitentiary.

So Ouseley set out to develop sufficient probable cause to put a Title III at the visiting room of Leavenworth prison where Nick transmitted his orders. He did. This coverage extended into 1980 and yielded more valuable evidence.

The next task for the agents was to put everything together, to prepare a summary of the evidence they had developed and give it to Dave Helfrey of the Strike Force. That was no easy task in view of the mass of information compiled by then.

In November 1981, Carl DeLuna, Nick Civella, Carl Civella, Charles Moretina, Peter Tamburello, Carl Caruso, Anthony Chiavola, Carl Thomas, Joe Agosto, Donald Shepard and Billy Caldwell were indicted in Kansas City for maintaining a hidden interest in and skimming from the Tropicana.

The first big break came when Joe Agosto agreed to cooperate and testify. He was a super witness and provided invaluable information that opened other avenues of investigation about other LCN families.

Before the case could go to trial, Nick Civella, who had been the LCN boss in KC for some thirty years, died.

After a nine-month trial all the remaining defendants except Tamburello were convicted. All the principal Kansas City LCN leaders were sentenced to lengthy prison terms, a crippling blow to the Chicago family. For instance, Carl Civella and Carl DeLuna each received thirty-year sentences.

Let me tell you, Bill Ouseley, Lee Flosi, Gary Hart, Dave Halfrey and the rest of the agents and attorneys in Kansas City had done one hell of a job! If you disputed that this was the most successful case in our history of investigation of La Cosa Nostra, then you would get one big argument from those guys. And I would understand why.

But it was not over yet. Flosi transferred to Rome, Italy, but Ouseley was about to commence Strawman II—where Tony Spilotro would become directly involved. Of course, Tony had been involved indirectly in Strawman I because, as boss of the entire situation in Las Vegas, any crimp put in the flow of skim from Las Vegas directly affected his operation. And Chicago was directly affected by Strawman I. The Trop had gone down. The Kansas City family of La Cosa Nostra, like all others west of the Mississippi, was under the domination of the Chicago family. The Civellas couldn't even go to a Commission meeting. They were represented there by Chicago. And, more to the point, Kansas City shared its cut of the skim with their mother family. Anything, therefore, that affected Kansas City affected Chicago. And anything that affected Chicago's interest in Las Vegas affected Tony Spilotro.

Of course, Tony could not be censured by his bosses in Chicago for the fact that FBI agents Ouseley and Flosi had done such a good job in Kansas City. Tony was not responsible for allowing them to penetrate the Kansas City family But he was held responsible for one major item in the Strawman I case. The defection of a guy who was supposed to be under his control out there in Las Vegas. A guy who played a major role in the skim from the Tropicana. That man, as I have stated previously, was Joseph Vincent Agosto.

40 Joe Agosto

Joe Agosto was not even his real name.

Vincenzo Pianetti was born in Italy in 1927. The real Joe Agosto was born in Cleveland in 1921 and died in Italy in 1951. Within a matter of months after the death of the real Joe Agosto, Vincenzo Pianetti appeared in Canada and then came into the United States using the identity of the deceased Joe Agosto. The father of the real Joe Agosto had been killed in gangland style in Cleveland on June 11, 1929. Since the son died in Italy in 1951 just before Vincenzo Pianetti assumed his identity, there is some speculation that Pianetti may have played a part in his death.

In any event, the new Joe Agosto arrived in Seattle in 1971. In view of his background, the Seattle field office of the FBI began to take a good look at the guy. They talked to Interpol, which found that in 1967 he seemed to have been involved in organized crime activities in Italy. INS reported that he had established some roots in Kansas City and that he was involved with such mobsters there as the Evola brothers and a man named Porrello. Then it was established that Pianetti was a nephew of Sadie Porrello whose son, Joe, was a small-time hood in Kansas City who had been killed in what appeared to be a typical gangland slaying. And that the real name of the father of the true Joe Agosto was Salvatore Todaro. Still more mystifying, it was then learned that the new Joe Agosto was the subject of an attempted hit in Anchorage, Alaska, by the

Evola brothers of Kansas City, but that Agosto was saved through the intervention of his aunt, Sadie Porrello.

A pal of Pianetti from Italy was apprehended by the INS in New York City, arriving there after engaging in Mafia activity in Italy. He was using the name Frank Agosto although his true name was Santo Librici.

After being baffled by all this, the Seattle FBI office pulled Joe Agosto in for questioning. He claimed that he was born Joseph Vincent Agosto on August 20, 1921 in Cleveland, Ohio, where he attended elementary school. After his father's death, his mother took him to Sicily in 1932. He claimed to have attended the University of Palermo where he received a law degree. He said he then practiced law in Northern Italy and came back to the United States in 1947, first going back to Cleveland and then to Kansas City, where he settled in with his nearest relative, Sadie Porrello, and her two sons, Angelo and Joseph. (Both were known to the Kansas City FBI as members of the Civella Crime Family.)

Agosto then claimed to have gone to Alaska to work for the U.S. Army in 1949 and remained there until 1954. The FBI's Identification Record for Joseph Vincent Agosto shows that an arrest of this man was made by the Kansas City Police Department for "investigation, larceny" on August 13, 1954.

Agosto then claimed he returned to Alaska, working for the military in Fairbanks and in Anchorage, and that he attended an Army school to learn contracting, construction, catering and food purchasing, which, if true, would hold him in good stead for future endeavors in Las Vegas.

In 1964, after a brief time in Tacoma, Washington, Agosto was involved in constructing a shopping center in Las Vegas as the president of a company called Golden West Enterprises. Later a fire destroyed the shopping center. Arson was suspected, but the insurance company made good on its policy.

Then Agosto went to San Diego, where he opened a nightclub, The Stars of Seven Nations. The San Diego Office of the FBI looked into it and found it had been financed by the Chicago and Kansas City families of the LCN.

Agosto would be arrested for "exhibit of a deadly weapon

with threat." When Agosto was interviewed by the FBI in San Diego he advised that his partner in the nightclub, David Verdusco, got drunk one night and argued with Agosto. Agosto had a kitchen knife in his hand and Verdusco called the police, charging Agosto with assault. "That was all there was to it." Verdusco was influenced to withdraw his complaint against Agosto and when he did the charges were withdrawn. In 1966, The Stars of Seven Nations went bankrupt.

Agosto then returned to Anchorage. There on June 15, 1966 he was indicted by a federal grand jury for furnishing false statements to the Federal Housing Authority. He was convicted but only fined and put on probation.

He then abandoned Alaska for Portland, Oregon, where he was again arrested, this time in a fraudulent check scheme using the name Enzo Joe DiPaola. On this occasion he was not so lucky. He was sent to the McNeil Island Federal Penitentiary on January 24, 1967 to begin serving a one-year sentence. He was released from McNeil Island on October 6, 1967.

Then he moved to Yelm, Washington, where he formed Agosto Building and Development Company, Olympic Bail Bonding and Olympic Building Corp. With a $1 million investment on his part, he began to build a motel and a restaurant. The Seattle office of the FBI suspected this money came from an organized crime family but were never able to substantiate that. Agosto, however, had obviously made a large leap forward.

Now he made a quantum leap! He returned to Las Vegas in 1972. One day he visited the Valley National Bank and made an offer of $2.4 million for a parcel of land located across the street from the Stardust. He told the bankers that he had the cash to make a full payment then and there and that he came from Sicily where he was "connected." That meant something to bankers in Las Vegas, especially at the Valley National, the source of more loans to casinos than any other bank in the city. Agosto also claimed "contacts" with Yale Cohen, one of Chicago's insiders at the Stardust. This deal was never consummated.

Then the Kansas City *Star* dug something up that was interesting. On August 30, 1972, they reported that when Agosto lived in Yelm, an attempt was made on his life in what appeared to be a would-be gangland slaying. While driving his car near his home, Agosto was the target of five shots, causing him to crash. Agosto claimed to have no idea why someone would want to kill him.

In 1973 more questions arose. Agosto purchased the Caravan Hotel in the state of Washington. He took out insurance with a close pal, Phil Damiano. The hotel thereafter burned down. Arson was again suspected but again the policy paid off. Damiano would be murdered in gangland fashion in Fort Lauderdale, Florida, in August 1975.

Also in 1975, Agosto was involved in a prepaid Legal Defense Fund scheme. One of his associates in the scam was a man known as John "Angel" Amaro. On February 19, 1977, Amaro was gunned down near his home in Kansas City.

On March 27, 1974, Agosto was observed, during a surveillance by Bill Ouseley and his crew in Kansas City, meeting Nick Civella, the Kansas City mob boss, at the Columbus Park Social Club.

On July 30, 1974, Ouseley and other members of the KC FBI observed Agosto arrive at Kansas City International Airport carrying a briefcase. He was met by John Amaro and taken to the residence of Angelo Porrello, a capo in the KC mob. When he left Porrello's residence it was observed he was no longer carrying the briefcase he brought to Kansas City.

On January 15, 1975, Agosto was now living in Las Vegas full time, attempting to construct a new hotel-casino called the Dutch Mill. Finally, in 1977, Joe Agosto made the biggest leap of all. He became the producer of the Folies Bergere, the famous show in the then mobbed-up Tropicana Hotel.

It didn't take long for the Las Vegas field division of the FBI to uncover Joe. They reported as early as 1978 that "Joe Agosto is a La Cosa Nostra associate who is responsible to Nick Civella and the Kansas City La Cosa Nostra family. Agosto's job is to receive and distribute to Kansas City all skim monies taken out of the Tropicana Hotel-Casino."

In April 1978 Carl DeLuna was surveilled by Ouseley and his guys in Kansas City. After he boarded a flight to Las

Vegas, they contacted Charley Parsons, the lead FBI organized crime agent there. Upon arrival DeLuna headed for the Tropicana. There he sat down with Joe Agosto.

From August 4, 1978 through February 14, 1979, St. Valentine's Day, the Las Vegas field division of the FBI, working closely with the Kansas City division, conducted continuous Title III surveillance, which resulted "in voluminous evidence linking Agosto to the Kansas City Organized Crime Family headed by Nick Civella, through Carl Angelo 'Tuffy' DeLuna." St. Valentine's Day in 1979 was the culmination of Strawman I.

Joe Agosto was the guy Bill Ouseley would use his powers of persuasion on. Joe spoke very poor English, but that was no problem because Bill was fluent in Italian. He got to Joe Agosto and turned him. He brought him over.

The Kansas City mob didn't have a chance. With all the evidence from the Title III and from the mouth of the main guy, Joe Agosto, the entire upper echelon leadership of the Kansas City family of La Cosa Nostra went down. Obviously, it was a mortal blow to that family.

It may not have been a mortal blow to the Chicago Outfit, but it sure did hurt. I didn't think they cared all that much about the Civellas and DeLuna, although they should have since Kansas City was run so efficiently, but they sure as hell cared about the serious diminution of the skim from the Tropicana.

41 Bugs!

In my opinion, some of the very best work ever done by the FBI was done in the Pendorf case and the two Strawman cases. Maybe the very best. I am very proud that I am always given some credit by those who did that work,

mainly Pete Wacks, Art Pfizenmayer, Bill Ouseley and Lee
Flosi. Not for any participation in those cases, because I had
none, but because I was the pioneer on the very first electronic
surveillance ever accomplished in an organized crime case.

The agents who followed me had climbed the ladder of success above what I had done. I am very proud of them. Not
only are they great agents but really high-class guys. And now
their generation of agents will soon pass the baton on to a new
group of fine agents. The FBI under J. Edgar Hoover was a
great organization, no matter what some poorly informed skep-
tics might think, and it is still a great organization under Louis
Freeh today.

We have already learned how agents can penetrate mob
meeting places. I want to describe here some of the exceptional
conversations which were intercepted in Pendorf and Strawman.

I have a very clear recollection of one conversation in the
Pendorf case as it was relayed to me. Joey Lombardo was conferring with Allen Dorfman on May 23, 1979, three years before Lombardo would either kill Dorfman or have him killed.
They were discussing the holdings of Morris Shenker, the ostensible owner of the Dunes, and how they helped Shenker get
the Teamster pension fund loan to buy the Dunes. They focused
on the fact that he had not made any effort to repay the loan.
At Dorfman's request, Lombardo made a phone call from
Dorfman's office to Shenker at his executive offices in the
Dunes. This is part of what Lombardo said to Shenker that day:

"It's twelve years and we're tired of this bullshit. You know
where you belong and he knows where he belongs and the
other guy knows where he belongs. [Talking about Shenker's
partners in the Dunes, such as Major Riddle of Chicago.] We
all belong to certain people you account to. It's a big world.
If they tell me to come back and give a message to pay, you
could fight the system if you wanna. But I'll tell you one
thing, you're seventy-two? I assure you that you will never
reach seventy-three."

That conversation was not difficult to interpret. Shenker belonged to the mob and he'd not live another year if he forgot

that. It was very similar to the message Murray Humphreys once delivered to Sidney Korshak over Little Al.

On another occasion, Lombardo had this to say: "Allen [Dorfman] is not that type of guy, but the people that got a piece of him are that type of guy. Allen is meek and Allen is harmless. But the people behind him are not meek and they are not harmless. Do you understand what I mean?"

That put to bed any illusions about the status of Allen Dorfman as far as control of him by the mob was concerned. Not that anybody I ever knew had any such illusions. It also was a good indication of why the mob would soon thereafter kill Dorfman. He was "meek" and "harmless." They did not want some sweet-talking FBI agent taking a run at Allen to make an informant out of him.

I think another great observation picked up on the Title IIIs at this time was one I have already mentioned, the one where Nick Civella observed: "In time, everyone out there [in Las Vegas], the fishes out there, gets corrupted. They can't help it. They live right in the middle of it." No comment.

Another outstanding effort was the Kansas City FBI's intercept of what became known as the "Marlo Tape." Again it was a last-minute effort. The Civellas in KC were a very alert crew. They took very few chances.

In 1978, Joe Agosto came into Kansas City from Las Vegas, where he was running the casino at the Tropicana. He brought Carl Thomas with him. Thomas was the master of skim who was convicted in Strawman I. At the last moment, Agosto and Thomas were instructed to meet with Nick and Cork Civella and with Tuffy DeLuna—the boss, the acting boss and the underboss, the three top leaders of the KC mob. They were advised to go to the basement of the residence of Josephine Marlo, a relative of the Civellas.

Ouseley and his guys had a couple of hours. They repeated just what Wacks and Pfizenmayer had done in Chicago. They located the residence, prepared the affidavit of probable cause, took it to Dave Helfrey in the U.S. Attorney's office, obtained the court order and rushed to Josephine Marlo's basement.

They quickly installed the bug. They had just cleared the area when the mobsters arrived. What they heard then was a classic in the history of mob intercepts. Thomas, with help from Agosto, gave the three mob bosses a primer on how to skim. I won't repeat it all, but here are pertinent parts, verbatim. If you didn't know how to skim before, you will now.

THOMAS: See the cashier's with us, you follow me? You grab the cashier's keys from the cashier. That's the guy we got in the cage. We take the key, open the box and snatch the money. Now what they been doin' in the past, which is very dangerous, is the fucking fill slips. You make a fill for $10,000, make a fill for $7,000 and then you got to get back there and get the fill slip in the box, but see, Tropicana hasn't had that much cash in the past to snatch.

So they would put the fill slip in there and take $10,000 cash. That's why we need the cashier, to get the money. Now once he can get back there, once the drop start goin' up, and just grab the cash, like this, there's no record of anything, but he's got to get the keys unless we go some other way. But the way I'd like to go. I could do it in my own joint because my joint's small and everybody belongs to me.

What Thomas was explaining here was the "fill slip skim." A fill slip is a triplicate slip of paper which the dealer uses when he needs more chips at his table. He signals his floor-man, who then signs the slip as does the dealer. Then the slip is taken to the cage where a cashier in on the scam pockets the slip without supplying chips.

The fill slip skim was exposed at the Stardust in 1982 when the FBI and GCB put undercover operatives at the tables as players. They made note of each fill slip transaction and then compared the fill slips with the cash in the counting room. When they didn't tally, the goose was cooked.

The conversation then continued.

THOMAS: Up until the scam in Argent [the exposure at the Stardust] everybody was making money.

AGOSTO: That's true. OK, let's say tonight is the time.

THOMAS: OK. They come in and take the fill book and they gonna grab $7,500. They make a fill slip . . .

AGOSTO: They gonna grab $7,500.

THOMAS: Sure, they make a fill slip for $7,500. They take it over to our cashier . . .

DELUNA: Nick, ah, Carl, maybe you'd better tell us all what is a fill slip.

THOMAS: Oh, I'm sorry. When a table gets short on money, you got to get money to the game. You just can't go get chips. So you make out a fill slip and you fill the table up. You're making fill slips every ten, fifteen minutes.

N. CIVELLA: In other words, you go to the cashier, get chips.

THOMAS: Right.

CIVELLA: What do you do with the fill slips, legit?

THOMAS: Fill slips, legit? Three copies.

DELUNA: All right, but what do you do with it?

THOMAS: You make three copies for $7,500.

DELUNA: All right. All right.

THOMAS: You sign it, the other guy signs it, the floor-man, you take it to the cashier. He takes it, time-stamps it, boom, all three copies.

CIVELLA: Time what?

THOMAS: Time-stamps it. He stamps it like a bank's got a time stamp, boom, 11:17.

CIVELLA: OK.

THOMAS: And the cashier signs the slip. The cashier then legitimately pushes out $7,500 in chips. That is a legit fill. Now, when they do it illegitimately, you go through the same thing, take the three fill slips . . . go to our cashier, he signs it, keeps a copy, no chips, nothin' leaves the cage.

AGOSTO: He don't give you no chips.

THOMAS: No chips.

Obviously, there have to be at least three crooked employees in this scam. The dealer has to be in on it, and the floorman who signs the slip, and the cashier who takes the slip and pockets it without giving chips to the floorman.

Thomas also discussed with the Civella brothers and DeLuna the easy way to skim—just by stealing cash from the drop boxes as they are carried from the tables to the counting room or in the counting room as they arrive. All large casinos have cameras in the eye-in-the-sky but there have been ways to conceal the theft from the cameras.

This was the famous conversation wherein Thomas referred to the "twenty-one holes in the bucket," twenty-one methods of skimming.

It was obvious that Nick, Cork and Tuffy were not practiced skimmers. Otherwise they wouldn't have needed the education Carl Thomas was giving them. They didn't need to be. That's what they had Thomas and his crew for. I'll bet Tony Spilotro didn't know the "twenty-one holes in the bucket," either. Getting two-bit buys to skim was not his job. It was not his function to fully understand how it was done, but to make certain it *was*.

It might not have been Tony's function to understand all the niceties of the gaming business, but now he was going to pay for that major portion in which he was involved. As Metro would report in 1984, "Anthony Spilotro has been long regarded as being the moving force behind the Chicago mob's interest in Las Vegas. He has been able to extend his influence to every quarter of Las Vegas society. Chicago, represented by Spilotro, rules with an iron hand in Southern Nevada." Wow! Strong words! "Every quarter of Las Vegas society!" Tony would probably consider that some kind of accolade. I can imagine that when he saw the report he sent a copy home to the Chicago mob. What an efficiency report!

Then came another. Preston E. Hubbs, the commander of the Intelligence Unit of Metro, was quoted also in 1984, as saying: "Let there be no doubt that we consider Tony Spilotro to be the lowest form of . . . human life. This hoodlum, who thrives off the weaknesses and misery of our citizenry, offers nothing but a disgrace to this community." Following that blast, Commander Hubbs went on to say: "150 persons actively associated with Spilotro's Chicago faction are involved in every aspect of criminal behavior in Las Vegas."

No wonder that Tony was the number one target of law enforcement in Nevada in 1984!

Tony might have been riding high in Las Vegas, but few would trade places with him that year. First of all, he was under indictment in Las Vegas for the activity of the Hole-in-the-Wall Gang. A new trial was imminent.

Then the stress really got to him. He complained of chest pains, then an accelerated heartbeat, then some nausea. All typical symptoms of heart problems. He went to his doctor and discovered he had suffered a heart attack. He was advised to slow down. Slow down? He'd like to but that was hard for a guy in his position.

One thing he could do, however. He could think of when he *might* be able to slow down. And I'll say this for Tony, he sought to insure the future of Nancy and his son.

He bought some land in southern Nevada, enough to make it a large investment in the future. After all, land near Las Vegas was then worth a great deal with every promise of increasing in value. He also made sure he put money on the street, a lot of it. At six-for-five each week, $11,000 for every $10,000 each week the loan is not repaid in full. You can't get better return on investment than that!

Then came another blow. To his heart. This time there was no doubt, no hesitation. Tony was rushed to the Houston operating room of the famous heart surgeon, Dr. Michael Ellis DeBakey, reputed to be the best. Tony was not his first Chicago mobster patient. Sam Giancana had seen him on a few occasions, once in the early summer of 1975, just before Sam returned home, only to be killed that same night by his own people. A sad legacy.

Tony was operated on at opulent Methodist Hospital in

Houston. It was a coronary bypass procedure, one that Dr. DeBakey had perfected and performed thousands of times.

Tony recovered quickly and at forty-seven now seemed to be able to pull things back together. He bragged to his pals that he felt "like a bull."

At the time I thought about Tony's "legacy." Sam Giancana had been killed by his own. Mad Sam DeStefano had been killed by his own. Milwaukee Phil Alderisio died while jogging in the federal prison in Marion, the country's toughest. Those were Tony's mentors. I wondered just which route Tony might follow. Would the stress get him or would it be something else, something experienced not only by such as Giancana and DeStefano but oh, so many others.

42 Strawman II

In October 1983, U.S. Attorney General William French Smith announced that he termed "one of the most far reaching indictments a federal grand jury has ever returned." Sometimes such pronouncements are hyped. Not in this case. If anything, AG Smith may have been guilty of a little understatement.

Fifteen underworld figures from five cities were indicted!

They were not just *any* fifteen. Some of them were the very top echelon of the leadership of La Cosa Nostra.

Tony Spilotro was one of them,.

Others indicted were Joey Aiuppa and Jackie Cerone, the two top guys in Chicago; capo Angelo "The Hook" La Pietra; capo Joey Lombardo, who was already convicted in Strawman I and who was now spending his days in the federal pen at Leavenworth; Frank Balistrieri, the boss in Milwaukee, along with his sons, Joe and John; Carl Civella, Carl DeLuna and Peter Tamburello from Kansas City; Carl Thomas, the master of skim in Las Vegas; and Milton Rockman of Cleveland.

Named as conspirators were four dead men: Nick Civella, the former boss in Kansas City; Jimmy "Turk" Torrello, a former capo in Chicago; Allen Dorfman and Joe Agosto.

The announcement by Smith, who was joined in making it by William Webster, the director of the FBI, charged the defendants with skimming $2 million from Las Vegas casinos. The casinos were those owned by the Argent Corporation: the Stardust, Fremont, Marina and Hacienda.

I was quoted in the press as saying that "this indictment looks like a who's who of organized crime in the Midwest!"

The indictment reflected the work of five years by several FBI field offices, but especially Kansas City. It alleged that the defendants conspired during the past nine years to establish and maintain hidden interests in gambling operations in Las Vegas casinos owned by Argent Corporation, which was headed by Allen R. Glick of La Jolla, California. Glick was not indicted and a spokesman for him stated that "he was not a willing partner with the defendants."

The indictment charged that Aiuppa, Balistrieri and Lombardo "used their influence with trustees of the Teamsters Central States Pension Fund on matters relating to Glick."

Pat Healy, executive director of the Chicago Crime Commission, said: "In one fell swoop, it's pretty well gutted the top hierarchy of the mob, not only in Chicago, but in Milwaukee and Kansas City."

Strawman II was actually just another phase of Strawman I. It was based on much of the same evidence, especially from the bugs that Ouseley and his fellow FBI agents had originally placed in accordance with the court order in Strawman I. The success of Strawman I allowed Ouseley et al to capitalize on it with the result that some of the participants in the Las Vegas skimming were prevailed upon to become government witnesses—some very important participants! When that happened, the great one-two punch of the government bugs and witnesses was delivered. Witnesses who were not available during the prosecution of Strawman I now became a vital part of the government's case, with the result that much more evidence became available, allowing the FBI and the Justice Department to proceed against a whole new category of defendants.

The top guys in Chicago and Milwaukee were charged in Strawman II together with the Kansas City leaders from Strawman I. A whole new area of the mob's operation in Las Vegas was exposed. After all, the Argent Corporation hotel-casinos were the major hotel-casinos the Chicago-Kansas City-Milwaukee mobs had going for them.

Probably the prime example of how the investigation of Strawman I fed the prosecution of Strawman II was the bug placed in the home of Chicago PD patrolman Anthony Chiavola, assigned to Area 6 traffic. This achievement was a great example of the close cooperation between the Chicago and Kansas City FBI offices, a sterling case of the best in law enforcement.

The KC FBI had a tap on a telephone utilized by Nick Civella, the boss there. On October 18, 1978, Civella placed a phone call to Chicago where he requested that his nephew, Officer Chiavola, make the arrangements for a meeting he wished to hold—to set up a meeting room and another room with a table and wine where he could hold private discussions outside the earshot of other conferees.

The KC FBI immediately contacted the Chicago Bureau. Agents Pete Wacks and Art Pfizenmayer immediately prepared an affidavit requesting a Title III elsur at the home of Officer Chiavola. James B. Parsons, Chief Judge of the U.S. District Court of Northern Illinois, approved the bug, making any evidence acquired from it admissible thereafter in any prosecution. The court order authorized the hidden microphone for five days only. That was enough.

The Bureau in Washington assigned Ed Tickel, then the master sound man, to the job. He entered the Chiavola home at 1452 West Barry on the northwest side of Chicago and accomplished his work in the early hours of October 22, while the police officer's family slept peacefully.

Sure enough, that day the agents spotted Anthony Chiavola,

Jr., also a police officer, assigned to the Foster Avenue District of the Chicago PD on the far north side. He was at O'Hare International Airport picking up Nick Civella and his wife. Young Officer Chiavola chauffeured Civella to the meeting site.

Other agents were watching the residence on Barry Street. At 12:23 in the afternoon they were rewarded. What did they spot but the arrival of Angelo LaPietra, a capo in the Chicago LCN. He was driving. His passengers were the two top leaders of the Chicago mob: Joey Aiuppa and Jackie Cerone.

The agents kept their distance. After all, they wanted the mobsters to believe they were home free. Civella, driven by young Chiavola, arrived at 1:13 P.M. The sit-down lasted until Aiuppa, Cerone and LaPietra departed at 5:26 P.M. Civella left five minutes after the Chicago threesome had cleared the area.

When the agents returned to the federal building in the Loop and bounced into the tech room they found all their work had been highly rewarded! The meeting had been about the proposal of the Kansas City LCN to buy out the interest of the Chicago family in the Stardust and the Fremont. The bid of Civella for the hotels was $10 million. It was rejected. The skim over the years would amount to much more. Or so it was believed at the time.

The conversation also clearly indicated that Tony Spilotro was running things for both mobs in Las Vegas. He was their enforcer!

Although this evidence was developed in the fall of 1978, it would be several years before it was utilized in court. Since it involved the Stardust and the Fremont, it was not disclosed in Strawman I. Since Act One concerned the skimming of the Tropicana, the evidence would not be used until Act Two played out.

(There was one immediate development, however. John Otto, then the SAC of the Chicago office of the FBI, called Sam Nolan, then the acting superintendent of the Chicago Police Department. An investigation of both Chiavolas was quickly instituted by the Internal Affairs Division of the CPD. The two officers would soon go on medical leave and, after being indicted and convicted in Strawman II, would go to prison.)

Modern technology helped Ed Tickel in placing the mike at the residence of Chiavola. The mike he worked with was the size of a fingernail. And it was wireless. The old mikes we worked with were the size of a pineapple and we had to string wires from the site of the mike to a spot where we could monitor it. A large difference. But in no way did that detract from the success of Ed Tickel. How many guys would take the chance that a Chicago cop, awakened by the appearance of a perceived burglar in his home in the wee hours of the morning, would not shoot the burglar? Tickel had guts! And a very special ability. As stated previously, he later succumbed to the stress of his job and wound up in jail. Nevertheless, my hat goes off to him. I know what it takes.

Tony was arrested. Once more. He complained of his heart condition, but at the time law enforcement officials felt that he was claiming the usual "mob illness." So many mobsters, such as Joe Bonanno, complain of some major illness when they are about to be subpoenaed or arrested. It has become so standard that it is not ordinarily believed, even when the defendant's personal physician files what is looked upon as a self-serving statement.

Before the trial could begin, Tony filed a motion for severance. When it became clear that his doctor was the famous Dr. DeBakey, the judge ruled in his favor. Tony would be tried separately when he was sufficiently recovered from his heart surgery to be able to withstand the rigors of a trial and fully cooperate with his attorneys in preparing and presenting his defense. Like all the Bureau agents who had assisted in the investigation over nine years, I was disheartened over Tony's severance. Not knowing just how legitimate a claim he had, I felt that he was resorting to the usual mob illness.

Nevertheless, the defendants included some real heavyweights. I have always considered Jack Cerone to be the real brains and brawn of the Chicago Outfit in the Seventies and Eighties. I had gotten to know him well and I recognized the capability of the man. He had done it all—all that a mob leader could accomplish: kill, organize, corrupt, lead with the utmost respect of his underlings and operate one of Chicago's top gambling crews. My fellow agents listened to reports of informants who claimed that Joey Aiuppa was the boss and Cerone was the underboss. That may or may not have been true. If it was, I believe Jackie wanted it that way. He did not desire the nuisance of the day-to-day operational problems. He had been boss once before, all by himself, in 1970 before we put him away in the Lou Bombacino case, and he knew about the headaches. I believe he was content to let Aiuppa deal with the mundane problems.

I had only one talk with Aiuppa. He did not impress me. When comparing Aiuppa to Cerone, there is no doubt Jackie has the far superior intelligence. Perhaps I am swayed by a conversation in the early Sixties I heard courtesy of Little Al. Sam Giancana told his underboss, "Frankie Strongy," Frank Ferraro: "If Joey Aiuppa comes whining to you tell him to go to hell. He says he's broke. We gave him Cicero. Cicero is a great territory. If he can't make it there he can't make it anywhere." I guess forever after when I heard that Aiuppa had ascended all the way to the top, to become one of Giancana's successors, I can't help but be reminded of that conversation.

When the trial commenced in the late summer of 1985, three high-powered witnesses took the stand for the government in the early stages. First came Ken Eto, the Chicago mob's man in Chinese gambling in Chicago, the guy they shot three times in the head at close range but who amazed them by running off and calling the police. The two shooters in that episode, one a Cook County Sheriff's deputy, paid dearly for their ineptitude. They were both killed. Now Eto was in Kansas City. It was a grisly reminder to Cerone, Aiuppa, Lombardo and LaPietra just how much the failure to put Eto away was costing them.

Eto testified that when Tony Accardo was the top boss in Chicago, Cerone and Aiuppa worked for him. Eto said that later they took over the Chicago mob and that Angelo LaPietra was a "gunman for the Outfit." He identified Vince Solano, Al Pilotto, "Turk" Torello, Joe Lombardo, Angelo LaPietra and Joe Ferriola as "territorial bosses" in the Chicago mob. He tes-

tified that one day "I was ordered by the Outfit to meet with
Johnny Gattuso and Jay Campise, which I did on February 10,
1983. I was shot three times in the back of the head. The hit
was ordered by Vince Solano after permission was received
from either Joey Aiuppa or Jackie Cerone." He added: "It is
my belief that my murder was ordered because the Outfit did
not think I could do my time [he had been indicted in Chicago
on gambling charges] and that therefore I would cooperate
with the government."

Eto also testified that on one occasion he was told by Turk
Torello "that he was going to Florida to kill a union guy. But
while they were there they noticed a guy on a telephone pole,
and a guy on a garbage truck, and various other things that
made them suspicious or which did not seem right, so they
passed up the hit. Torello later said that he was sure glad that
they passed up the hit because they found out these men were
law enforcement officers and the planning of the hit had been
bugged. The order to make the hit had come from Jackie
Cerone, who was also in Florida at the time."

I sure recognized the hit Eto described. We had learned in the
early Sixties that Sam Giancana had ordered Jackie Cerone to
hit Frankie "The X" Esposito, an official of the International La-
borers Union, who was vacationing in Hollywood, Florida. We
heard Giancana discuss it with Cerone on our bug, "Mo."
Cerone reported to Giancana that he had gone to Miami, rented
a house and would use it as his headquarters while he performed the job. Fortunately for us, he gave Giancana the address of this house. Two of the top guys on C-1, John Roberts
and Ralph Hill, then hastened to Miami where, with the assistance of two top agents from the New York office, they installed
a hidden mike in the house. At the same time they alerted the
Dade County Sheriff's Office who put men in the vicinity to
guard Esposito. I called Esposito to discuss the situation with
him when he returned to his home in Chicago, but he refused
to recognize that he had been a target of the Chicago mob.

Eto also testified that he knew "Milwaukee Phil" Alderisio.
He knew Alderisio to have a "very violent temper and he was
very hot-headed and dangerous. He would kill in an instant."

Another defendant Eto testified against was Joey Lombardo. He said that Lombardo was just below Aiuppa and Cerone in the organization hierarchy and that he was made. Eto said that Lombardo performed hits for the organization. In talking about how Lombardo was made, Eto said that to become a made member of the Outfit, it was necessary "to participate in violent acts including breaking arms and legs and killing."

Eto also testified against defendant Angelo "The Hook" LaPietra. He identified him as a "vicious and sadistic killer." He believed that LaPietra had killed a man who had threatened Eto. He said that LaPietra had been "provided for me by the Outfit as security for my gambling operation" and that LaPietra had been a hit man for Fifi Buccieri, another Chicago *capo*. When Buccieri died, LaPietra became a "territorial boss of one of the biggest juice operations in Chicago" and he collected a street tax from any gambler operating in his territory.

Another key witness was Aladena "Jimmy the Weasel" Fratianno. Neither he nor Eto actually testified during the trial. Rather, they were affiants during the detention hearing which followed the trial. Their testimony would be key to immediately incarcerating the defendants without bail.

Fratianno swore that he knew Aiuppa and that it was Aiuppa who had ordered the murder of "Ray Ryan, William Holden's partner in his Kenya venture. Ryan's car was blown up. He was ordered killed because he had testified against Johnny Marshall Caifano, an organized crime operative. I was also advised by Frank 'Bomp' Bompensiero that Joey Aiuppa had ordered the murder of Tamara Rand, a San Diego housewife and Las Vegas casino financier. Anthony, 'The Ant' Spilotro did the killing along with some other persons. Joey Aiuppa also ordered the murder of Rick Manzi, the husband of Barbara McNair. Spilotro also carried out that killing."

Then Fratianno swore that Joey Aiuppa "also ordered the murder of Johnny Roselli. Roselli was found in a barrel floating in Key Biscayne."

Fratianno also stated that he knew Jackie Cerone to be the underboss of the "Chicago organized crime family, or Outfit.

I also knew Joseph Lombardo to be a capo in the Chicago Outfit. If anybody wanted a killing done, Lombardo would do it, if ordered by the boss, Aiuppa. Also, once Joey Lombardo refused to make or post bond or to move for a bond reduction because to be safe he wanted to show that he could do his time without talking, as anyone who could not would be killed." As we have seen.

Jimmy had been made into the Chicago family and had been one of their top people in California for decades. He had even been the acting boss of the Los Angeles family for a short time. He proved to be a damaging witness. Jimmy was an articulate guy. If I were casting a movie and I needed an actor to play a top mobster, I'd go get Jimmy. He looked like what he was and he talked like what he was. Jimmy testified in about a dozen mob trials and did an outstanding job in each. I don't recall a single case in which Jimmy testified that resulted in an acquittal. I liked the guy. It was too bad he felt that his government had deserted him by removing him from the witness protection program.

Another witness the government rolled out was Frank Cullotta. Oh, how Tony Spilotro now wished he had never known Frank! He wasn't going to hurt Tony in this trial, but Tony was next.

Then came three more powerful witnesses. First, Roy Williams, the former president of the Teamsters Union, the successor to Hoffa and Fitzsimmons. He testified at length about his role as the mob's man at the helm of the Teamsters. He told the jury he had even been code-named "The Rancher" by the mob for reasons of protection from discovery. (He owned a farm in Missouri or Kansas.)

Williams made a great witness for the government. First of all, he traced his career in the Teamsters. He admitted that he had received a total of $117,000 *before* he became president of the Teamsters as his share of the skim of the Stardust!

Testifying after a grant of immunity for Strawman II but not with any deal on his ten-year sentence in Strawman I, which was handed down only days before the Strawman II trial commenced, Williams admitted he had lied during his testimony at the first trial. Williams testified that he received payments of $1,500 a month from Nick Civella beginning in late 1974 until mid-1981 when he asked that they be stopped. He told the jury that he had been approached by Nick Civella in 1973, when he was a trustee of the Central States Pension Fund and before he became president of the Teamsters Union, to approve an initial loan of $62 million to Allen Glick for the Stardust and then another for $40 million.

Williams also told how pervasive was the influence of organized crime. He said, "Civella knew many of my superiors in other parts of the country, including Jimmy Hoffa when he was Teamsters president." He also said, "If there was an argument between me and Civella, my superiors in the Teamsters would ask me to comply with Civella's request." Williams went on to testify that Civella met often with Hoffa, Frank Fitzsimmons, Billy Presser (a high-ranking official of the Teamsters and the father of Jackie Presser who would become president of the Teamsters) and Allen Dorfman.

Obviously, the testimony of Roy Williams was very damaging to the defendants. "The Rancher" would become a prime witness for the government in years to come while he spent some time in the medical facilities of the federal prison at Springfield, Missouri. He would later die of acute emphysema and heart problems.

Perhaps the greatest surprise witness at Strawman II, however, was Angelo Lonardo. You couldn't get a higher guy in the Cleveland family of La Cosa Nostra than Lonardo. He had been the acting boss, the underboss and just about everything else in the Cleveland mob. Lonardo had been convicted of a drug violation and then began cooperating as a witness for the FBI. He testified at Strawman II that he had come to Chicago from Cleveland with defendant Milton Rockman, an older killer for the Cleveland mob, to meet with Jackie Cerone and Joey Aiuppa. The nature of the sit-down, Lonardo testified, was to discuss who would be the next president of the Teamsters Union. At the time of the meet, Frank Fitzsimmons, the current president, was dying from lung cancer. Several mob families were pushing their own candidates for the presidency of the union. Cleveland had theirs, Jackie Presser. But they realized that he was not quite ready. They had made a deal with Roy Williams. If Cleveland would support him for the presidency, Williams would give Presser a top spot in the Teamsters, probably replacing Williams as director of the Central States Conference of the Teamsters. Lonardo further testified that the Kansas City family of the LCN had vouched that they had Williams under control, "that they could talk to him."

There was a problem, however. The Chicago mob had their own candidate. Lonardo could only recall that his first name was Ray. Many speculated that the reference was to Ray Schoessling, the president of the Joint Council of the Teamsters in Chicago and the general secretary-treasurer of the international union at one time. Further, Cerone and Aiuppa indicated at the meeting in Chicago with Lonardo and Rockman that they "did not trust Presser." (Their instincts were right on target because at the time, and until his death, Jackie Presser was a CTE, a top echelon informant, developed by a fine Cleveland FBI agent, Bob Friedrick.)

Lonardo testified further that following their meeting in Chicago with Aiuppa and Cerone, he and Rockman then traveled to New York where they met with "Fat Tony" Salerno, the boss of the powerful Genovese family. Salerno approved the selection of Williams and told Lonardo and Rockman that Tony "Pro," Tony Provensano, a New Jersey mobster and Teamster leader, would also approve Williams. Then, Lonardo said, Cerone and Aiuppa were swayed to accept Williams, probably after conferring with Salerno. Shortly thereafter, on May 6, 1981, Fitz died and on May 15 the Teamsters executive board met in Las Vegas (where else?) and elected Williams president. A week later, however, a federal grand jury in Chicago indicted Williams in Strawman I. A year later, he was convicted. Although Jackie Presser did not surface as a witness in Strawman I, the information he supplied sub rosa to Bob Friedrick was critical. However, it was in the interest of the FBI to keep Presser covered for the greater good of law enforcement. As a CTE he was in a great position. In fact, on April 20, 1983, with Ray Schoessling as his opponent, Presser was elected president of the Teamsters. Cerone was known to oppose Presser, but mobsters from the other LCN families supported him and that assistance won Presser the post.

I think that the following affidavit supplied by Angelo Lonardo at the detention hearing of the defendants on January 17, 1986 gives an accurate picture of Aiuppa and especially of Cerone and how they ran the Chicago mob when they were its bosses:

"As a member, and eventually underboss, of the organized crime family in Cleveland, Ohio, I became acquainted with Joseph 'Joey' Aiuppa and John 'Jackie' Cerone. I knew them to be underbosses and eventually bosses in Chicago. It was their reputation that anybody who did anything wrong, including providing information to the authorities, would be killed. At one point, Jackie Cerone said the Chicago organization was getting rid of at least one guy a day to keep the people in the organization in line. Part of Jackie Cerone's responsibility was enforcement: to get organized crime family members and associates to stay in line. Joey Aiuppa was known to demand that the organization be run according to the rules and he had a reputation of being a very tough disciplinarian, which included using force and death as necessary. One rule which was enforced in the Cleveland family, as well as in other families such as Chicago, New York and Milwaukee, was the rule of silence or *omerta*. Those who testified or provided information against the family would be silenced, including by their death."

At the time Lonardo provided this affidavit, he was the highest-ranking La Cosa Nostra leader ever to turn. Later there would be one or two others, such as Sammy "The Bull" Gravano, the underboss to John Gotti in the Gambino family of the LCN in New York City, who were of material assistance in downing their bosses like Gotti and "Little Nicky" Scarfo. But at the time Lonardo was a breakthrough and a real credit to the good work being done at the Cleveland office of the FBI under Joe Griffin, who had been a clerk in the Chicago office when I was on C-1.

Also on the witness list was another friend of mine, this time a most legitimate guy, Dan Shannon. Dan was a former

All-American football player at Notre Dame, and more recently the Executive Director of the Central States Pension Fund when $160 million in loans were made to Allen Glick and Argent. Dan took no part in approving those loans, placing the blame where it belonged, on the late Allen Dorfman.

Then came two witnesses who, along with Cullotta, were supposedly under the control of Tony Spilotro. Two guys who, in the opinion of Cerone and Aiuppa and Tony Accardo, never should have gotten this far.

The first was Allen Glick! No wonder he hadn't been indicted! Glick had a lot to say. He had been the front for the mob in Argent, controlled four hotel-casinos for them. Obviously, Glick, fully cooperative, could hurt the defendants, especially the four Chicago defendants. He did. Glick lives today in La Jolla, with a full private security force including, at one time, former FBI agent Bill Fleming.

Then came another guy who could hurt the defendants. The master of skim. The guy who the Kansas City and Chicago mobs employed to skim the four casinos of interest to this trial. This was the guy who was right down in the muck, so to speak, the guy who handled the on-the-spot skimming. One of the defendants who now was promised some leniency if he would turn on his fellow defendants and testify against them. Carl Thomas. The man on the "Marlo Tape."

Of course, the government also produced the "Marlo Tape" in conjunction with Thomas's testimony. And so many other transcripts of conversations. The transcript of the meeting at the home of the cop in Chicago, where Ed Tickel had performed his derring-do, was again introduced.

The Chicago defendants were represented by some good members of the Chicago defense bar including Joe DiNatale, Santo Volpe, Frank Oliver and Louis Carbonaro. The trial was heard by a jury of six men and six women. When it concluded they were out thirty hours. Some of the defendants like the Balistrieri brothers were discharged after their father, Frank, the boss in Milwaukee, plea-bargained. His guilty plea included the dismissal of charges against his sons.

On January 20, 1986, the FBI arrived at the luxury suites of a high-priced Kansas City hotel. The four guests there were placed in handcuffs. Aiuppa, Cerone, LaPietra and Rockman. They would soon join Joey Lombardo at Leavenworth. They had been found guilty!

When the sentences later came down it was clear that Auippa, then seventy-eight, and Cerone, then seventy-one, would probably spend the rest of their lives in prison. I have been in contact with Cerone at his prison near Austin, Texas. Jackie has been a health nut like myself all his life. While running the Chicago mob he worked out twice a day. He jogged in the morning around his neighborhood in Elmwood Park and worked out with weights in the late afternoon at the Regency Club at the Hyatt-O'Hare. But now he is feeling the effects of advancing age. I wonder if those guys feel it was all worth it.

Many observers believe that the victory for the government in Strawman II was the biggest blow to the Chicago mob since 1944 when Paul Ricca, Johnny Roselli, "Little New York" Campagna and others were convicted in New York in the "Hollywood Extortion Case" for extorting millions from every one of the Hollywood studios of the time. Since Frank "The Enforcer" Nitti committed suicide after his indictment in that case, these observers had a point. The big difference, in my opinion, was that in Strawman II not only did the top guys in Chicago go down, as in the Hollywood Extortion Case, but so did the chief mobsters in satellite cities answering to Chicago: Kansas City and Milwaukee. Therefore, it is my opinion that if you combined the three associated cases—Pendorf, Strawman I and Strawman II—you can easily argue that they, as a group, were the most successful cases in history against La Cosa Nostra and its extended family.

Tony had been very lucky to avoid being with his bosses in any of the three cases. That is, *if* it is lucky to suffer from his heart bypass to escape prison. I imagine there might be those who would rather go to prison.

However, in Tony's case, lady luck was not to continue on his side. The government had yet another shot to take at him.

43 A Short Reprieve

The year 1986 started out badly for the Spilotro family when the "good Spilotro," brother Pat, was indicted for two counts of filing false income tax returns. Dr. Spilotro, then forty-nine and living in Northbrook but practicing dentistry in Des Plaines, both northwestern suburbs of Chicago, was charged with failing to report interest earned on bank accounts held in his children's names. Dr. Pat had twelve children. The amount of interest involved was small, and it appeared that had the good doctor not been a brother of Tony he might have escaped detection. Pat argued that he had not raised twelve kids in order to use them to cheat the government.

At almost the same time, the Hole-in-the-Wall Gang trial began. Tony and eleven other defendants were on trial for burglary and racketeering. If convicted, Tony faced ninety-seven years in the penitentiary and a $95,000 fine. Even if he were to be acquitted he faced still another trial for the 1979 contract murder of Sherwin Lisner. After that, still another, the Strawman II case from which he had been severed. Could he win all three cases and stay out of prison?

Tony's attorney, Oscar Goodman, argued that he was "not on trial for his reputation," after the 1984 Metro report was introduced describing him as "the lowest form of representation of a human being."

Pat Healy, the executive director of the Chicago Crime Commission, was quoted as saying, "This trial would be the main event if it were held here in Chicago." Healy went on to say that, "there is an excellent chance that if he is not taken off the scene with a conviction, then he could be the heir to the Chicago crime syndicate."

The prosecutor in the Hole-in-the-Wall Gang trial was Larry Leavitt. He had also grown up in Chicago. He was a capable guy, educated at the University of California at Berkeley. In the Sixties, he had joined the U.S. Attorney's office in Las Vegas and had won acclaim when he obtained murder convictions against the two men who had murdered Al Bramlet of the Culinary Union in Las Vegas. Bramlet had previously hired the men to bomb some Las Vegas nightclubs that were resisting the efforts of the Culinary Union to organize them.

Two of Tony's old pals, who had joined him from Chicago, were the primary witnesses against him—Frank Cullotta, the more important of the two, and Sal Romano.

The material evidence consisted of the Title IIIs the FBI had installed in Gold Rush Ltd. and in many of Tony's other hangouts, including his home and the home of brother John.

Perhaps the most interesting *defense* testimony was that of another old nemesis, Detective William Hanhardt, then retired from the Chicago Police Department. He was the detective who, with his partner, John Hinchey, had rousted Tony on several occasions when he was a top moper at the start of his criminal career. Bill Hanhardt had also arrested Frank Cullotta on several occasions. He knew both Tony and Frank as young burglars very well. So well that he was subpoenaed to Las Vegas to give testimony on Tony's behalf. He testified that Frank Cullotta was well known to him and that he considered him to be "unreliable as a witness." If the jury did not believe Cullotta's testimony, then Tony might well escape conviction.

The trial lasted for twelve weeks and, after eleven days of deliberation, the jury announced that it was deadlocked on several of the thirty-seven counts of the indictment. Then one of the female jurors sent U.S. District Court Judge Lloyd George a note. She had overheard two of the jurors conversing on a stairwell, discussing money. She believed that at least one of them had been offered a bribe!

Judge George called the prosecution and defense attorneys into his chambers to discuss the situation. Then he declared a mistrial, even though four of the defendants had pleaded guilty. All that work for nothing! Now the defendants would have to be retried.

One of the defense attorneys working under Oscar Goodman would later say that, according to what he inferred during the conference in Judge George's chambers, the juror in question had been offered $10,000.

During the next few days, the media went into a wild frenzy speculating about the future of Tony "The Ant," now that he had beaten the government. Although the case would be retried—this time, hopefully, without any jury tampering—the newspapers, television and radio reporters in Chicago and Las Vegas speculated about Tony's future. Phil La Velle, the fine reporter then with the *Las Vegas Review-Journal*, wrote an article with a headline at the top of the front page entitled "Spilotro Stock Goes Up!" La Velle quoted many law enforcement officials who thought that the mistrial "gives the mobster a fighting chance of becoming the boss of the Chicago mob." The article also quoted a top organized crime expert in Chicago as saying that Spilotro could now challenge any other leader of the Chicago Outfit for the top spot and "probably beat him."

I was quoted in the article as stating that the top position was open now that Joey Aiuppa and Jackie Cerone, the two top leaders of the Outfit, had been convicted in Strawman II. But I expressed the opinion that it would go to a more qualified man than Tony, the more likely choice being Joe Ferriola, known to his pals as Joe Nick and to some as Joe Negall. I went on to say that I believed Ferriola and Spilotro would work in tandem. Ferriola had been on the scene in Chicago and had been groomed for the position. He'd done all the things an heir apparent is supposed to do and done them well. I have spent time with Ferriola and I know he's a very capable guy and that he's held in high esteem by the right people. I did not share the opinion of others who felt that Tony was then in a position to take over the Chicago mob. But it was a time of crisis in Chicago and anything could happen.

* * *

In Las Vegas, Judge George set a new trial date of June 16.

Before that, however, Tony would fulfill one more contract killing. One of his people in Las Vegas was Emil "Mal" Vaci. Vaci was seventy-three years old but he was not to be allowed to reach seventy-four. He had been implicated with Jay Vandermark, the slot skim expert who had cheated the Chicago mob by diverting some of the skim to himself. I have described how Vandermark's son was killed and how the father had disappeared never to be found, apparently slain. Now it was Vaci's turn. The bad example could not be left to fester, to tempt others who might follow in his footsteps. We'll never know whether Tony did the job himself or whether he subcontracted it out. Vaci had fled to Phoenix, where he was the maitre d' of Ernesto's Back Street, a well-known restaurant. After being contacted on the phone there, he told the employees that he had to leave for a while. He was never again seen alive. On June 7, 1986, Vaci's body was found wrapped in a tarpaulin in a drainage ditch by a couple hiking in the desert. He had been shot in the back of the head.

In November, Pat would be acquitted of the tax charges in Chicago. His attorney, Allen Ackerman, would claim that the only thing Pat was guilty of was "being a Spilotro." Ackerman pointed out that Pat was an Air Force veteran, active in the Knights of Columbus, the Kiwanis Club and Little League baseball. The jury was out just over lunch before returning with its not guilty verdict. Pat was now free of all charges; he even had his seat on the Merc. Ackerman told the press: "Do you realize the IRS had two men on this for five years, the FBI had two agents, and the U.S. Attorney's office put two lawyers on the case. If you can figure out the cost of this prosecution to the government you're better at figures than I am."

Dr. Pat was still the good Spilotro. The jury had heard the evidence and returned a reasoned judgment. That's good enough for me. I fully accept Dr. Pat as a respected member of our society.

But not Tony. Or John. Or Michael. Or Victor. I never did know what ever became of the oldest Spilotro, Vincent. He must have been law-abiding because I never heard otherwise.

The New Boss

44 The weather in Chicago in January can be a bitch, and January 1986 was no exception. But at least it was not snowing.

Tony was glad to be in the desert, but in Chicago the mob had gathered. They took over a private dining room in one of their favorite spots, the Czech Lodge in North Riverside, a cozy suburb. The entire upper echelon of the Chicago family of the La Cosa Nostra had convened; its *consiglieri*, Tony Accardo, would preside. Others present included Gus Alex, the leader of the "connection guys"; Vince Solano, in charge of mob activity on the north side; Al Pilotto, in charge of the southern suburbs; Rocky Infelice, John "No Nose" DiFronzo and Sam "Wings" Carlisi, in charge of the west side and the western suburbs; Toots Palermo from the southside; and Butch Blasi, the mob's appointment secretary. Sitting up at the head of the table with Accardo was Joe Ferriola.

Missing were some key figures. And that was the reason for the meet this day. Joey Aiuppa, Jackie Cerone and Joey Lombardo had gone off to prison. Lombardo, of course, had been in prison since 1983 when he was convicted in the Pendorf case. Now, once more, he had gone down in Strawman II. He would be spending the next ten years in prison. Aiuppa and Cerone, the boss and the underboss, would spend the rest of their lives in confinement, Aiuppa in Minnesota and Cerone in Texas. The boss had to be replaced. And then there would be one other important item on the agenda.

The *consiglieri* took the lead. Even when Chicago had a boss there was a man above him. Unlike any other family, at any time, the *consiglieri* in Chicago had the first recommendation and the final veto. The boss might run the day-to-day operations of the Outfit but final say was in the hands of Tony Accardo.

We didn't have a mike in the room, but I did have a highly placed CTE who was present. So it is known what Accardo talked about. He was usually a man of few words, but today he felt he should deliver the story of the history of the Chicago Outfit. He talked about how Al Capone had built the organization only to be sent away on tax charges. About Frank Nitti, who took over until the Hollywood scandal caught up with him. He discussed Paul Ricca's brief reign, and his own years at the top until he stepped down.

He talked about Sam Giancana's public visibility while boss and what happened to him. Then Sam Battaglia, Philly Alderisio and Jackie Cerone, until Accardo returned with Alex and Aiuppa. He described Cerone's release from prison, and his own chance to step down once more.

He paused to observe his audience. Everybody was paying rapt attention. Nobody was inattentive when Tony Accardo talked.

Joe Batters then continued by reviewing with them the devastating effect that the Pendorf and Strawman cases had had on the Outfit. That was why they were all assembled, he said. To regroup and to pick a new boss.

He said that the guy he and Gussie had talked about for the top spot was right here. And he laid his hand on the shoulder of Joe Ferriola. He was their choice to be the next boss. Was there anybody who wanted to say something about that?

Accardo gave them all a moment or so to comment. None did. If Joe Batters had put the mantle on Joe Ferriola, that was good enough for all concerned. Besides, Joe Ferriola was a popular choice. He had done it all. He had killed, he had run much of the Outfit's gambling operations for several years, their lifeblood, and he had corrupted the cops who stood in his way.

Accardo kept his hand on Ferriola's shoulder, keeping him down for a few more minutes.

"Now, one of the reasons I have gone to all this trouble to

make sure you guys all know about the history of our thing is this. Think back what I told you. How many of the top bosses in our Outfit have stepped out on their own or died in their own bed? How many have not been hit by the G and gone to prison! Think about it. I'm the only exception. When a guy these days agrees to become the top guy he's lookin' at a few good years and then the rest of his life in prison. Most guys don't want that, it ain't worth it. So when we find a capable man who has the loyalty to us and to our thing and agrees to take the top job, then, by God, we got to count this guy as one hell of a man. We got to understand he's sacrificin' for the rest of us. And we got to give him every fuckin' thing we got. He's gonna keep his head down. Work like hell to keep it from getting to the G that he is the top man. Then the whole world comes down on this guy. The G and the Strike Force put all their guns on the guy. So before I let him up, I want every one of you to pledge to Joe Ferriola that you will work your ass off for him and that you will keep him as protected as you can. Do I have your understanding on that?"

He did. None of the assembled thought himself ready to step over Joe Ferriola. It was at this point that Joe Batters took his hand off Joe Ferriola's shoulder and sat down.

Now the mantle had passed. The great Tony Accardo had stepped aside once more and now another in the long line of successors to Al Capone had been anointed.

"First of all, I got to say this," Ferriola began. "Joe has agreed to stay on as *consiglieri*. He's still the *man*. I may be the boss but we all understand his is the final say. We're all clear on that. And then also, Gussie has agreed to continue as head of the connection guys. Both of them will spend a lot of time at their places away from Chicago but both will be available whenever we need them."

Ferriola made sure that was clear. Then he resumed. "Now we get down to our first problem. Joe and Gussie and I have discussed this. We wouldn't be in the mess we are now in if it weren't for one thing. The way that asshole out there in Las Vegas has ruined us."

Ferriola then launched into an angry account of Tony

Spilotro's years in Las Vegas. First he reminded those present of the good years at the beginning, when millions in skim was making its way to Chicago. But then he listed everything that had gone wrong recently. All those court cases. Tony's sponsorship of Geri Rosenthal. Dealing dope. Burglaries. Ferriola let everyone know in no uncertain terms that such activities would not be acceptable under his leadership.

Ferriola then began on all those who had turned against the Outfit. Cullotta and Romano. Glick. Agosto. Thomas. All guys working out there for Spilotro.

Ferriola had really worked himself up to a fever pitch. Spittle came onto his lips. He was hot about this. He had already conferred with Accardo and Alex about the situation. He knew what his course of action would be. But he wanted the support of his capos. He wanted them to clearly understand why what would follow would follow.

"OK, do you understand what I'm sayin'?" Ferriola asked. All nodded. "So what do we do about it?"

Rocky Infelice was the one who replied for the group, articulating the consensus that had formed. Rocky is an unusual mobster. He had been a member of the 101st Airborne in World War II and had parachuted behind the German lines in Operation Overlord, the invasion at Normandy, as one of the Screamin' Eagles. A real-life war hero. "Hit him," Rocky said, softly.

Ferriola looked at the rest of his capos. All seemed to be in complete agreement. He looked at Accardo. Accardo said nothing, didn't move a muscle.

"OK, that's it, I got nothin' else," Ferriola announced. The first meeting of the new regime of the Chicago family of La Cosa Nostra had come to an end.

45 Finitu!

Aware that Joe Ferriola had taken over as the top boss in Chicago but entirely unaware of the major item on his agenda, Tony Spilotro went about his business in warm, sunny Las Vegas.

With the assistance of his top aide, Herbie Blitzstein, he had been spending the last year or so putting over $1.5 million on the street in juice loans. This business, along with the land he was buying up, was to be Tony's insurance policy for the years, or even decades, down the line when he would no longer be active. There might come a time when he'd need an ace in the hole.

Tony was fully cognizant of all the major hurdles before him. The second trial of the Hole-in-the-Wall Gang case was to start on June 16. Since the mistrial, the FBI in Las Vegas under John Schrieber had assigned ten agents to investigate the possibility of jury tampering. And there was still the Strawman case. He had been severed from the first trial, but now that Tony was back on his feet, in reasonably good health, the judge in Kansas City would schedule another Strawman trial with Tony as the only defendant.

But Tony Spilotro could live with the devil he knew. After all, hadn't he beaten the M & M Murders and the case against him for which he had killed Mad Sam so as not to be associated with that "pazzo"? And the Deming, New Mexico, case when he killed Daniel Seifert, the prime witness against him? Tony was no virgin when it came to beating court cases against him—one way or another. You bribed the jurors or you killed the witnesses or you got highly regarded character witnesses who would demean the witnesses against you or you murdered your high-profile co-defendant. You did whatever it took. For the Hole-in-the-Wall Gang case, it might be he could locate Frank Cullotta and/or Sal Romano before June 16 so they would not be available to testify.

These vital concerns were in Tony's mind between April 9 and June 16. Tony was now forty-eight. He had lived an exciting, rich life. He had a pretty wife who closed her eyes to his peccadilloes and his life of crime, seemed to thrive on it. He had a nice home, everything money could buy. He was coveted by dozens of showgirls and playgirls in the Sin Capital. With a snap of his fingers he could have the car of his associate blown up, the throats of anybody who got in his way slashed. This world, at least, was still his oyster. Sure, he had to beat a couple more cases, lose a little of the girth that had accumulated around his waist as Dr. DeBakey had ordered, and take a little better care of his health. But, Christ, what top executive in any business didn't have these problems. In Tony's mind, he was sitting on top of the world. Or, at any rate, the part of it on the Strip and in Glitter Gulch, downtown.

In Chicago, way beyond the neon lights of Las Vegas, thoughts of Tony were not so tranquil. Joe Ferriola had taken a few months in 1986 to get his house in order, to get his ducks in line. Now, as spring turned into summer, Joe Nick got to the major item on the agenda he had announced at the Czech Lodge in January.

The first thing Joe did was order Tony back to Chicago. Tony protested. The Hole-in-the-Wall retrial would start on Monday and he was busy looking for Cullotta and Romano. Tony's pleas fell on deaf ears. Ferriola had had enough from his man in Vegas. He had inherited the guy and now had seen nothing in the Las Vegas *Review-Journal* or the *Sun* but stories about Tony Spilotro this and Tony Spilotro that. The fucker wouldn't keep his head down. Roy Kozial, then the Chicago *Tribune*'s man in the west, and Art Petacque, the ace crime reporter of the *Sun-Times*, were devoting column after column to the man they called by his familiar nickname, "The Ant."

So it was that on June 13 Tony traveled to Chicago, pissed. He and Nancy were picked up at O'Hare by kid brother Michael and his wife, Anne. They drove in Anne's Lincoln to Michael and Anne's home at 1102 Maple in Oak Park, the former home of Tony and Nancy.

Michael filled Tony in. As three different informants would advise the FBI in subsequent years during the investigation that would follow, "Black Sam" had taken over many of the duties of the everyday functions of the Chicago Outfit. Ferriola was the boss but Sam Carlisi was his powerful *underboss*, his *sotto capo*. And directly under Black Sam, called "Wings" in the press, was his driver, Jim Marcello. One of these informants would later tell the FBI that he was advised by Michael that in the event an emergency occurred and Michael could not be reached, Jim Marcello should be contacted.

Another informant would later tell the FBI that he had been with Tony and Michael after Tony arrived in Chicago. He advised that Michael received two phone calls that day from "Jim." Michael considered them "very important." After the second call, Michael told his informant that he had to attend a meeting the following day, June 14.

This same informant later advised that he had been with Tony and Michael shortly before they left for this "very important" meeting and that they acted "in a very unusual fashion." The informant advised the FBI that this was the meeting which had been arranged during the telephone calls from "Jim" on the previous day.

One other informant was developed by the FBI during the intensive investigations that would follow. He had also been with Michael on June 13 and 14. This informant advised that for some time before June 13, Michael had been in touch with Jim Marcello and that Marcello "always identified himself as 'Jim.' " Michael had told him on June 14 that he and Tony had to attend a meeting that day with "Sam." This source told the FBI that he knew from prior conversations with Michael that "Sam" was Sam Carlisi. Before he left for the meeting with Sam, Michael told this informant that if he did not come back from the meeting that "it was no good."

I have never personally confronted Sam Carlisi. He had grown up in upstate New York and had been closely associated with the Buffalo family of La Cosa Nostra before he came to Chicago. I recall, however, that several years before Sam Giancana was killed we had him under surveillance in Boca Raton, Florida, and took photos of him meeting with Carlisi. For many years, Carlisi was the driver for Joey Aiuppa, first when Aiuppa was the boss of Cicero and then when he became the boss of the whole Outfit in the early Seventies. We suspected that Carlisi had been carrying a message from Aiuppa to Giancana when we spotted them in Boca Raton. In Chicago he was not only closely associated with his mentor, Aiuppa, but with another fast-rising mobster about his own vintage, Rocky Infelice, with whom he had a partnership in JEP Leasing, a truck-leasing operation. In 1986 Carlisi had recently been released from the Metropolitan Correctional Center on Clark Street in Chicago.

Although Sam Carlisi had taken over many of the day-to-day functions of running the Outfit, it was Joe Ferriola who was still the boss. However, Joe had physical problems at this stage of his life. He had incurable cancer. He could and did function, but he anointed Carlisi, on the recommendation of Aiuppa, to take over the mundane duties of running things.

When Michael received the final phone call, he and Tony were instructed to proceed to the Howard Johnson's Hotel near O'Hare. Before Michael left he told Anne, "If we're not back in time for the kid's game, you'll know we're in deep trouble." He hoped it would be a routine meeting with Ferriola and that he would be back in time for the six o'clock Little League game. He and Tony then took off in Anne's Lincoln.

When they arrived at the Howard Johnson's, they spotted the two guys they expected would be there. We'll probably never know just who they were. Was it "Jim" and/or "Sam"? The FBI investigation has never conclusively developed their identities. Betty Tocco, the wife of Al Tocco, the capo in charge of the southern suburbs of Chicago, would later testify that Al was involved, but this was never confirmed.

The two guys told Michael to leave his car in the parking lot at Howard Johnson's and get into theirs.

One of the guys was in the back with Tony, while the other drove onto the Tri-State Tollway and headed south. Tony looked at the guy beside him quizzically. Tony was told they were going out to Joey Aiuppa's hunting club, located sixty miles south of the city. This was not a great surprise. He had been there before. But it was somewhat unusual since Aiuppa then was in prison following his conviction in Strawman II. However, Tony figured that the lodge was still used from time to time for sensitive meets when the mobsters were taking no chances of being observed in Chicago.

"Looks like we won't make that Little League game," Tony said to Michael. Michael groaned.

When Tri-State turned hard east, the driver exited onto U.S. 41, heading directly south. Still Tony would not have felt any particular concern. He would also consider it within the mob's modus operandi for the driver to make a sharp U-turn and head back north on U.S. 41. After watching his rearview mirror closely for five minutes and finding that no one had U-turned after him, the driver turned east into Indiana and then checked once more to make certain he was not being tailed. Nobody of any suspicious nature. With that the driver made another sharp U-turn and drove at ninety miles an hour back to U.S. 41. There he pulled into the parking lot of a McDonald's, where the foursome, desiring no surveillance, watched carefully for anything that might be the least bit suspicious. Tony understood all this. This was his method of operation whenever he went anywhere, even to a normal shack-up with some broad. If he was to meet Ferriola this afternoon, he would be shocked and upset if his driver acted any other way. Again they headed south on U.S. 41.

As the car approached the village of St. Anne, Indiana, Tony would have realized he was in big trouble. One might suppose that he would think first of what he had gotten Michael into. But not if you knew Tony.

The cause of Tony's sudden realization was quite simple. The guy on his left pulled out a big old .38 with a four-inch barrel and stuck it in Tony's ribs. Not a word was spoken. None had to be. The pretext was over.

When the car was about twelve miles east of St. Anne, heading away from Aiuppa's hunting lodge, the driver turned onto Newton County Country Road. He then pulled off the rural road and onto a cornfield alongside the Willow Slough Preserve, 12,000 acres of state-owned land located ten miles into Indiana. Two other thugs were waiting for them. The driver exited the car as these two opened the doors for Tony and Michael, covering both with .38s and .45s. A hole about six feet long and five feet deep had been dug into the cornfield. Tony reacted immediately. He turned to throw a punch. But the thugs were ready for that. For his trouble Tony got the butt of a .45 across his face. One of the other thugs stepped forward and brought his gun down swiftly onto the top of Tony's head. It was the last thing Tony would ever recall.

When Tony and Michael had not returned to her Oak Park home by June 16, Anne Spilotro realized there was cause for alarm. It was not unusual for Michael to spend a night away from home, especially when he was under the influence of his big brother, but at least he would call and let her know what was up. Anne didn't always believe him, but at least she knew he was alive and well. Now she recalled what would be the last thing he ever said to her. Against the advice of Nancy, who had gone through this kind of thing numerous times during her turbulent marriage, Anne called the Oak Park PD. Since the subject was Tony Spilotro, the Oak Park PD called the FBI. The FBI had already begun to search for Tony after getting a warrant for him based on his failure to show up for his trial that day in Las Vegas. They had had no luck.

Mob experts were asked by the press for comments. One, a retired FBI agent who had tracked Spilotro for decades and was then an investigative attorney living in Tucson, Arizona, mustered all his credibility and opined that Tony "had done a Bonanno. That, like Joe Bonanno, the mob boss from Brooklyn, he had voluntarily disappeared in order to escape his trials." That guy is still wiping the egg off his face.

The corn was now four inches high in Indiana. Farmer Michael Kinz, who had leased the land adjacent to the Willow Slough Preserve, decided on June 23 that it was time to put some weed killer in the field. When he came to one spot he found that the soil had recently been turned over. That was unusual. Kinz had had some experience with things like this, however. Once before, a poacher on his land had illegally killed a deer and, after he had taken the parts he wanted, buried the remains in a shallow grave. So Farmer Kinz called the Indiana Game and Wildlife Agency. They sent a biologist named Dr. Hudson to the site. He began digging.

What he discovered were two badly bludgeoned bodies, clad only in their underwear. Dr. Hudson immediately called the Newton County sheriff. He called the resident agent of the FBI in Hammond, Indiana, who called Ed Hagerty, the SAC of the FBI in Chicago. Hagerty, widely recognized as an organized crime expert from his days as an agent in Philadelphia, hustled to the cornfield and took charge of the crime scene. Since everyone was aware of the disappearance of the Spilotro brothers, Hagerty immediately suspected that these were their bodies. But their faces were so disfigured that they were unrecognizable.

They were not identified until their dentist was located and x-rays of their teeth obtained. The dentist, a distinguished oral surgeon who just happened to have the appropriate x-rays, was Dr. Pasquale Spilotro.

The retired FBI agent in Tucson quickly reversed his story. Now, he explained, it was very clear that Tony Spilotro was killed because he caused problems for his bosses in Chicago and that Michael was included in the hit because he had become deeply involved in Tony's affairs in recent years.

Joe Ferriola, of course, hadn't left home on the afternoon of June 14. He made sure he conversed with his neighbors on both sides of and across the street from his luxurious home in the affluent suburb of Oak Brook. Nothing could be linked to Ferriola. Nor to anybody else. The abductors were obviously known to the Spilotro brothers, or at least to Tony, but they were never identified. Not yet.

The case remains today what it was when Farmer Kinz discovered the bodies. Just another unsolved mystery. Just another gangland murder among the thousand that have been tracked by the Chicago Crime Commission since the days of Al Capone. As a matter of fact, Scarface would have been proud of his successors on this one. The big man in glitzy Las Vegas winds up far from the madding crowd, the neon lights, the noise of the revelers? In a cornfield yet? Near some hick town in rural Indiana? Come on. Who could write stuff like that?

Epilogue

Reverend Thomas Paprocki, the Vice Chancellor of the Archdiocese of Chicago, conducted an investigation after the double-slaying and made the decision to bar Tony and Michael from receiving a public Roman Catholic funeral mass or burial service. Such services were recommended by the pastor of Michael's parish, St. Bernardine's in Oak Park. The Reverend John Fearon stated that he "was not too pleased with the decision of the archdiocese since Michael was an active, contributing parishioner. The whole neighborhood was crazy about him. We feel a person is innocent until proven guilty. Michael has never been convicted of anything." St. Bernardine's was also the parish of Angeline Giancana, Sam's wife, who died in 1954. In her memory Sam Giancana donated tens of thousands of dollars for stained-glass windows and marble in the church.

Sister Joy Clough, the archdiocese spokeswoman, said the archdiocese acted because of "the danger of giving scandal to the general populace and faithful." She said that public ceremonies can raise questions "in the minds of many" on how a notorious gangster can be buried within the church.

As the FBI investigation into the killing of Michael and Tony progressed, it became obvious that Michael had been taken out due to the ever-increasing role he seemed to be assuming during the Eighties in the affairs of his brother. Whereas it was brother John who was closely allied with Tony in Las Vegas in his early years there, it seemed that it was Michael who became closer and closer to Tony as the years went by. Michael, of course, was the youngest Spilotro and it took him some time to mature to the point where Tony felt he was "ready." It was Michael's bad luck to reach that state at the moment in Tony's life when things had begun to go downhill for him. I never had a reason to meet Michael. His apparent ascension in Tony's activities seemed to commence about the time I left Chicago. From what I understand, however, Michael was the most personable of the Spilotro brothers. Those who knew him when he ran Hoagie's found him to be a "real nice guy." He also may have been the second most intelligent Spilotro, second only to Pasquale.

For all these reasons, it seems apparent that when the mob took Michael out, they were nipping in the bud his progression in the affairs of the Chicago Outfit, in general, and of Tony in Las Vegas in particular. Some informants have recently speculated that had Michael not "gotten crosswise" with the leadership of the Chicago mob, he might have exceeded the success of his brother in the mob. We'll never know.

Although the murder of Tony and Michael Spilotro has never been solved, Jack Bonino, the ace FBI agent assigned to the investigation, has advised that Betty Tocco, the wife of Albert Caesar Tocco, furnished him with some interesting information. In 1986, Al Tocco was the capo in charge of the mob's activity in the southern suburbs of Chicago. Subsequently, he was sentenced to two hundred years in prison and will very likely spend the rest of his life there. But Betty told Bonino in October 1989 that when Tocco left his home on the evening of June 14, 1986 he told her that he had to meet three men. He identified them as Dominick "Toots" Palermo, his underboss, Nick Guzzino, another of the mobsters who worked under Tocco, and Al Roviaro, an associate.

Betty advised Bonino that she saw nothing of her husband until early the next morning when she received an excited phone call from him asking her to come to Enos, Indiana, and pick him up. Enos is located about two miles east of where Tony's and Michael's bodies were found.

Tocco was "hysterical" when she arrived in Enos, according to Betty. He was wearing work clothes covered with dirt. As the couple sped away, Al Tocco advised his wife that he had been digging the grave of the Spilotro brothers and that something had caused him and his helpers to panic. All of the men ran off in different directions without completing the digging of the grave site and they were unable to locate each other in the darkness. Tocco blamed Toots Palermo for poorly organizing the dig and worried that his fingerprints might be found on the wooden handle of the shovel he used. Tocco told his wife that he feared that Joe Ferriola, the mob boss at the time, might have him killed for incompetence. Betty advised that Tocco was fearful for weeks afterwards. He fled to Florida to escape Ferriola's wrath and stayed there until he received word from an intermediary that Ferriola had forgiven him and that it was safe to return to Chicago.

Bonino does not claim that Betty has implicated her husband in the murder of the brothers—only in the burial. When it became known to Al Tocco that she was talking to the FBI and eventually would testify, Betty was placed in the witness protection program where she remains today.

In May 1990 another witness would come forward. William L. Bauer of Peoria, a convicted career thief then serving a sixteen-year sentence for armed robbery, was a cellmate of Al Tocco in the Metropolitan Correctional Center in Chicago while Tocco was on trial. Bauer disclosed that Tocco "ranted and raved and hollered about how Betty had helped the government. He said he would like to have his hands around her neck." He talked about killing Betty, the FBI agent who elicited her cooperation, and an assistant U.S. Attorney who prosecuted him. He also talked about having been involved in nine "hits." Bauer gave his testimony during a sentencing hearing before U.S. District Court Judge James Holderman.

During the sentencing hearing of Tocco, a court memo was introduced stating that the Spilotro brothers, according to pathology reports, had been "beaten with fists and feet about 11 P.M. on June 14, 1986 and that each was buried unconscious but still alive."

The major hotel-casinos in Las Vegas I have described as having been mobbed-up are now owned by legitimate concerns. Organized crime no longer has a hold on them. These include the Tropicana, the Stardust, Desert Inn, Circus-Circus, Caesars Palace, the Fremont, the Aladdin, the Sands, the Riviera and the Sundance. The Dunes and the Marina have been torn down.

In my opinion, concerns remain about three other hotels in Las Vegas, the owners of which were involved with the Tropicana when that hotel-casino was being heavily skimmed. However, the Nevada Gaming Control Board has issued licenses to those owners, finding them acceptable. Obviously, therefore, the presence of organized crime in Las Vegas, and throughout Nevada, today, is nowhere what it was when Tony Spilotro ruled the roost there.

When Spilotro was killed, the Chicago family of La Cosa Nostra replaced him with Don "The Wizard of Odds" Angelini. Angelini is a huge cut above Spilotro. He achieved capo status in the Chicago mob because of an unusual intelligence rather than the ability to perform the heavy work. He was recognized as the Outfit's prime gambling expert. However, Donald has had nothing but troubles with the law since 1970. I arrested him twice. He is now in federal prison after having been convicted on a RICO case in San Diego in 1993. In view of the mob's vastly diminished involvement in Las Vegas, Angelini has not been replaced. There is no current *representato* of Chicago in Las Vegas.

The charges in the San Diego case included an attempt to gain control of the gaming on the Rincon Indian Reservation near San Diego, and extortion. Convicted with Angelini was John "No Nose" DiFronzo, one of the two top bosses of the Chicago mob. The other, Sam Carlisi, was acquitted. John Spilotro pleaded guilty. The extortion charges involved the attempted collection of the juice loans which Tony Spilotro had put on the street in Las Vegas before he was murdered. The debtors had declined to pay up after Tony's death until they were threatened by some of the defendants in the San Diego case. One of the debtors involved was Joe Pignatello, the former driver for Sam Giancana. Joe Pigs had opened a restaurant in Las Vegas and had needed an infusion of cash, which Tony supplied him.

Sam "Wings" Carlisi, generally acknowledged to have been the boss of the Chicago mob in the late Eighties and early Nineties, was convicted on December 16, 1993, along with seven of his top underlings, of racketeering, gambling, loan-sharking, extortion, arson, tax violations, and of plotting the murder of Anthony Daddino, whom Carlisi and the others suspected of being a potential government informant. Included among those convicted was Jim Marcello, involved in the abduction of Tony and Michael Spilotro. At the time of this writing, Carlisi, seventy-two years old and ill with throat cancer, faces seven to ten years in prison and the confiscation of millions of dollars in illicitly gained assets, including his homes in Florida and in the Chicago area.

Tony Accardo died of natural causes in May 1992.

Lefty Rosenthal is alive and well, living in Florida.

Gus Alex is spending the rest of his life in federal prison after being convicted of extortion in 1992.

Pat Marcy suffered a heart attack while on trial in Chicago in early 1993. He died soon thereafter.

Joey Lombardo was released from federal prison on November 13, 1992 and is currently living once more on the west side of Chicago in the same home where his wife treated Johnny Bassett and me so well when we went there to arrest him. Many in Chicago expect Joey to become the top boss of the Outfit since it is a widespread belief he is the most qualified. I believe he is waiting for the term of his parole to expire to do so.

I have been informed by an investigator of impeccable credentials that Lombardo may be using a cousin who is currently an upper-echelon leader of the mob in Chicago—Joe Andriacci, called "The Builder"—to pass on his orders and instructions to members of the Chicago mob. My source thinks that Lombardo is very hesitant to become actively involved as the Chicago boss in view of "the paper on him," his parole status. If he were surveilled meeting with mobsters, his parole would be jeopardized and he could be remanded to serve out the rest of his sentence in the Pendorf case. However, if he is observed meeting with his cousin, at least he has an argument that he was discussing family business. Not the family of La Cosa Nostra but his personal family. It may be a thin argument, but it's better than nothing.

Joey Lombardo is nobody's clown. He is a savvy, sharp guy. Shortly after he was paroled, he took notice of the several items in Chicago newspapers commenting on his return and the suspicions of law enforcement that he might be resuming his activity as a top leader in the mob. Joey thereafter placed the following public notice in the classifieds of several newspapers in Chicago during the week of December 8, 1992: "I am Joe Lombardo. I have been released on parole from Federal Prison. I never took a secret oath with guns and daggers, pricked my finger, drew blood or burned paper to join a criminal organization. If anyone hears my name used in connection with any criminal activity please notify the FBI, local police and my parole officer, Ron Kumke." Quite a ploy. Who would suspect that a person publicly announcing that he is not "connected" was? Joey is an interesting personality.

Frank Cullotta and Sal Romano remain in the U.S. Marshall's witness protection program. Alive and well.

Jimmy "The Weasel" Fratianno died of natural causes in the summer of 1993.

Allen Glick is alive and well in La Jolla, California.

Carl Thomas moved to southern Oregon following his release from prison after serving his term for his conviction in Strawman I. He had been refused a gaming license in Las Vegas despite his cooperation with the government when he testified in the Strawman II case against the Chicago and Kansas City mobsters. Thomas died of natural causes in November 1993.

Paul Lowden, who was a mid-level executive at the Tropicana when it was fronted for the Kansas City mob by Joe Agosto and was being heavily skimmed by Carl Thomas and his crew under the aegis of Agosto, now owns the Sahara and the Hacienda, one on each end of the Strip.

Frank Fertitta, who was a one-time partner of Carl Thomas, now owns the Palace Station, a favorite of Las Vegas locals, just off I-15 behind Circus-Circus.

Moe Dalitz died of natural causes in the late Eighties.

Joe Ferriolo died of natural causes in March 1991.

Dominic "Butch" Blasi died of natural causes in 1993.

Marshall Caifano is alive and living in Florida.

Johnny Roselli's body was found in a drum, floating in Biscayne Bay in Florida, in the mid-Seventies.

Gerry Denono is still in federal prison.

Meyer Lansky died of natural causes in Miami in the mid-Eighties.

Chuckie Crimaldi is alive and well in the U.S. Marshall's witness protection program.

Murray Humphreys died of a heart attack in late 1965 on the evening of the day he was arrested for contempt of a federal grand jury, my case.

Sam Giancana was killed in the basement of his home in Oak Park in June 1975.

Jackie Cerone continues to be incarcerated in a federal prison near Austin, Texas.

Joey Aiuppa continues to be imprisoned in a federal correctional facility in Minnesota.

Nick Civella died of natural causes in Kansas City in the early Eighties.

Carl "Cork" Civella and Carl "Tuffy" DeLuna continue to serve their sentences in federal prison after convictions in Strawman I and II.

Chris Petti is in federal prison.

Roy Williams died of natural causes.

Frank Fitzsimmons and Jackie Presser both died of natural causes.

Sidney R. Korshak resides in Palm Springs and in Bel-Air, California.

Doc Stacher was deported to Israel, where he died.

Bob Matheu is living in Las Vegas. He wrote the best-selling book, *Next to Hughes*, detailing his experiences as the high hand of Howard Hughes and his involvement with Sam Giancana, Johnny Roselli and Santo Traficante in the CIA plot to kill Fidel Castro among other most interesting episodes in his life.

An attempt was made on the life of Joey Cusamano in Las Vegas but he escaped, served a prison sentence and is now living in Las Vegas, where he hangs out at the Sahara.

Richard Bryan continues to be a U.S. Senator from Nevada. The other senator is Harry Reid, who jousted with Lefty Rosenthal when Reid was a member of the Nevada Gaming Control Board.

Joe Blasko was released from prison and was last known to be working as a bartender in a topless joint in Las Vegas.

Tommy Parker died of natural causes after he retired from the FBI and from the Valley National Bank in Las Vegas.

Scores of Chicago judges, including Judge Thomas Maloney, have been convicted in recent years in Operation Greylord and Operation Gambat. Maloney is the judge who acquitted Tony Spilotro in the M & M Murders case.

None of the killings in which Tony Spilotro was the main suspect has ever been solved. These would include the murders of Danny Seifert, Emil Vaci, Marty Buccieri, Tamara Rand, Sam DeStefano, Frank Bompensiero, Billy McCarthy, Jimmy Miraglia, Sherwin Lisner, Allen Dorfman, and six or eight of Sam DeStefano's juice victims. The one partial exception was the killing of Leo Foreman.

Pete Wacks continues to be a Chicago FBI agent assigned to the most complicated organized crime cases.

Bill Ouseley is retired in Kansas City but is very active as the security representative of the National Football League there, as a private investigator and as a lecturer.

Lee Flosi retired from the FBI in December 1993 to become the Director of Security in Chicago for the 1994 World Cup soccer tournament.

Art Pfizenmayer is the supervisor of the organized crime squad in the San Diego Office. He supervised the case in

which John Spilotro pleaded guilty and "No Nose" DiFronzo
and Donald Angelini were convicted.

Mike Simon is living in retirement in Carson City.

Johnny Bassett is living in retirement in Florida.

Duncan Everette died of natural causes.

Joe Yablonsky is living in his retirement in Cincinnati. He
has written his autobiography, which I highly recommend.

Dr. Pasquale Spilotro continues as a highly regarded Chicago area dental surgeon. He was never known to have been
involved in any criminal activity.

The Nevada Gaming Control Board is much more efficient
than in the past. It now rivals the Casino Control Commission
of New Jersey. Part of the reason is its close cooperation with
the FBI now that it is deemed trustworthy. The good working
relationship between the two agencies has been fostered by
Ron Asher, a former Las Vegas FBI agent who is now a top
official of the GCB.

Pat Healy resigned from the Chicago Crime Commission
and is now associated with a prominent Chicago security firm.

John Jemilo resigned from the Chicago Crime Commission
and is now practicing law in Chicago and teaching at the University of Illinois–Chicago.

Bob Fuesel, Jerry Gladden and Jeannette Callaway are currently the top officials at the Chicago Crime Commission.

No Atlantic City hotel-casino has ever been suspected of
being "mobbed-up." This is primarily due to the extreme dil-
igence of the New Jersey Casino Control Commission and its
Division of Enforcement with employees like Greg Kowalick.
That is not to say, however, that the mob is not in Atlantic
City. They are there through ancillary services owned by the
mob, such as suppliers and purveyors, and are able to find
work for employees through the Hotel and Restaurant Employees Union, known as the Culinary Union. Several Atlantic City
mayors have been convicted of corruption.

Frank Sinatra continues to entertain in Las Vegas.

Phyllis McGuire, Sam Giancana's former mistress, continues to reside in her mansion in Las Vegas. The McGuire Sis-
ters continue to entertain. I caught their act a couple of years

ago at the Fairmont Hotel in San Francisco and thought they were just great.

Antoinette Giancana, the "Mafia Princess," the daughter of Sam Giancana, continues to live in a Chicago suburb with her husband, Bob McDonald, the former attorney for Mad Sam DeStefano. Toni and I are creative consultants to HBO, which is developing one of my books as a two-hour movie.

Ed Hanley, who got his start with Local 450 in Cicero, which was chartered by Joe Aiuppa, continues to be the president of the Hotel and Restaurant Employees Union.

Long after the murder of the Spilotro brothers, the situation continued to boil in Newton County, Indiana, the location of the burial site. Newton County submitted a bill for $575 to the Spilotro brothers' estates. That was the cost, billed to Newton County, for transporting the bodies via ambulance to Indiana University's forensic laboratory in Indianapolis for the autopsy. The estates refused to pay. Newton County Attorney Daniel Blaney wrote to Allen Ackerman, the Chicago criminal attorney who handled the estates, but the county has never received reimbursement for the ambulance fee. As a result, members of the Newton County Sheriff's Office held a fund-raiser, offering green T-shirts emblazoned in bold white letters: "Spilotro Brothers Fertilizer Company." They were a big hit, no pun intended.

The Chicago mob continues to be a dangerous entity. It still exerts tremendous influence in Chicago. Its income from illegal gambling in Chicago and its environs continues to provide sufficient funds to keep the Outfit machinery operating at a fast speed. However, not at the speed that once was. Investigation by the FBI and prosecution by the U.S. Attorney's Office in Chicago has put a serious crimp in the Chicago family of La Cosa Nostra. Most of the capable leaders of the Chicago mob have been incarcerated. Since 1986, just about every top leader of the Chicago mob has been disposed of, one way or another. Accardo himself died. Ferriola died. Capos like Vince Solano died. Al Tocco was convicted, sentenced to two hundred years. Lenny Patrick became a government witness and helped convict Gus Alex. He also testified in the San Diego case that put away "No Nose" DiFronzo and the successor to Tony Spilotro, Donald Angelini. Rocky Infelice became a top boss. The FBI put him away. Sam Carlisi, another top guy, skated in the San Diego case but now looks to spend the rest of his life in prison. Sal DeLaurentis, Lou Marino and Bobby Bellavia were convicted. Joe DiFronzo, "No Nose's" brother, was indicted and is now a fugitive.

Are there any good men left in the Outfit? Sure. Guys like Joey Lombardo, who is smart enough not to get materially involved until his parole runs out, and Dominic "Large" Cortina, Angelini's long-time partner. Dom, who I know well, would make a very capable leader. However, he's been imprisoned twice in the past twenty-five years, once just recently, and, knowing him, I think he's smart enough to know there is no future in taking over the Chicago mob, not when the FBI focuses so much of its investigative attention on the top guys. There are other capable, experienced guys who are available. Guys like Joe "The Builder" Andriacci; Marco D'Amico; Jimmy D'Antonio; Pete DiFronzo; Jimmy Inendino; Angelo LaPietro, now that he is about to get out after Strawman II; Joe and Larry Petitt; Al Pilotto, now that he is out again; Bobby Salerno, now that he beat a big case; and old friend Joe Spadavecchio. They and several others have at least the minimum amount of experience and ability to become bosses and capos.

There is no way one can believe the Chicago Outfit is *finito*. No way. A lot of progress has been made along that road, but the road is long. We see the light at the end of the tunnel, but we are not there yet. We are in a fifteen-round world's championship prize fight. We are winning the later rounds after losing the early ones. But we can't quit now. Joe Louis knocked out Bill Conn in the thirteenth round after losing most of the early rounds. We are now approaching round thirteen. We've got to keep punchin' and keep the faith!

After I had completed the first draft of the manuscript of this book, Jeannie and I were visited by John and Elaine

Bassett on the last legs of their seven-month odyssey, travelling in their RV from their home in Florida to Vermont to Alaska and then down through California, Arizona and Texas enroute home. As the reader will recall, John was a member of the C-1 Squad, working organized crime cases in Chicago with me for some fifteen years before he succumbed to the temptation of advancement in the Bureau and became a top official of the Bureau with an office in the executive suite of Clarence Kelly, then the Director of the FBI.

John perused my manuscript. He then told me: "I have two suggestions. One, you didn't get into the depth of the brutality of the killers in the Foreman murder (when the DeStefano brothers, Spilotro and Chuckie Crimaldi tortured and then killed Leo Foreman) and two, you forgot to mention one other time when you confronted The Ant."

John reminded me that on the Sunday morning when we arrested Milwaukee Phil Alderisio, while we were still in his home searching it, Tony Spilotro had arrived. It is recalled that Spilotro was working under Alderisio at this time, July 1969, as a "hit-man."

I have just a slight memory of that. Johnny Bassett tells me the reason is that "you were so interested in finding the bodies that may have been buried, one way or another, in the basement of Alderisio's house. You thought since he was a killer that, like the basement at Mad Sam DeStefano's house, there might well be some secrets down in Alderisio's house. I was upstairs with Alderisio and when Spilotro arrived, you immediately told him 'sit your ass down in that kitchen chair and stay there' and then you went down into the basement. I had to deal with those two assholes after that."

That is obviously true if Johnny Bassett says so. But since I am after him to write his own book, his autobiography, I'll leave the details to him for his own use. I'm sure John would do a better job since he recalls the details so much better than I do.

Author's Note

The mania for gambling has swept through the country like wildfire during the past several years.

Just while I was writing this in the fall of 1993, there were more hotel rooms *added*, opened, in Las Vegas than there are hotel rooms *in existence* in the city in which I live, Tucson, Arizona. When Treasure Island, the Luxor and the MGM Grand opened in late 1993, 10,500 hotel rooms were added to Las Vegas. We don't have that many in all of the "metropolitan" area of Tucson, not a hick town by any means. A "resort" city to boot.

It is expected that some twenty-five million visitors will come to Las Vegas in 1994. I can see the grin on Bugsy's face! What an inspiration he had!

It is not just in Las Vegas that the gambling bug has bitten the American public, however. In 1987, shortly after Tony Spilotro was buried, gross gambling revenue in the United States was roughly 18 billion dollars. In 1992 it reached 30 billion. It will undoubtedly go much higher.

In 1990 there were 20 gambling stocks on Wall Street. In 1992 there were 50—with many more about to be offered to the public.

Forty-eight states offered some form of gambling in 1993.

The state of Minnesota, with its Indian gambling halls, has more casinos than Atlantic City.

The most insidious statistic to me, however, is this one: compared to the 30 billion dollars that Americans wager, a mere 8.8 billion dollars is spent on books! Almost four times as many Americans would rather stick a quarter in a slot machine than read a good book! What does that say about our society?

As a matter of fact, six times as much money is gambled as is spent at movie theaters. Five times more is spent by people gambling than is spent on recorded music.

More money was spent in 1992 on gambling than on books, movies, amusement attractions and recorded music—*combined*!

I'm not talking just Nevada and Atlantic City, of course. I'm talking about horse and dog racing, riverboat gambling, Native American casinos, bingo, state lotteries, offtrack betting parlors and card clubs, now legal in almost every state in one form or another. And the boom is expected to explode even further in the next several years. So much so, I wonder if Nevada and Atlantic City might be imperiled. For instance, why travel several hours to Atlantic City when a resident of Boston, Hartford or New Haven can travel an hour or so to Foxwoods, the Indian casino so luxurious in southeastern Connecticut, and find and ambience there just as plush as the casinos on the Boardwalk? With the same odds, almost all of which are universal?

For that matter, why hike, bowl, golf or play tennis when the same spirit of adventure can be satisfied by sitting at a blackjack table, or if people want some exercise, why not just throw dice at the crap tables? You'll sweat just as much and your heart will beat just as fast at the MGM Grand as it will in the Grand Canyon. And at the MGM Grand, with all its recreation, especially for the kids, with the Luxor and Excalibur right across the strip—also great playlands for the youngsters—why travel to Disneyland or Disney World? The kids can enjoy the days just as well while the grownups enjoy the nights.

I say this with tongue in cheek. But there are hundreds of thousands of families who take such counsel very seriously. Especially the mommas and the papas.

As I think I've made clear, I have serious problems with this phenomenon. Will organized crime overcome the best efforts of the regulatory authorities to keep them out? Will the gambling addiction that is bound to take root cause great social problems? Will street crime—the pickpockets, the muggers, the prostitutes, the burglars and the thieves—proliferate? Even if organized crime is kept out, will illegal gambling spread because the addicted gambler will not be able to gamble in the casinos due to his lack of cash and credit as I have explained herein? Will the social agencies of the cities be able to cope with the homeless and the welfare people who will be attracted to the areas where gaming flourishes—just like everybody else?

Somebody once said there is never a free lunch. We're going to find out. Will the additional revenue to the cities, states and Indian reservations be worth the social problems and the crime problems? We'll see. Tony Spilotro may be turning over in his grave, wishing he could be there to get his hand in one more time.

INDEX

Don't miss

ACCARDO
The Genuine Godfather

by William F. Roemer, Jr.

William Roemer was the first FBI agent to face Tony "The Big Tuna" Accardo, America's most dangerous criminal for forty years. Drawing on secret wiretaps and inside information, ACCARDO chronicles bloodshed and mayhem for more than six decades—as Roemer duels against the most powerful don of them all. . . .

ACCARDO
The Genuine Godfather
by William F. Roemer, Jr.

Published by Ivy Books.
Available in bookstores everywhere.

Look for

WAR OF THE GODFATHERS

by William F. Roemer, Jr.

Featuring the battling godfathers themselves—Joe Bonanno and Tony "Joe
Batters" Accardo—plus a rogues gallery
of high rollers, professional hitters,
capos, underbosses, and soldiers, here
are the strategies, the setups, the take-
downs, and the double crosses in the real
words of the men who cut the deals—and
the throats—in the biggest, deadliest
power play in the history of the mob and
the annals of crime.

WAR OF THE GODFATHERS

by William F. Roemer, Jr.